THE WORCESTERSHIRE REGIMENT
1922-1950

5251421 PRIVATE K. HUNT, D.C.M.
1st Bn. The Worcestershire Regiment
(*From the painting by Eric Kennington now in the Regimental Museum*)

THE
WORCESTERSHIRE
REGIMENT
1922-1950

BY

LIEUT.-COLONEL LORD BIRDWOOD
M.V.O.

ALDERSHOT
GALE & POLDEN LTD
1952

First published February, 1952

PRINTED AND BOUND IN GREAT BRITAIN
BY GALE AND POLDEN LIMITED AT THEIR
WELLINGTON PRESS, ALDERSHOT, HAMPSHIRE

TO

THOSE OFFICERS AND MEN OF
THE WORCESTERSHIRE REGIMENT

WHO ARE DESTINED

IN FUTURE YEARS

TO INHERIT THE CUSTODY OF THESE TRADITIONS

"Get you the sons your fathers got and God will
save the Queen."

A. E. HOUSMAN : *Shropshire Lad.*

FOREWORD

by

LIEUT.-GENERAL SIR R. N. GALE, K.B.E., C.B., D.S.O., M.C.

Colonel of the Regiment

THE position of the infantry regiment in the Army as a whole is unique. The infantry regiment is, and always has been, by comparison with the other corps, small. It is, in the majority of cases, tied by historical association and by deep sentiment to the county whose name it bears, and in whose lands its home and depot are situated. It is, in fact, a very personal and rather exclusive family. It is proud of its great past and of its traditions ; it is deeply conscious of its obligations and its duty to live up to those great traditions and, indeed, to build on them. Its spirit animates all its members whether they are regulars, territorials, short service or war-time officers and men.

The regimental histories are the libraries of the past achievements of the regiment. In these books are the records of moves, of experiences, of battles, of achievements and endeavour. The study of regimental history and a consequent knowledge of what the regiment has done, where it has been and how it has conducted itself, are essential to any good regimental officer or man.

A regimental history is a most difficult book to write. This is so because those who will read it—in fact, those who should read it—are so varied in their outlook and their viewpoint. There are those who were there, in the battle, in the cantonment, or on the march. Details of what transpired will be very vivid in each mind, but these details will for each person be of some different event. The historian has to remember this : these readers will be his most critical. It may be that an event, quite vivid to their recollection, is missing or merely apparently glossed over. Yet if full justice is to be done and all these events in their detail are to be faithfully recorded, the book would become so bulky, the mass of detail would be so immense, that few would ever have the time to read it. In our present times, too, the cost of production would be prohibitive. Finally, the time that it would take to compile such a book would result in its publication so many years after the events that few would still be alive to read it. The official histories of the First World War are a case in point.

There is also another field of readers who must be considered. These are the mothers and fathers, wives and other relations, of men who fought and died in the regiment. These people are nearly always non-military in their background and unversed in those detailed techniques which are common ground to the professional soldier. It is right and fitting that a regimental history should cater for these readers: their sacrifice alone demands it; and their love for the regiment, which so many of us know to be so real and so deep, demands it. The style of writing must therefore be such as to be intelligible to this field and minute detail, technical in its nature, reduced to a minimum.

There are finally those who come after: the younger generation of soldiers-to-be in the regiment. The history must be true; it must be factually correct; it must show in clear relief great occasions; it must attempt to portray life as it was and events truly as they were.

The task, then, of the writer of a regimental history such as ours is a difficult one. Lord Birdwood, our author, a soldier himself, has overcome these difficulties and given us a book readable in style, reasonable in size and, in so far as it is humanly possible to check and cross-check all detail, factually correct.

Richard N. Gale

Lieut.-General.

Colonel, The Worcestershire Regiment.

CONTENTS

ILLUSTRATIONS

MAPS

INTRODUCTION

WHEN the privilege of writing the History of the Worcestershire Regiment in recent years came my way, I was eager to accept as attractive a literary proposition as a retired officer could wish to find. It seemed then just a matter of collecting the records and getting down to work. But as time passed I realized that I had underestimated the difficulties. An author's excuse for inflicting an Introduction on his readers is therefore first his own apology. He wishes to find space to explain the nature of some of those many small problems which confronted him as he sifted the mass of evidence available ; while, secondly, he welcomes his only opportunity to say "thank you" to many officers of the Regiment who offered so much friendly assistance and advice which formed the hard core round which this story was written.

As I conceived it, the task was to write a story of a length acceptable to the average reader rather than a detailed record for the student of history. There is therefore no attempt to compete with Captain FitzMaurice Stacke's monumental work of research. Nevertheless this work claims to be a historical record and as such it must deal with facts and be faithfully accurate in doing so. Yet in a book which it was hoped might not only appeal to many hundreds who have served in the Regiment but also to those whose sons and relations fought in its ranks, only the more prominent facts could be recorded ; which immediately confronted the author with the most intractable of problems—the choice of what to omit and what to include. The most difficult chapters to write were those concerning the First Battalion in France, and the Second and Seventh Battalions in Burma, while those chapters for which there was little available data and which were constructed from interviews with officers proved comparatively straightforward. I would therefore ask the indulgence of the reader if he is irritated at the omission of any episode or situation which he considers might have received a mention and ask him to believe that many hours were spent in the process of selection.

Having chosen what should be included, the next difficulty which faces a military historian is to avoid a mere recitation of the facts selected. This is easy enough for the writer who sets out his own experience, since the personal touch can so readily lend flesh and substance to the dry bones. In Lieut.-Colonel O. G. White's splendid story of the 2nd Battalion the Dorsetshire Regiment in Burma, the author is able very effectively to impose his colourful style over the bare narrative because he can fully exploit the "first person singular." No such happy circumstance is available to one who writes from outside and must therefore draw on the memories of others and to some extent on his own imagination. It would at least have been very pleasant to have been able to have written the word "we" rather than have to repeat many hundreds of times the words "the Battalion." But since there would have been eight "we's," the book, as the record of one Regiment, could hardly have read as logical history. It was paradoxical that much colourful history of vital importance, such as the exploits of the 2nd Battalion in Burma, proved to be the type of narrative which most readily slipped into a monotonous repetition of moves from A to B and B to C. Yet another difficulty was that not infrequently two accounts of the same episode would not agree.

In the matter of abbreviations I have tried to select the most logical system from many alternatives. The result is that the first time a unit or formation is mentioned it receives its full title, thereafter being written in the shortest possible manner. The same principle is applied to names. No set formula, however, could be found to the selection of names, and so there may well be some "who have no memorial" and who yet were prominent in their sphere in peace or war. I have tried usually to mention the departure of a Commanding Officer and the arrival of his relief. Apart from this, I admit that names appear in haphazard manner as they were represented either in conversation or in official records. In general an attempt was made to reduce names to a minimum without entirely abandoning the attraction of the personal reference. While in recording dates, names, units and formations I hoped to write according to a system, those who look for complete uniformity in these matters will be irritated to note many exceptions to the rule.

Often the context seemed to make one form more appropriate than another, and sometimes a title is in full while on other occasions an abbreviation is used.

In recording the names of places I am very conscious of the

inadequacy of a name without a map from which to identify it : and it would certainly have been very satisfactory to have included more large-scale maps. Time and finance, however, were not unimportant factors in writing this story. Maps and photographs add to the expense of production and a voluminous and expensive book could only appeal to the few.

The method of giving separate chapters to separate Battalions seemed to carry the great advantage that any one chapter can be read as a separate story, but it will be seen that the allotment of chapters has not resulted in an even distribution of written material to Battalions. In the luck of the draw some were destined for a more crowded life than others and in such circumstances their record must inevitably claim more space. We all, I think, appreciate that in modern war the role of spectators is often as exacting as that of holding the stage.

Apart from the War Diaries buried in the bowels of the earth in the old War Cabinet Offices under the Foreign Office, I consulted the Record Office at Preston, while, nearer home, many copies of *Firm* were invaluable ; as were also Major D. Y. Watson's History of the 1st Battalion in 1944 and 1945, Captain F. G. Thompson's account of the 7th Battalion in Burma, Lieut.-Colonel O. G. White's book already referred to, and the "War History of the 64th Indian Infantry Brigade," by Major E. H. C. Davies (1/6th Gurkha Rifles). In reconstructing material from various accounts it was frequently found that the first author's choice of words or expression was the obvious best, in which case they were unashamedly reproduced.

My thanks are also due to many officers who gave their time in London and elsewhere, often undertaking detailed research which made me very conscious of an obligation not to disappoint them in the final presentation. Colonel S. W. Jones, the administrative officer, and Major Dean and his staff at the Depot were ever ready to meet my detailed needs in the search for material and have been of the greatest assistance with both suggestion and correction. To these, and indeed to all officers and men of the Worcestershire Regiment, I am indebted for the rich experience of a year or so in the compilation of this record. My cherished hope is that the story may do justice to so great a theme.

C. B. B.

CHAPTER ONE

THE FIRST BATTALION, 1922-1939

Meerut, Allahabad, Shanghai, Plymouth, Aldershot

IN the days when the Indian tour was not only essential **1923**
education for a battalion of the Line, but also something
of an adventure, Nasirabad was hardly one of the stations
regarded as meeting all requirements. It was therefore
with few regrets that the 1st Battalion left the arid wastes
of Rajputana for the greater attractions of Meerut in
January, 1923. Nevertheless, the subsequent years in
Meerut are hardly remembered for any outstanding event
or achievement in the record, save for the winning of the
Durand Cup at Simla in 1924. Previously the Cup and
the Calcutta Shield had been won by the 3rd Battalion in
1921, so the football reputation of the Regiment stood
high. The best Indian and British teams came to Simla
for the Durand Cup, which was generally regarded as the
reward of the champion team of India. For several years
the standard of hockey had also stood high. But finance
did not permit of teams entering major tournaments for
both hockey and soccer ; and in these circumstances
soccer won first claim. Nevertheless, the semi-final of the
Army Hockey Championship was reached in 1925.

An exacting task which fell to the Battalion in Meerut
was the organization of the annual meeting of the Army
Rifle Association, when for ten days in March all ranks
were busy acting as hosts to some hundreds of visitors to
the Meerut ranges. Our District Commander at this
time was Major-General Deverell,[1] an infantry soldier
who drove his District hard, but whom all respected as a
great leader and humanitarian. Under his constant eye
no one could afford to relax.

---

[1] The late Field-Marshal Sir C. J. Deverell, G.C.B., Chief of the
Imperial General Staff.

1923   Meerut was the Mecca of pig-sticking, and several officers joined the Tent Club. The competition, however, was high and it was not until later, in Allahabad, that officers could derive full benefit riding after pig and taking to polo, when, away from the critical eye of a Cavalry Brigade, they felt free to tackle the sport of horsemen in their own way. Every year in the spring parties left Meerut for Ranikhet, while as an alternative Naini Tal, with its lake, was available for a few pleasant days to break the depressing monotony of the heat of an Indian summer.

In July, 1923, the Battalion came in for the familiar communal riots and detachments were called on to keep the peace in the bazaar. It is recorded that on one occasion the smallest private in the Battalion successfully held up a crowd about to overwhelm his post, and when later the Cantonment Magistrate asked how it had been done, he was told that it had been accomplished by raising the hand and saying "bas": to which was added the explanation, "and they bust"!

For the rest, life in Meerut passed happily with two race meetings in the year, with pagal gymkhanas and a memorable Torchlight Tattoo when a detachment of the Battalion carried out some spectacular physical drill and club swinging with illuminated dumb-bells and clubs.

One administrative development deserves recognition. For the first time since the days of the Corps of Black Drummers, coloured personnel formed an integral part of the Battalion, and an Indian officer and a platoon of Hindu "gujar" sepoys were recruited for transport duties with the pack-mules of the Machine Gun Group. The platoon took the uniform of Indian Infantry with Regimental shoulder titles, hose-tops and green puggri-fringes. Those with education became thoroughly interested in Regimental history, and all identified themselves with the good name and interest of the Battalion. It is sad to reflect that such associations have passed away, never to be revived.

1926   In the winter of 1926 a move was made to Allahabad. A draft of 108 men which had just arrived from England entrained for the new station direct from Bombay, so that only a strength of 15 officers and 476 other ranks marched out of Meerut on 28th December. Since such a simple movement has now become to be thought of as primitive in comparison with the mobility of a modern mechanized unit, it will be of some interest to recall the story of the trek along the dusty Indian roads to Allahabad.

The total distance covered was 384 miles in 33 marches, averaging eleven or twelve miles a day. A day's rest was taken at Bulandshahr, Akrabad, Karauli, Cawnpore, and Fatehpur, while at Gursahaiganj, familiarly known as "Goosey Gung," a much appreciated four days' halt was called.

To speed the Battalion on its long trek, the bands of the Scots Greys and Dorsets played our men out of Meerut Cantonments, while Major-General Franks,[2] the District Commander at that time, rode out with the Commanding Officer for the first three miles.

The cavalcade of transport would indeed have been the ridicule of a new age of mechanization. Bullock and buffalo carts lumbered along piled up not only with the creature-needs of a battalion but also with an array of camp followers, and their pots and pans, chickens, dogs, and all the paraphernalia of a tribal migration ! The system was that of simple contract by which the transport changed as one District was left and another entered. The Battalion mules, three private cars, the contractor's lorry, a mineral water lorry and the Officers' Mess Ford accompanied the column all the way.

On most days the march would be completed by midday, leaving the afternoons for foot and rifle inspections. The transport then generally appeared, tents were quickly erected, serge donned, and dinner consumed, with time over for correspondence, sleep and shikar.

The men were accommodated in 160-pounder single-fly tents, and the allotment worked out at about fourteen men to a tent. Each day bolts were removed from rifles, and the rifles then buried in pits dug under each tent, the tent orderly sleeping over the rifles. Hay was provided

---

[2] Major-General G. McK. Franks, C.B.

1926 to sleep on, but few men bothered to fetch it and all soon were accustomed to sleeping on the bare ground.

Shikar, though not plentiful, provided pleasant relaxation. The eventual bag covered nilghai, blackbuck and gharral as well as every conceivable species of game bird. Many of the men had long dogs and made good use of them after hare.

No description of the march would be complete without reference to a certain "pi-dog" which fell in with the column early on, and, in spite of every discouragement from the Adjutant, the Sergeant-Major, Company guides and others, marched into Allahabad serenely determined to establish himself as a permanency. Accordingly he was accepted and promoted to the dignity of a collar. There will today be many pi-dogs in India who must miss the dog-lovers of the British Army along the Grand Trunk Road.

One of the invisible assets of a dusty march of 400 miles in India was that it enabled the country folk to see the troops and the troops to see the country, an aspect of soldiering to which perhaps higher authority never gave sufficient attention. Soon after arrival at Allahabad a change of command saw the departure and arrival of two officers whose names have become very familiar in the annals of the Battalion, Lieutenant-Colonel L. M. Stevens handing over to Lieutenant-Colonel W. F. O. Faviell.

For the next two years the Battalion led a settled life in Allahabad. The city had formerly been the capital of the United Provinces. It is situated at the junction of the Rivers Ganges and Jumna and with its municipality and Cantonments boasted a population of 300,000. The site of the river junction known to Hindus as "Prayag" attracted an immense annual pilgrimage, in connection with which the Battalion was called on to perform duties in crowd control involving more tact than arduous force. Within the Fort was a shrine, and the task of our men was to prevent the over-zealous from overrunning the object of veneration.

The Cantonment area was well laid out, clean for an Indian station, with electric light and fans and a good piped water supply.

A large civilian population based on the High Court of 1928
Justice lent variety to social life, as did also the University.
The Fort of the Moghul Emperor Akbar, which lay some
four miles from the lines, proved a mixed blessing, since
companies had to take spells of six weeks on duty guarding the Fort and the civil Treasury. The latter duties
involved an elaborate system for the custody of the
Treasury keys. The safety of lakhs of silver rupees in
bags was at stake, which involved the sentry having to be
locked in behind the grille.

Recreation facilities, apart from station polo, included
blackbuck shooting and pig-sticking, the Tent Club being
revived in 1928. The Battalion Rifle Club afforded
shooting parties the opportunity to shoot buck, but owing
to the encircling rivers in the immediate neighbourhood
there was only a little mugger shooting and some in-
different fishing.

Within the Cantonments the other units stationed with
the Battalion were a battery, an Indian Infantry Battalion and Ordnance personnel. For much of the time
their companions were the 4/19th Hyderabad Regiment,
who used the "Royal Windsor" as their march and whose
musical interpretation of our own Regimental March was
not necessarily appreciated by those with sensitive ears
for tone. Nor did it appeal to the 1st Worcestershire's
legitimate sense of possession.

In October, 1929, the Battalion sailed from Bombay for 1929
Shanghai in the *Neuralia*. Much early practice led to a
particularly smooth embarkation, for which the Battalion
received a commendation from the embarkation authorities.

Shanghai seemed a new world after Allahabad. From 1930
the quayside the Battalion marched six miles up to the
lines in freshly starched drill, and received a great reception. Headquarters and two companies were at Great
Western Road, while the other two companies were at
Jessfield Park, both sites being hutted camps.

The role of the two British battalions in Shanghai was
the protection of British commercial interests. In other
words, both battalions were tied to the great city with
little opportunity to see the countryside and with no

1930 prospect of collective training in open country. Since it
was forbidden to go outside the international settlement
in uniform, only individual training in the camp area
could be undertaken. T.E.W.Ts. for officers were conducted in mufti. It was forbidden to enter Chinese
territory, but certain roads were international.

In these circumstances it is easy to see how such
exceptional conditions of confinement encouraged British
troops to exploit the pleasures of Shanghai, with its
astonishing night life : its cafés, bars, night clubs, and
super-cinemas ; and British regiments had to reckon with
a certain loss of efficiency and vitality after two or three
years in the China station. To add to the indigenous
temptations, lavish British and American civilian hospitality was readily at hand. Great efforts were made to
offer sport as the antidote to good living. Football both
soccer and rugger, was played intensively, while officers
could play polo or ride the miniature Chinese ponies on
the race-course. A strenuous paper hunt ran points of
twelve to fifteen miles. A climate which was hotter than
Bombay before the monsoon and colder than the Punjab
in winter was another enemy to physical fitness.

One duty outside the Shanghai boundary, however, did
fall to the Battalion, and it represented a welcome change
from the close city life. Chinese piracy was still an element of uncertainty in the Yangtse river trade, and the
anti-piracy guards, seldom more than one section at a
time, furnished on the ships of British trading firms, were
eagerly accepted. Sometimes, too, the larger ships of the
C.P.R. on the Hong Kong and Manilla run applied for a
guard up to platoon strength, and there was always keen
competition for the trip.

Apart from a close liaison with the other British battalions on the station and with the American Marines,
little contact was made with other international forces in
the city. The French, who had their own concession,
were in particular given to isolation.

In 1930, on the occasion of "the Glorious First of
June," when the Regimental Colour was trooped for the
first time since its presentation in 1913, the ceremony
was watched by a cosmopolitan audience which, apart

from the Chinese, included representation from the **1930**
French Army, the Italian Navy and, of course, the
popular American Marines. The demands on hospitality
were frequent, and equally frequent were the invitations
in return. On one occasion a Russian General, a former
light of the Russian Imperial General Staff, was entertained. The old Imperial Russian anthem not being
available, at the General's request the "1812 Overture"
was substituted. The full overture takes some twelve
minutes to play, and the records do not state whether the
assembled company were expected to remain at attention
throughout the overture !

In one activity at least our men were able to test out
their ability against other national Forces, and in the
International Cross-country Run the two teams entered by
the Battalion took first and second places.[3] At musketry
in 1930 the Duke of Connaught Cup for revolver shooting
was captured. Only once was the more fundamental
aspect of a British battalion's association with Shanghai
in evidence. On that occasion the 1st Worcestershire,
together with the 4th U.S. Marine Corps and Shanghai
Defence Corps, manned the boundary of the International Settlement in preparation for an assault by a
Chinese Communist Army. The army, however, was of
another vintage to that of 1950 and melted away on
reaching the boundary.

It was with few real regrets that in January, 1931, **1931**
the 1st Worcestershire handed over to the Royal Scots
Fusiliers and set sail for England on the old *Nevassa*
after a march to the docks behind the magnificent
band of their old friends, the U.S. Corps of Marines.
Three weeks later one of those rare chances in
Regimental history was to give the two Regular Battalions
of the Regiment the opportunity to meet in Malta for an
hour or so, when, as can be imagined the short time
available was put to the best purpose ! The 2nd Battalion
had already prepared a great reception. But when the
great moment came, the ship had only a few hours to
spare and there was no time for parties to go ashore.

[3] That fine runner, Capt. J. J. Abbott, who was later missing in
Norway, took first place.

1931 Representative parties of the 2nd Battalion therefore
came aboard and were welcomed with vigorous traditional hospitality. The Admiral in command stretched a
point, and a complete precedent was created when the
band and certain officers of the 2nd Battalion proceeded
to sea in H.M.S. *Worcester* from the reserve Fleet and
played the *Nevassa* into Malta for two or three miles.
The ship was not ready for sea at that time, but it was
felt that the occasion was such as demanded very particular measures and official restriction was sympatheti-
cally waived.

At Gibraltar the Battalion found another welcome
ready from "our cousins," the Royal Lincolns. The
officers accordingly dined ashore and the ship sailed in
the early hours of the morning.

On 17th February, 1931, the Battalion disembarked at
Southampton and entrained for Crownhill Barracks,
Plymouth, where, after settling in, all ranks dispersed on
a month's leave. At Plymouth there was a great reception,
the 2nd Battalion Norfolk Regiment and 2nd Battalion
Wiltshire Regiment having sent their bands to play our
men up from the station to the barracks, and thus providing a very happy ending to a journey of 10,000 miles.
The 2nd Wiltshire had been recently played out of
Shanghai by the Battalion band and it was pleasant now
to have the gesture returned.

In a sense Crownhill Barracks represented something
more than accommodation, for the 2nd Battalion had
only moved out earlier in the year. Previously, away back
in 1896, the 1st Worcestershire had once before marched
in on their return from foreign service.

The routine of Plymouth is referred to in some detail
in a later chapter when the story of the 2nd Battalion is
told ; and so the round of Crownhill Barracks, Fort
Tregantle, Wilsworthy Camp and Salisbury Plain is not
here elaborated at length. The 1st Battalion can, however, tell one story unlikely to be challenged when
competition in anecdote develops over a glass of beer or
the port has gone round on a guest night. On a certain
Sunday morning when the Battalion was at church, a call
came through from Dartmoor prison to the effect that a

mutiny had broken out, that certain prison buildings were   1931
on fire, and that the senior prison officials were prisoners
within their own prison. It took the Adjutant some time
to persuade the Commanding Officer and the Brigade
Staff that the call for assistance was genuine. One
company had then to be extracted from Divine Service,
and it is on record that under the emotional strain of the
moment, the hatless R.S.M. saluted the Padre in the
middle of his sermon, with all the precision of a ceremonial parade. The detachment was withdrawn next day
after a special party of the Plymouth police had dealt with
the affair. Two nights later, however, an emergency call
was repeated after "lights out," and so welcome was the
chance of novelty in the daily routine that sufficient fully
dressed volunteers were on parade before the R.S.M.
had time to order "Orderly Sergeants" to be sounded.
"Blimey, the troops !" was the comment of the prisoners
as the first working party left the prison in the morning.

Under Lieutenant R. E. L. Tuckey weapon training   1932
maintained a very high standard. In 1932 the Connaught
Cup (Revolver) was captured and the Battalion was well
up in the Victoria Trophy. It is of interest to note that
in the same year the 2nd Battalion were busy winning the
Victoria Trophy (abroad) in Malta. In the Individual
Revolver Cup the Battalion took 2nd, 3rd, and 4th places.
The year 1932 was indeed a "vintage" one, for at the
Western United Services Meeting Lieutenant M. E.
Newman won the Rifle Championship Challenge Cup,
while at the Southern Command Weapon Training
Meeting no less than four prizes were captured.

For the sportsman, every taste was satisfied. The
officers could enjoy tennis and cricket at the U.S. Club,
Mountwise, and golf at Yelverton. The fishermen could
catch sea-trout and salmon in the Tavy and Meavy rivers,
and the Battalion ran a syndicate near Launceston. A
most enthusiastic cricketer, Lieutenant A. T. Burlton,
initiated the "Molehills" Cricket Club at Mountwise.
All three Services used it and it had a list of good fixtures,
the club flourishing up to 1939.

At Plymouth the Battalion, under the command of
Lieut.-Colonel J. F. Leman, was a unit of 8th Infantry

1932 Brigade, which was fortunate in having at this period
two successive Brigadiers, Liddell and Brooke, who
were in later years to achieve fame ; the former as
Adjutant-General, the latter as Chief of the Imperial
General Staff.

1935   In January, 1935, the Battalion left the less exacting
life of Plymouth for the more intense conditions of
Aldershot, where it entered the 2nd Division, then under
the command of Major-General Wavell.[4] It was an era
of experiment, for the power of new support weapons
was beginning to be appreciated and mechanization was
emerging from the suspicion which had hampered progress. At the beginning of 1937 the Battalion received its
first Morris 15-cwt. trucks and 30-cwt. lorries, while
tactically the possibilities of that new element in co-
operation, the Support Company, were being explored,
the fourth rifle company being eventually sacrificed to
allow for the new set-up. The carrier, too, made its
appearance, originally as a vehicle for the .303 Vickers
machine gun.

Training at Aldershot worked to a rigid cycle of which
the Commanders of 1950 might well be envious. Days in
September were mapped out in January. The first two
months of the year were devoted to individual training,
March was allotted for sections and platoons, the company
got together in April and May, and the Battalion trained
in June.   From June to August the Tattoo took precedence over all other considerations, though somehow
Brigade Training also received attention.

At Aldershot an average rather than a brilliant standard
of sport was maintained, although there were some good
athletes, Private Benton winning the Army Mile in 1936.
But once again it was on the range that the Battalion won
distinction and full teams went to Bisley in 1935 and
1936   1936. In 1936 the Battalion won the London and Middle-
sex Rifle Association Meeting and at Bisley captured the
Roupell Cup, Sergeant G. Jones winning a silver medal.
1937 But the full triumph came in 1937, when at the Aldershot
Command Small Arms Meeting the Battalion won no less

---

[4] The late   Field-Marshal Viscount Wavell, G.C.B., G.C.S.I.,
G.C.I.E., M.C.

than ten events, with a wealth of competitors placed high 1937 up in other events. In that year Captain R. E. L. Tuckey won the Officers' (Individual) Challenge Cup and the "Best Shot of All Ranks" Challenge Cup. C.S.M. Shrimpton, who had been shooting consistently for many years, was second in the Warrant Officers' and Sergeants' Match, while the Battalion team won the Aldershot Command Match and Challenge Cup.[5]

Shooting for keen officers was not confined to the range. A syndicate shoot at Bordon was formed and there were good days after pheasant and woodcock and a few rabbits. Transport drivers acted as beaters on Wednesday afternoons in Alice Holt Wood, and on one occasion a roedeer was added to the bag.

The year 1937 was memorable as Coronation year. The Battalion was called upon to furnish a detachment of one officer and seven other ranks to march in the procession, a party of two officers and forty-three other ranks to line the streets, and a third party for less spectacular and more exacting work in connection with the camp which was to hold the "Duty Troops" in Hyde Park. The patience of the members of "J" Group in Hyde Park was certainly tested to capacity ! Small boys pulled up the pegs which had been carefully plotted to lay out the camp. It is reported that one young optimist approached the Sergeant-Major for an autograph on his peg. There is no record of the answer. A civilian walking through the lines set a tent on fire with a lighted cigarette end, and pelting rain on consecutive days churned the ground round the cook-houses and dining tents to muddy soup.

The party to line the streets camped in Kensington Gardens near the Albert Memorial. Leaving camp at 10.30 a.m., they took up position on both sides of East Carriage Drive not far from Hyde Park Corner, where for two or three hours the humour of the dense London crowds, the occasional activities of the ambulance men

---

[5] Capt. R. E. L. Tuckey, Capt. J. O. Knight, Capt. P. O. C. Ray, Lieut. J. C. Home ; C.S.M. Shrimpton ; Sergts. Hanson, Jones, Wright ; Cpls. Thacker, Hobbs ; L./Cpls. Wilson, Bird ; Pte. Bingham ; Dvr. Wyatt.

1937 and the Abbey service coming over the loud-speakers
helped to pass away a weary wait. But the great procession itself, culminating in the splendour of the Royal
Coach, was more than compensation for any physical
demand of endurance.

From the Coronation the Battalion turned to sterner
stuff and was engaged in the large manœuvres held in
Cambridgeshire, details of which never found their way
into *Firm*! It was the Coronation Tattoo at Aldershot
which next occupied their concentrated attention : and
indeed over many years the Aldershot Tattoo had come
to be regarded as a public pilgrimage equal in status with
the Royal Show, the British Industries Fair and other
events of nation-wide significance.

The Battalion contribution to the great spectacle was
to furnish a party of about 150 officers and other ranks to
take part in a scene entitled "Lodging the Colour." This
was exacting work which at one stage involved no less than
thirty-five words of command to load and fire a musket !
It seems that the Pikemen and Musketeers of good King
Charles's golden days were men of retentive memory. It
was all good fun and the "Green Company" always drew
a laugh from the spectators when such commands as
"Blow off your loose corns" and "Have-a-care to cock
your matches" sounded across the arena.

1938   In the spring of 1938, the Battalion moved to London
to take over custody of the Tower. Very appropriately, it
was at a time when a former commanding officer of the
Battalion, Colonel Faviell,[6] was Governor, while later
Field-Marshal Sir Claud Jacob,[7] our Colonel, took up the
appointment of Constable of the Tower.

Indeed, the instalment of the Field-Marshal was made
the occasion for a ceremonial parade on 24th May. Inside
the three sides of a square formed by the Battalion, the
Yeomen Warders in their full dress of knee breeches, red
coats, white frills, swords and halberts had formed up and
lent colour to a ceremony full of historic association and
interest. The King's Keys of the Tower were handed
over by the Lord Chamberlain, who was received with a

---

     [6] Lieut.-Colonel W. F. O. Faviell, D.S.O.
     [7] Field-Marshal Sir C. Jacob, G.C.B., G.C.S.I., K.C.M.G.

The Installation of Field-Marshal Sir Claud Jacob, G.C.B., G.C.S.I., K.C.M.G., Colonel of the Regiment, as Constable of The Tower of London on 24th May, 1938. The 1st Battalion, under command of Lieut.-Colonel S. A. Gabb, O.B.E., M.C., which was stationed in the Tower, was on parade. The Resident Governor and Major of the Tower was Lieut.-Colonel W. F. O. Faviell, D.S.O.

Royal Salute. The Coroner read out the King's Patent appointing Sir Claud Jacob as Constable, and the custody of the Tower was presented to him on His Majesty's behalf by the Lord Chamberlain. Such is the bare outline of a very memorable ceremonial occasion.

No account of the responsibilities at the Tower would be complete without a note of that ancient and engaging ceremony which daily marked the taking and handing over of the "Keys." The Yeoman Warder, having locked the gates of the Middle and Byward Towers, is challenged on his return by the sentry on the main guard outside the Jewel House. Then follows a dialogue which has survived the centuries.

"Halt ! Who goes there ?"

"The Keys."

"Whose Keys ?"

"King George's Keys."

"Pass, King George's Keys ; all is well."

The Guard and Escort present arms and, with a final "God preserve King George" from the Warder, answered by "Amen" from all, the Keys are taken to the house of the Resident Governor.

Life at the Tower was certainly an experience. There were constant demands for the band in full dress. On a few occasions they played outside the Tower on the wharf for the delight and entertainment of city clerks and others enjoying their sandwich lunch. But three months of little else but intensive guard duties is too much of a good thing, and the Battalion was ready enough to return to Aldershot for a short and hurried preparation before sailing for Palestine.

The Battalion notes in *Firm* at the time fully reflect the last rather crowded days at Aldershot, when a new Weapon Training Course had to be tackled, some Bren Gun Training being thrown in with the Brigade Commander's annual inspection and a month's embarkation leave for all.

In a sense 15th September, 1938, when the 1st Worcestershire sailed in H.T. *Neuralia*, marked the close of one era and the opening of another. For the Coronation, the Tower of London and the Aldershot Tattoos bore

1938   little relation to a new phase which set in with the departure for Palestine and which was to cover the next six years.

Among a great assembly gathered at the quayside were our Colonel, Sir Claud Jacob, and Brigadier-General Grogan[8] to wish our comrades God-speed and good fortune in the days to come.

---

[8] Brigadier-General G. W. St. G. Grogan, V.C., C.B., C.M.G., D.S.O.

CHAPTER TWO

THE FIRST BATTALION, 1939-1942

Palestine, Sudan, Eritrea, North Africa

FOR more than two years previous to the move to **1938**
Palestine, the situation in that very delicate corner of the
world had merited the title of "the Arab Rebellion";
and it was to participate in spasmodic operations against
the Arabs that the Battalion, under command of Lieut.-
Colonel Gabb,[1] sailed from Southampton on 15th September, 1938, disembarking eleven days later at Haifa.
No one within the unit nor among those many friends and
relations who waved their farewell at the quayside could
know that for many it would be six years before they again
set foot in England and that others were never to return.
During those years many a boy under eighteen was to
kill his first enemy, while many another was to lose his
life on the rocky heights of Eritrea or in the wind-driven
sands of North Africa.

The year in Palestine acted as a very appropriate
curtain-raiser for the sterner events to come. The Battalion found itself quartered in Bethlehem with companies
scattered about in Hebron, Deir Sha'ar and the surrounding hamlets. The daily round developed into a campaign
of clearing road-blocks, searching for arms and the
occasional skirmish with parties of Arabs. It was a war
of small but hazardous adventures. The cordoning and
searching of villages in the hills, crossing deep wadis
and ferreting in caves, combing Jerusalem, Hebron and
Bethlehem—these were the tasks which were to encourage
quick thinking and initiative, and which provided a
sufficiently exacting preliminary for the grim days ahead.
It proved extremely difficult to bring the bandits to a

---

[1] In August, 1939, Lieut.-Colonel S. A. Gabb, O.B.E., M.C., handed
over command to Lieut.-Colonel E. L. G. Lawrence, D.S.O., M.C.

1938   formal encounter and they were adepts at slipping away
before they could be engaged. Only on three occasions
could it be claimed that rebel bands were properly engaged, but as a result of these actions the Battalion was
rewarded by three M.Cs. and several M.Ms. and mentions in despatches. In addition a reward of ten shillings
for every captured rifle had its sporting appeal, and some
companies managed to accumulate as much as £80 for
their Games Funds. It was also a sniper's war, with the
enemy under the cunning leadership of one "Mansour."
Casualties were suffered and given in full return. Yet
as unlicensed arms and ammunition were captured in
many an isolated encounter, it became clear that this
curious warfare with brigands was not without its in-
trigue : for by and large the Arab was a clean fighter.
In between the shooting there was time for conducted
parties to study the Palestine of the Bible, and in particular Christmas in Bethlehem was a memorable experience.

1939   In view of the international situation, the subsequent
move to the Sudan was hardly unexpected. In May,
1939, two officers had gone to the Sudan on reconnaissance. In August the Battalion was stationed at Hebron,
with "A" Company in Jerusalem, and it was on a hot
August night that the Divisional Commander, General
O'Connor, sent for the Commanding Officer [1] and
warned him to be ready to move.

Accordingly, the Battalion embussed for Lydda in the
early hours of the morning of 25th August and entrained
for Cairo. Here a busy day was spent in the Abbassia
Barracks. Since the 1st Worcestershire was additional
to the normal Sudan establishment, a mass of "barrack"
equipment had to be picked up in Cairo and packed into
the one train which was to carry the Battalion down to
Shellal, the limit of the journey by the Egyptian railway.
At Shellal the journey on into the Sudan was by river.
The train ran alongside the three flat-bottomed paddle-
steamers, and on a hot afternoon on 30th August the
Battalion set to and transferred itself and all its equipment, including transport and barrack furniture, from
train to ship.

The next three days were spent slowly steaming up the

River Nile at a speed of three to four knots in much the **1939** same manner as Kitchener had moved some forty-two years previously.

Wadi Halfa was reached at 0100 hours on 3rd September. Once again a long-suffering quartermaster was called on to cope with a sudden situation, for information was received that two companies were to be dropped at Atbara and this entailed re-sorting out all the barrack equipment and furniture. Accordingly on 4th September "B" and "C" Companies remained at Atbara under the command of Major Knight.[2] This officer had stayed on in Jerusalem to bring on the heavy baggage, which was three days behind; for in the peculiar conditions at the time the Battalion was still in a hybrid state of war preparation on a peace-time scale.

The journey continued on by train to Gebeit, which was reached in the early hours of 5th September. Progress had been full of interest in spite of the administrative headaches. The original orders in Palestine had given no hint as to whether the route lay by land or sea, and in Cairo the sea voyage had been considered too precarious. The overland journey, however, had its compensations.

Gebeit is a bleak, unimposing township standing a thousand feet up in the hot Red Sea hills. The train journey by rail up from Wadi Halfa was not without incident. All along the line news of the war in Europe had spread and the local inhabitants had ridden in, in large numbers, on camels and donkeys to cheer the Battalion on its way. Indeed, their enthusiasm was at one point to prove an embarrassment, for they held up the first train and insisted on presenting the Commanding Officer with a large bull. The bull was hardly an appropriate passenger in the "personnel" train and he therefore was left to be picked up by the second train. Installed in comfort he then proceeded to sit down on a case of helmets, which could not have contributed to the peace of mind of a harassed quartermaster. He was stabled for several weeks at Gebeit and finally, due to

---

[2] Lieut.-Colonel J. O. Knight, D.S.O.

C

1939   the difficulty of reconciling him to Europeans, he was
       added to the menu.

1940   For the next few months until the end of March, 1940,
       the Battalion was based on Gebeit and the time was spent
       in acclimatizing, in getting to know the country and, above
       all, in inculcating the spirit of independence and the faci-
       lity to go long distances and fend for oneself. Small
       parties would disappear for days on long-distance recon-
       naissances and individually men were learning to rely
       on their own resources.

         In 1938 the Battalion had left Aldershot with its full
       equipment of Brens, mortars and anti-tank rifles. The
       Brens of the A/A Platoon were mounted in trucks ; but
       it was a new experience to mount the mortars on camels,
       a measure which was taken to bring the Battalion into
       line with the Sudan Defence Force, with whom a close
       liaison had developed. In Palestine puttees had already
       been exchanged for hose-tops and short puttees. Tunics
       or shirt-sleeves with shorts, and trousers for night wear,
       prevailed, battledress not yet having appeared. There
       was rough shooting and a few officers procured ibex.
       Shikar, always a happy medium of introduction to a
       strange country, ensured a correct and friendly relation-
       ship with the inhabitants.

         In April, 1940, "B" and "C" Companies moved from
       Atbara to Port Sudan. Later, in July, they moved on to
       Suakin, when the remainder of the Battalion moved up
       to Port Sudan, a small detachment being left behind at
       Gebeit. Italy had now entered the war and for a time
       the role was that of mobile defence with the possibility
       of Italian raids by land, sea or parachute. Responsibility
       for the defence of Port Sudan was curiously shared with
       three companies of the Egyptian Army, which apparently
       were prepared to ignore their *de jure* status of neutrality !
       In addition, at this period, in order to deceive the Italians
       as to our real strength, there was constant liaison with
       the Sudan Defence Force on distant reconnaissance.
       Ingenious efforts were made to advertise our movements
       to the full ; and this with other exaggerated subterfuges
       would, it was hoped, deceive the enemy into a belief that
       they were faced by at least a division.

Hitherto the Battalion had come directly under the 1940
G.O.C.-in-C., Sudan, Major-General Platt, while for
a period in July and August, together with the 2nd West
Yorkshire and 1st Essex, they comprised Brigadier
Marriott's 21st Infantry Brigade. In September, however,
the 5th Indian Division less 9th Brigade began to arrive
and the British Battalions were then distributed. The
Battalion came into the 29th Indian Brigade, the other
units being two fine Indian battalions, the 6/13th
Royal F.F. Rifles and 3/2nd Punjabis, the whole under
the command of a Guardsman, Brigadier J. C. O.
Marriott.[3]

During this period there were constant moves with 1941
detachments at Tokar and Suakin. The Carrier Platoon
have reason to remember Tokar as an isolated station
which must surely deserve notoriety for its habit of sand-
storms. The one unfortunate British official entertained
our officers to meals eaten out of the drawers of a table,
and he frequently had to grope his way along the hundred
yards to his office by a rope put up for the purpose.

At the end of December the whole Battalion concentrated at Gedaref, and the war diaries from 1st January,
1941, were for the first time written up with the caption
"In the Field." The 5th Indian Division under Major-
General L. M. Heath[4] were now concentrating in the
area. By day all troops dispersed and lay up hidden in
the scrub, making use of small knolls. Our planes testified to the success of the secret concentration so far as
air observation was concerned.

To follow the Battalion in its subsequent Eritrean
campaign some description of the general situation which
faced the 4th and 5th Indian Divisions at the time will
be helpful. It was clear that the mountain fortress of
Keren was the key to Eritrea, with its peaks dominating
the main road through to the coast at Massawa. Briefly,

---

[3] Brigadier J. C. O. Marriott, C.V.O., D.S.O., M.C. Later as
Major-General Sir John Marriott he commanded the London District
after the war.

[4] Major-General L. M. Heath, C.B., C.I.E., D.S.O., M.C. ("Piggy"
Heath). A former commander of the Wana garrison in Waziristan. On
12th April he left to command a corps in Malaya and was succeeded by
Brigadier A. G. O. M. Mayne, D.S.O.

1941   the plan was first to secure the line Barentu–Agordat. Barentu was the objective for 5th Indian Division, the 4th Indian Division being directed on Agordat. Once the line was in our hands, reconnaissance forward to Keren could be made.

On 19th January the Battalion embussed and crossed the Eritrean border to Tessenai, after which the Barentu road became the axis of advance. Movement was by night with tail-lights, a form of driving which in the Eritrean dust taxed the staying powers of drivers to the full. On 25th January the Brigade fought its first deliberate battle at El Gogni.

El Gogni was a small hamlet near which a low range of three knolls ran out at right angles to the Barentu road and provided the Italians with an admirable opportunity to fight a rear-guard action. The approach to the position had to be made over thorn-scrub country which afforded little cover for "C" and "D" Companies, who were to share the attack with 3/2nd Punjab.

The plan involved a right approach to the position with an attack after supporting fire on the objective from a troop of the Sudan Defence Force. In the darkness and featureless scrub direction was lost; so that when dawn broke it was revealed that "D" Company on the left was becoming involved in the attack of the Indian Battalion! On the right "C" Company had occupied a small feature some distance from the main position in the belief that they were on their objective. In the first hours of daylight, however, individual initiative and leadership were able to exploit a tricky situation. An improvised shoot on the objective by the gunners at the last moment turned the scales and the El Gogni position was taken with some forty prisoners. It was through initiative at platoon level such as that shown by Sergeant Kelly and Private Sheldon of "D" Company that the day was won, the latter receiving a Military Medal for his courage and skilful use of a Bren gun. The leadership of Major P. H. Graves-Morris was recognized with the award of a Military Cross.

From El Gogni the advance continued down the main road to Keren. On 28th January features at Tauda

and Alamah were reported as being held in strength. **1941**
The Frontier Force were accordingly directed to attack
Tauda with artillery support (6-inch howitzers), the
Battalion following 2,000 yards in rear. At Tauda the
attack was successful, and resistance which was effective
at first at Alamah was overcome by a turning move from
the south carried out by 3/2nd Punjab.

The fighting advance continued, for considerable opposition was expected at the village of Barentu. On the
evening of 29th January the Battalion moved by M.T.
to concentrate by the ridge west of the village. Barentu
lay some forty miles down the road from Tessenai. Here
the road took a sudden bend to the north round a small
rocky feature (the Fort) which the enemy had prepared
for a determined defence. To the south of the bend
the one landmark of note was a white house by a road
junction.

At 11.30 a.m. on 30th January two platoons of "A"
Company under Captain R. B. Frith first encountered
the enemy on the ridge south of the road. Two armoured
cars were sent forward and during the afternoon the ridge
was cleared. "A" Company then switched north-east
to attack the Fort, which was finally taken at the point
of the bayonet. They then settled down for the night.

At 10.30 a.m. the following morning "A" Company
were attacked by fourteen light tanks which came down
from Barentu east of the road.   But they received such
a warm welcome that they beat a hasty retreat, having
achieved nothing. Yet to advance was impossible in
face of well-dug-in machine-gun posts only 200 yards
from the Fort.

On 1st February, Captain T. J. Bowen with two platoons (from "A" and "B" Companies) attacked the posts
and successfully cleared them.   His action won him a
M.C. and Corporal Miller with him won his M.M. Meanwhile the general picture was one of a determined enemy
who had for the moment succeeded in halting the advance.
"Enemy sticking it well," was the entry in Brigadier
Marriott's diary. But the local Italians appeared not to
have realized that away to the north the 4th Indian
Division was about to capture Agordat, while 10 Brigade

1941   had moved into Biscia and had now set across country,
making for Barentu from the rear. On 2nd February our
forward patrols found Barentu deserted. The pressure
from the north had decided the matter and the Italians
left behind every evidence of a very sudden decision.

Barentu had been "A" Company's battle, and the
harassing conditions of heat, thirst and the ubiquitous
and hateful thorn bushes which they had so gallantly
withstood served as a warning of things to come.

The first phase of the operations had been successful
and the defeated Italians retired to their mountain fortress. The task of storming Keren was now given to the
4th Indian Division which was to capture the heights,
after which 29 Brigade from the 5th Indian Division
was to push through to Keren itself, which was some four
miles beyond.

Against an enemy superior in numbers and entrenched
in as formidable a position as could be found in any
mountain campaign, the attack, staged early in February,
failed.   29 Brigade was accordingly withdrawn to
Tessenai on 14th February. Here several days of intensive training in mountain warfare with supporting artillery
were put in previous to a second and final attack. Both
Divisions were now to be used, the 5th on the right of the
main road, the 4th on the left. The town of Keren, lying
some 4,300 feet above sea-level, is guarded on three sides
by mountainous country. From the direction of Agordat
a barrier of mountains lay across our line of advance
through which only the narrow Dongolaas Gorge permitted entry. Through the gorge the road and railway
climbed and twisted up to the Keren plateau. To the
left the features Cameron Ridge, Sanchil, Brigs Peak
and Mount Amba guarded Keren from the west. To the
right Happy Valley ran eastwards to the steep Acqua
Col skirting the great mass of bleak mountains which
were to test 29 Brigade; Dologorodoc, Falestoh and
Zeban.[5]

---

[5] See sketch map, p. 27. For the battle of Keren and much of the
action in Eritrea the author made constant use of "Ball of Fire," the
history of the 5th Indian Division (Gale and Polden Ltd.). He was
also extremely grateful for the use of Brigadier Marriott's personal
diary.

A major problem which three weeks of intense training had helped to solve was to bring assaulting troops
to grips with their enemy in a fit state to fight and inflict
defeat. The physical effort of climbing on soil which
crumbled under the feet, the prickly bush which cut and
tore, the weight of equipment, lack of water and the heat—
these were the enemies which first had to be met and
resisted before ever the garrison of Keren were encountered and defeated.

The new plan aimed at the capture of Fort Dologorodoc, with exploitation towards Falestoh and Zeban,
by the 5th Division while the 4th Division kept the enemy
preoccupied on Sanchil and gained the heights on the
left. It was an ambitious plan which subsequently had
to be adjusted as the battle developed. Dologorodoc was
overlooked from Falestoh, Zeban and Sanchil. But it
appeared to have one topographical advantage. The
ground behind sloped away gently, depriving the enemy
of immunity from our artillery, which hitherto he had
so frequently enjoyed through the protection of steep
slopes.

On 11th March 29 Brigade arrived in the Keren area
and on the same day Lieut.-Colonel Bucknall from the
Black Watch arrived with the Battalion. Two days later
a very popular Commanding Officer, Lieut.-Colonel
Lawrence left, and Colonel Bucknall was to see the Battalion through the grim struggle for Keren.

During the night 14/15 March, 5th Division were
brought forward and deployed in the darkness. Meanwhile at 0430 hours, 4th Division on the left had
attacked, but had not succeeded in capturing all their
objectives. Sanchil and Brigs Peak in particular remained
in the hands of the enemy. Nevertheless, General Heath
obtained permission for his attack to go in, and accordingly at 1030 hours Brigadier Messervy's 9 Brigade moved
to the attack, the H.L.I. advancing to capture "Pinnacle."
They were met by very heavy fire and by noon were
pinned to the ground short of their objective. All their
courage and endurance were then to be tested as they
lay out, unable to move in the heat of the day.

During the afternoon General Heath had made a fresh

1941 plan to attack in the darkness up the steep west slope of "Pinnacle." After desperate fighting with wild firing by the enemy in the dark, 9 Brigade were able to claim the capture of Dologorodoc, and at 0630 hours on 16th March the 2nd West Yorkshires were in control of the Fort. With the key position in our hands the stage was set for 29 Brigade to move through to capture Falestoh and Zeban.

Accordingly, on the night 16/17 March the Battalion moved up to attack Falestoh, with the 3/2nd Punjab on the left making for Zeban. The original plan timed the move for 1230 hours but the Brigadier, who had moved forward early in the evening with his unit commanders, realized that the climb would never be accomplished in the time available; and so zero was postponed to 0230 hours.

Previously no daylight reconnaissance had been possible and plans were formulated from air photographs and a sand model. The air photographs, alas, proved deceptive, and ground which had appeared to be comparatively easy to negotiate turned out to be a yawning chasm. The Battalion was pinned to a single track. Crumbling stone turned to powdered dust and in the darkness inevitably the Battalion fell behind the artillery programme. By 0730 hours on 17th March our men were clinging valiantly but precariously to the western slope of Falestoh just short of a feature Point 1552. On the left, 3/2nd Punjab were within half a mile of Zeban minor. Brigade H.Q. had been heavily shelled at Dologorodoc and the cables had been cut. At 1030 hours Lieut.-Colonel Bucknall returned to Brigade H.Q. to report the position. The forward companies were isolated on the slopes of Falestoh and were suffering heavily from fire from Zeban and Falestoh itself. With great speed Divisional H.Q. improvised an air drop of supplies, but it fell wide of the mark and recovery was quite impossible. There was nothing to do but withdraw the forward troops, and so after nightfall the Commanding Officer brought back his men to the reverse side of Fort Dologorodoc. A party of 6/13th F.F. Rifles who throughout the operation had acted as carriers for ammu-

nition, water and rations now helped in the wounded.
The losses had been cruel. Two fine Company Commanders[6] had lost their lives and three officers were
wounded.

Although the attacks on Zeban and Falestoh had failed,
the possession of Dologorodoc was a very valuable
asset and it was imperative to hang on to the ground
won. On 19th March a fierce counter-attack by an Alpini
battalion was only halted 300 yards from Brigade H.Q.
At 1000 hours General Heath and Brigadier Messervy
paid the Brigade a visit, with the result that it was decided
to relieve 29 Brigade and 9 Brigade took over the forward
area successfully. The Battalion concentrated near
"Pinnacle" and on a smaller feature near by known as
"Pimple." For the next few days some slight relaxation
was enjoyed, though constant shelling, the heat and the
difficulty of man-handling up supplies and water destroyed any chance of real rest.

The issue of the immediate capture of Keren was
still at stake. Neither Division had made its objectives.
Previously 10 Brigade had been lent to 4th Indian Division on 16th March for a costly and abortive attack
through a supposed gap in the Sanchil position which
proved not to exist. The Brigade required several days
in which to be ready again for operations. It was in this
difficult situation that General Heath suddenly hit on the
only immediate solution of the problem. If the enemy
could be surprised at night by an assault where he would
least expect it, the features known as "Railway Bumps"
in the centre, it should be possible completely to ignore
the imposing defiance of the Sanchil position. "Railway Bumps," in fact, and not Sanchil were the key to
Keren. They overlooked the enemy's road-block in the
gorge below, but they could with care and skill be approached without opposition by the railway line from the
tunnel below Cameron Ridge. For this purpose 10 Brigade were to prepare and could be ready by 23rd March.

---

[6] Major P. O. C. Ray, "C" Company. Captain R. B. Frith, M.C.,
"A" Company. Two days later Captain P. W. Kerans (attd. Brigade
H.Q.) died of wounds. Total casualties on 17th March were : 2
officers, 21 other ranks killed ; 3 officers, 52 other ranks wounded.

1941   Finally, on 25th March, after an anxious wait of dramatic suspense in the tunnel, 10 Brigade emerged in
the early hours of the morning to creep forward and
secure their objectives. Simultaneously, 9 Brigade
pushed forward to capture three small features that lay
between Fort Dologorodoc and Mount Zeban. Meanwhile
the sappers had been working desperately to clear the
road-block in the gorge. So soon as the road was open
the mobile column (Fletcher Force)[7] were to push
through, the operation being completed by the capture
of Zeban and Falestoh by 29 Brigade. At 0430 hours
on the morning of 27th March, 29 Brigade moved
through 9 Brigade's positions. The night was dark and
the approach march difficult. But within an hour 1st
Worcestershire found themselves in possession of Zeban
minor. The same story was to be told at Falestoh and
by 0730 hours 6/13th F.F. Rifles had captured Zeban
major. The enemy had had enough and as the morning
progressed white flags fluttered from the tops of the great
heights. Keren was ours.

At 1000 hours Fletcher Force pushed through the gap
and entered Keren. The 6/13th moved on to Mount
Canabai and the rest of the Brigade concentrated south
of Keren.

A few distinctive features of this hazardous mountain
battle merit a record. Thus, leading troops discovered
that metal shields reminiscent of "bow and arrow"
warfare could once again be useful against the rain of
small Italian red bombs. Yellow patches on haversacks
were used for identity purposes on the mountain side.
The problem of supply was only solved by one company
in each battalion performing "carrier" duties for trans-
porting water, food and ammunition up the steep slopes.
Later, when the Cypriot Mule Company was available,
stampeding mules terrified by gun fire were as often as
not a menace to ration and stretcher parties using the
mountain tracks. Nevertheless miracles of fine leadership
had overcome both nature and a determined enemy
who had considered himself secure in an impregnable

---

[7] Under Brigadier B. C. Fletcher, D.S.O., M.C.

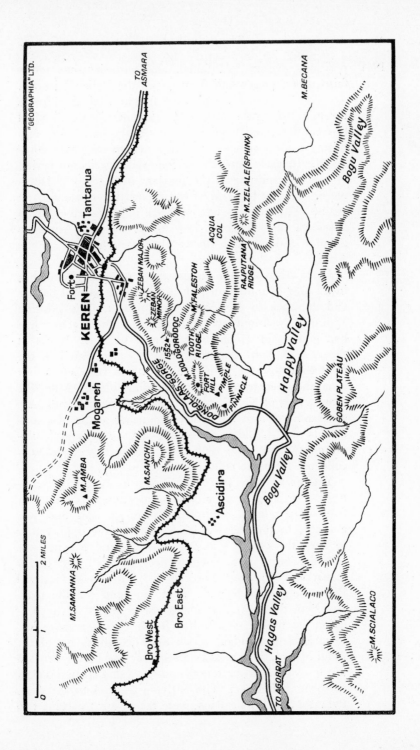

1941   position. Keren had fallen, and with it went much
faith in the boasts and promises of the Italian Dictator.

Colonel Bucknall, who had fought against sickness
through the battle of Keren, was now forced to yield
to treatment, and Colonel Knight², who had been away
raising a local camel corps, returned to take over command. In early April there followed a welcome period
of rest and training at the pleasant little town of Deca-
mere. But by the end of the month the chase was on
again. The enemy, having been quickly driven from
Massawa and Asmara, now retreated into Abyssinia
through Adowa and on to the stronghold of Amba
Alagi.

Amba Alagi was the largest and most precipitous peak
in a range of mountains which formed a natural barrier
and entrance to the Abyssinian plateau. The position
appeared wellnigh impregnable and the enemy had
had months in which to prepare its defence. It was at
the end of April that the Brigade concentrated in the
foothills below the main feature, which rises some four
thousand feet from the surrounding plain. After the
intense heat of Keren, rain and grass-covered slopes were
a welcome contrast. To meet the needs of the new conditions our M.T. drivers had suddenly to become "mule-
minded," and some 800 local donkeys were rapidly
collected from the countryside.

Yet the vast size of the position was in fact its weak-
ness. For heights of such natural strength covering a
front of ten miles required a larger garrison than was
available to the enemy. It also offered the opportunity
to keep the enemy guessing, and General Mayne⁴ was
able to deliver a thoroughly deceptive left and centre
thrust with Fletcher Force and 3/18th Royal Garhwal
Rifles before 29 Brigade were deployed for the main
attack on the right. On the night of 3rd May the Battalion assembled in a nullah just north of a long, low
feature, Sandy Ridge, which extended south up to the
Alagi Massif. The attack on 4th May had been entrusted
to the two Indian battalions, and well and truly did they
perform their tasks. The outlying features to the west,
Pyramid and Whale Back, were taken, but to attempt to

advance farther against the main position was considered   1941
too expensive. The Brigadier therefore postponed the
final assault until the early hours of 5th May. Before
dawn 3/2nd Punjab had secured Middle Hill, which
nestled under the northern slopes of Alagi. Half an hour
later Captain F. E. Baker led the Battalion to Little
Alagi. The first rays of the sun were on the hill-tops and
a gallant assault was stopped by wire and machine-gun
fire from two features to the east, Bald Hill and Little
Alagi. One platoon did in fact penetrate the wire, but
the Battalion was pinned to the ground, unable to move.
There on the slopes of Amba Alagi our men lay for the
rest of that day. It says much for their patience that
when within range of enemy mortars and machine
guns they were able to keep sufficiently still to prevent
the enemy from realizing the magnificent target which
lay in front of them. In the circumstances the casualties
were not heavy—8 killed and 28 wounded—and so at
1800 hours orders to withdraw went out. By midnight
the Battalion were concentrated on ground north of
Whale Back and the attack of 29 Brigade had been definitely checked.

During the engagement Captain F. E. Baker was
killed. He had served in the Regiment first as a Boy
and was one of the first Warrant Officers to receive his
commission. With his death the Battalion was deprived
of the last of its Company Commanders who had faced
the campaign before Keren, three having been killed and
one wounded.

In the subsequent fighting the Alagi position was
never really mastered, though for three weeks the Battalion was able to overlook the Italian line of communication from Amba Alagi up to Addis Ababa ; and it
was not until the 1st South African Brigade appeared
suddenly and established themselves on the far side of
the mountains, with their guns shooting into the enemy
gun positions from the rear, that the Duke of Aosta with
some 20,000 Italians and hundreds of vehicles capitu-
lated. From the Battalion came a contribution of 19
officers, 381 Italian other ranks and 18 colonials, all
M.T. personnel. On 20th May the Battalion had the

1941 privilege of forming the guard of honour for the Italian
viceroy when, rightly, he was allowed to lead his troops
out with the full honours of war.

"The Glorious First of June" was celebrated round
a camp fire with a sing-song and plentiful beer. A rifle
meeting was held and the R.S.M. was able to produce
a live sucking pig draped in the regimental colours !

For six weeks after Amba Alagi the Battalion was busy
mopping up, to be followed by a return to Asmara and
three weeks' rest and holiday. The opportunity was
taken to overhaul all transport in Italian workshops,
only to have to part later with vehicles urgently needed
elsewhere. In the meanwhile 5th Indian Division, leaving 29 Brigade in Eritrea, moved to Cyprus. Thus for
the 1st Worcestershire did the Eritrean phase end. It
had been a type of warfare and a struggle as different
from that which was to follow as was the North African
campaign from the later days in France. But it had been
no less exacting in its demands of endurance and leadership.

*   *   *   *   *

At the end of July the Brigade was transferred via
Egypt to the Western Desert, where at first it operated
as an independent brigade directly under Army H.Q.,
later coming under the 2nd South African Division. The
move to Egypt was made by sea, and after the heights
of Asmara a temperature of 120 degrees in the shade at
Massawa was not appreciated ! So intense was the heat
that fifty of the Indian ranks who had had to spend
the day lying-up on the ship in harbour suffered death
from heat stroke. There followed four hot, uneventful
days at sea and the Battalion disembarked at Port Tewfiq
on 5th August, and put in a month's intensive training
in the canal zone at Ismailia, entraining for Burq el
Aarab on 9th September.

Burq el Aarab lies some twenty miles down the
Matruh coastal road from Alexandria, and the thought of
regular sea bathing visibly sent up morale ! Indeed,
the introduction to the desert and its new conditions
was generally deceptively pleasant and by easy stages.
The next few days were spent in getting acquainted with

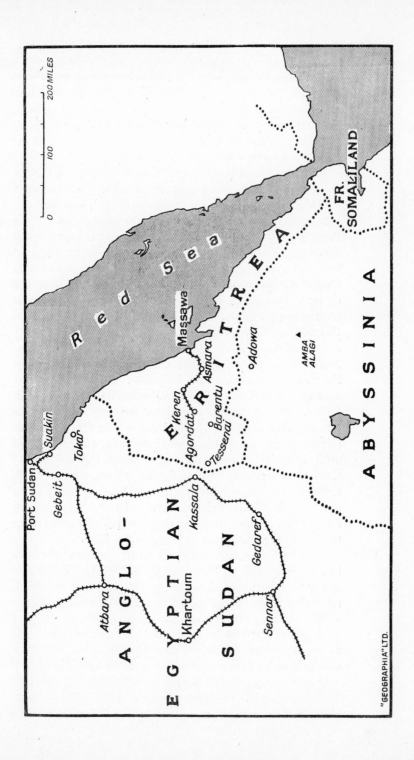

1941   the new conditions, and M.T. exercises across the desert were the basis of training. On 3rd October the Battalion moved to the area of the Siwa oasis and the month passed with officers away at the Middle East Training School, with inspections and, last but not least, an abundant variety of excellent dates available for all.

At Siwa the Long Range Desert Group had been formed with a sub-group in the Siwa oasis. In September 29 Brigade took on the role and title of "oasis group," with the Battalion at Siwa and the remainder of the Brigade forward at Giarabub. One company again was detached eighty miles to the west at Williams Pass, so that the group constituted a very scattered command. Desert exercises continued to be the order of the day and all ranks became thoroughly at home with the intricacies of the sun-compass. From Siwa a move was made to Giarubub, where desert operations consisting mainly of long-distance raids constantly demanded the application of those habits of quick thinking accumulated since the more leisurely days of Palestine. In mid-December a sudden order was received to move back to Mena, in Egypt. The move was completed by train on 24th December, and in order to allow more time for Christmas festivities the celebration of Christmas was postponed until 26th December. After the desert the delights of Cairo were welcome enough for a few days, with football, hockey, and cross-country runs to balance the joys of the city. But such brief relaxation hardly compensated for the loss of the entire transport, which was taken away to fill the gaps for units fighting in the desert.

1942   Back in Cairo rumours came in of German successes in the desert, and on 16th January the brief period of rest came to an abrupt conclusion. Vehicles of doubtful reliability were rushed up from a New Zealand Brigade on the Canal, a certain amount of stores were issued, and on an order franked "most immediate" a move was made to the outskirts of Alexandria. Thence, once again the course was set into the Western Desert, and a march of 400 miles brought the Battalion within thirty miles of Tobruk, where it rejoined its old brigade. The Brigade bivouac area lay in some scrub bordering the main

Sollum–Tobruk road and was consequently a happy 1942
hunting ground by night for enemy aircraft. Someone
in the Battalion ingeniously improvised an A/A mounting
for an anti-tank rifle and after shooting up a particularly
low-flying machine on the road there was little further
trouble. On 14th February the whole Brigade took over
the defence of Tobruk, with the Battalion widely dispersed and responsible for the defence of the Southern
face.

The Brigade role now changed. Though still an independent formation under Army H.Q., it was sent off to
the south-west to its old hunting ground, where it was
told to watch the left flank of the desert army. Thus
three months went by during which the Brigade
developed a high degree of mobility, with security as a
happy complement. Soon it was able to halt and put down
effective all-round protection, wired, mined and stocked
up with ammunition and water, within a few hours.
These "boxes" were, in fact, strongholds from which
mobile columns could operate against the enemy's
L. of C. if he should make a sudden sweep to the east.
Company columns were formed and officers and men were
attached to the various "jockols" which dominated no-
man's-land between our forces and the enemy.

May, 1942, found the Battalion at the extreme southern
end of our defences running through Agheila, guarding
the left flank which was held by the French Foreign
Legion. A Brigade Box had been formed at Bir el Gubi.

Such was the situation when in the second week of
May the German-Italian bid for the conquest of Egypt
was launched. Enemy columns moving far to the south
had outflanked our main position and carried out a daring
raid on our communications near Bel Hamid, some 200
miles behind our forward positions. The Brigade was
therefore hurriedly withdrawn from Bir el Gubi and
moved back to the Sollum area by Sidi Rezegh, where it
was hoped to contact the enemy forces. But a highly
mobile enemy had withdrawn and a defensive position
was therefore taken up, the Battalion sector lying along
an escarpment covering Sidi Rezegh. The first three
days in June were spent in preparing the rocky escarp-

D

1942 ment for defence. Nevertheless on 1st June once again
the traditional occasion was observed. Beer arrived in the
nick of time, and in the evening the officers entertained
the sergeants.

Meanwhile patrols in M.T. were combing the desert,
and it was one of these which returned to report that they
had discovered an A.D.S. which had been completely
wiped out by the enemy, the M.O. orderlies, ambulance
drivers and patients being found, shot dead. Round
about the area lay the black hackles of the Italian Ariete
Division.

There followed a few days when the Battalion was
shuffled between Bel Hamid and Sidi Rezegh, according
to the changing information of enemy movement and
intentions. The area round Bel Hamid contained large
petrol and supply dumps which constituted extremely
attractive objectives for a bold enemy. Sunday, 7th
June, was spent in the Bel Hamid area; but that night
orders were received to rendezvous south of Acroma.
The Battalion now left 29 Brigade and became a small
independent force with 62nd Battery, 3rd Field Regiment, "A" Troop, 3rd Light A/A Battery, "A" Troop,
"B" Battery, 95th Anti-Tank Regiment and a section
20th Field Company, I.E., all under command.

In general the situation in the Western Desert was
critical. Rommel's panzers were sweeping on from
Benghazi and we had lost more tanks than we could
afford. In these circumstances a decision, which, of
course, was not generally known, had been taken to
withdraw the Gazala line which ran from Bir Hakim
to the sea, eastwards to Tobruk. It was this phase which
was to furnish the 1st Worcestershire with perhaps its
most challenging opportunity to prove itself a worthy
custodian of the motto "Firm," an opportunity which was
fully accepted.

The line was being held by the 50th British Division
and 2nd South African Division, while away to the south
were the Free French and the Foreign Legion. The left
of the line was to withdraw first, the main covering position being Knightsbridge, which lay some twenty-five
miles south-west of Tobruk and had been organized,

among others, by the Guards Brigade. Generally the intention was that a series of boxes were to cover the retreat from the Gazala line, and accordingly the Battalion and its invaluable satellite units received orders to establish a box at Point 187, some six miles south of Acroma.

The Battalion arrived at 1800 hours on 8th June and a site was selected astride a small ridge running through Point 187, covering a strong gun line behind the ridge.

Away to the south the site commanded all the ground up to Rigel, four miles away, while behind the Rigel ridge, again another four miles beyond, was Knightsbridge.

To the north were some sandy patches which later proved invaluable, while beyond again lay a flat open plain for some six miles, running up to an escarpment 50 to 100 feet high, at the back of which ran the main road from our forward line to Tobruk.

The box constructed was a square, the sides being about 1,000 yards, protected by a minefield eventually all round to a depth of 500 yards with mines at a density of one every yard. Two dummy fields were constructed to run out from each flank. Inside the box, two forward companies, "D" and "A," held the southern face, the two supporting companies covering the sides and rear. The eight 2-pounder anti-tank guns were sited to cover the south, west and east faces with direct fire, while "B" Battery, 95th Anti-Tank Regiment, and the three Bofors of the 3rd Light A/A Battery covered the sides and rear. The battery of 25-pounders was located in the northern half of the box with the guns deeply bulldozed into the ground, making full use of the sandy patches with camouflage nets. Forward observation posts could cover the whole front of the position.

The defences of supporting companies were comparatively easy to construct, but those of the forward companies, in full view of the country to the south and in rocky ground, had to be dealt with by compressors at night. In particular, "D" Company were unable to dig deep. The average depth of a slit trench was about one foot, after which solid rock prevented digging. Sand-bags

1942 and stone sangars were built up to add protection, but
it was meagre and did not add to the comfort of the battle
to come.

On 11th June the Corps Commander visited the box
and stressed the seriousness of the situation. We had apparently lost large numbers of tanks and it seemed that
the enemy would soon be knocking at the door. Nevertheless 12th June passed quietly, save for large numbers of
enemy planes which flew over and seemed to ignore our
presence.

During the morning of 13th June fighting to the south
developed and heavy shelling and dive-bombing attacks
could be observed on the Scots Guards box at Rigel.
At 1400 hours the enemy attacked the Rigel position, and
by 1700 hours he appeared to have penetrated the defences. Some of our tanks came up from the east and put
in an attack, and as dusk fell our forward companies could
watch the fantastic spectacle of a modern tank battle in
a fading light, with tracer shells cruising lazily backwards
and forwards and occasional bursts of machine-gun
tracer ricocheting off the rocks, more reminiscent of a
public festival than a grim matter of life and death. That
night (13/14 June) the fog of war was on. Patrols
sent out to the south could not penetrate far owing to
enemy tanks. In the meanwhile the Battalion with troops
under command had come under 2nd South African
Division, and with only one W/T link with the Division
by key, news was scarce, while stragglers from the
Scots Guards and Sherwood Foresters gave contradic-
tory reports of the evacuation of Knightsbridge and
Rigel. At this stage two tanks of our 22nd Armoured
Brigade entered the minefield in front of "D" Company.
One was later salvaged, but the other was set alight the
following morning and, alas, acted as an excellent rang-
ing point for the enemy for the remainder of the action.
Hitherto in the night ranging shells had fallen in the
Battalion position and the sapper mine-laying parties
had some very uncomfortable moments.

With the dawn of 14th June it was clear that Knightsbridge had been evacuated and the box was now isolated.
Its fall would open the way for the enemy to our main

line of communication along the coast. It was therefore
with a grim realization of its heavy responsibility that
the Battalion met and held the attack of what proved to
be over sixty German tanks, supported by lorried infantry. The battle opened after breakfast. The enemy
tanks came forward cautiously and their tank commanders could be seen scanning our positions with their
field-glasses. They presumably had a fair knowledge of
what they were up against from air photographs taken
the day before. Their heavier guns sought out our gun
lines, whereas their leading tanks concentrated on our
small anti-tank guns inadequately dug in on the forward
slopes, though camouflaged as much as possible.

The anti-tank guns had orders to hold their fire until
the enemy tanks were at the outer perimeter of the wire.
Their first burst appeared to take the Germans by surprise and several tanks were hit. Simultaneously "A"
Company engaged the enemy, who replied with heavy
machine-gun fire all along the face of the box and the
battle developed fast and furiously. It was at this stage
that Major D. H. Nott, seeing a forward Bren gun of
"D" Company jammed, dashed 150 yards down the
slope of the position through a hail of machine-gun
bullets, got it firing and had some excellent shooting at
the Germans on the face of the mine-field. His very
gallant action resulted in a large number of enemy
casualties. Even so, in spite of many a heroic individual
encounter and a grim tenacious defence, more and more
German tanks swarmed around. With the wind getting
up from the south, a dust-storm set in, whilst dust from
enemy tanks twisting and turning outside the box increased the confusion. Our anti-tank guns were doing
magnificent work in spite of many casualties. Captain
F. N. Lynes, who was later awarded an M.C. for his
action, moved from gun to gun in the face of heavy fire,
exhorting his men to even greater efforts, but they had
little chance against the heavy Mark IV tanks, although
they managed to knock out a few. At 1000 hours Captain
Sargent arrived with a convoy of much-needed mortar
bombs and also the beer ration. He had driven some four
miles across the desert under heavy shell fire. Our mor-

1942   tars were now doing some splendid shooting. The enemy
appeared to be deceived by the dummy minefield and
averse to working round the flanks. Three of his tanks
which had found their way round were set on by the
25-pounders and two were immediately knocked out, the
third scuttling away through the dust haze.

By noon the German artillery had the measure of the
box and were searching out our 25-pounders. The area
reeked with smoke, bursting explosives and churned-up
earth from the heavy shelling. Some twenty tanks had
been accounted for by the anti-tank guns and 25-pounders.
But in the process nearly all our anti-tank guns had been
knocked out.

At 1300 hours a lull in the shelling gave an opportunity
for some platoons to snatch a meal, while a heartening
message of congratulations from the Army Commander
was some consolation for the lack of response to requests
for aircraft and tank support.

By 1400 hours the enemy had brought up more heavy
guns and the shelling again began. The sand-storm
still raged and the flying sand was keeping many L.M.Gs.
out of action. German infantry, taking advantage of the
heavy dust-storm, were now brought up and in the few
fleeting opportunities of clear visibility "B" Company
had some wonderful rifle and mortar shooting. Through
the storm glimpses of enemy tanks could be caught as
they profited from the cover of nature, with their mine
detector parties now working well into the southern,
western and eastern faces of the box. By the afternoon
the shortage of water and the terrible dust had brought
on intense thirst. "D" Company never had the opportunity to drink the beer ration so gallantly brought in by
Captain Sargent. The Commanding Officer, Colonel
Knight, visited the slit trenches of the forward troops
and himself directed the battle, exposing himself to heavy
machine-gun fire, and by his personal disregard for danger
instilling great confidence into his men.

At 1700 hours, with the shelling increasing and the
battle now raging on all sides, a mutilated message
in cipher came through from the 2nd South African
Division which closed with "leave immediately." But

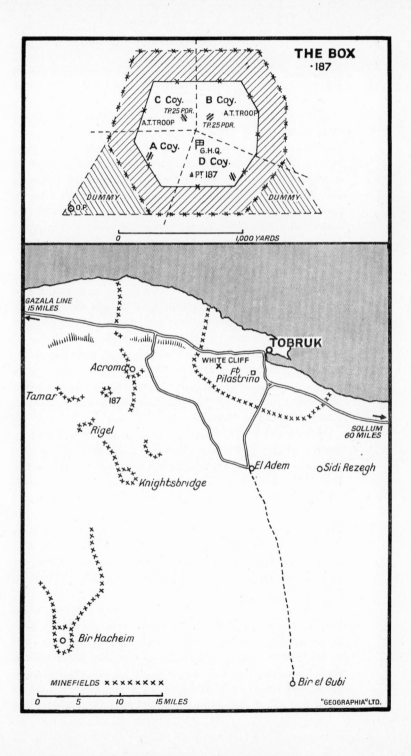

THE BOX
·187

C Coy.
TP. 25 PDR.
A.T. TROOP

B Coy.
A.T. TROOP
TP. 25 PDR.

A Coy.
G.H.Q.
D Coy.
▲ PT 187

DUMMY
DUMMY
△ O.P.

0   1,000 YARDS

GAZALA LINE
15 MILES

TOBRUK

WHITE CLIFF
Ft
Pilastrino

Acroma

Tamar
187

Rigel

Knightsbridge

El Adem
○ Sidi Rezegh

SOLLUM
60 MILES

Bir Hacheim

Bir el Gubi

MINEFIELDS ××××××××

0   5   10   15 MILES

"GEOGRAPHIA" LTD.

1942   with the battle at its height a message was sent back to
the effect that at that moment it was quite impossible
to break off the engagement.

As evening drew on it was obvious that it could be
only a matter of time before the box would be completely overrun. German tanks had penetrated well
within the wire and it was therefore decided to attempt
a withdrawal. Thus the last and most difficult phase of
the day was initiated, verbal orders being delivered in
most cases personally by the Adjutant, Captain R. L.
Dray, who was subsequently awarded a bar to his M.C.
for his extremely gallant conduct throughout the engagement. The final German assault of the box, which the
Commanding Officer was able to watch, was a timid
affair, the enemy being obviously shy of entering a trap
which had inflicted so much loss on his armour and
infantry. A very gallant rear-guard action by a platoon
under Lieutenant J. J. Horton contributed to a day of
heroism. By laying lines of booby traps in front of his
position, Horton was able to blow the first two or three
waves of advancing infantry sky high, and his platoon
accounted for most of the German casualties in the south-
east corner of the "box."

Within the scope of a chapter it is not possible to do
justice to the individual skill and gallantry with which
all ranks withdrew northwards to Acroma. So far as was
humanly possible all that could not be moved was destroyed. The majority of the wounded were evacuated
by carrier or ambulance. A certain number were too
severely injured to be moved, and the Padre, the Rev.
R. N. de B. Welchman, gallantly stayed behind to look
after them and accept the fate of a prisoner. Two platoons remained to cover the withdrawal and fought to
the end.

Companies withdrew in good order back to the main
road five miles to the north, where welcome M.T. took
them on into Tobruk. Colonel Knight was the last man
to leave the "box." Throughout the day his personal
leadership had been an inspiration to his officers and men.
Dusk had set in and, aided by the flying dust, casualties
were few since the ground northwards to Acroma was

covered. Thus the battle drew to its close and officers
who had watched throughout the day through field-
glasses expressed their amazement at the tough resistance
and orderly withdrawal. The final enemy losses were
totalled as thirty-five tanks, one large recovery vehicle
and very large numbers of infantry lorries. A year later
the debris of battle still lay around in grim evidence. In
the minefield alone 120 Germans and 60 of our comrades
lay unburied. In the years to come, Point 187 will surely
become a pilgrimage of faith for those of the Worcestershire Regiment who chance to pass that way.

Three or four miles to the north-east of Acroma lay
the village of Tobruk with its harbour, guarding the main
road east to Bardia. It was to Tobruk, then, that the Battalion withdrew passing under the command of 201st
Guards Brigade on 14th June, and once again coming
under its old commander, Brigadier Marriott. It had
originally been intended after the fight to withdraw into
reserve. But the Scots Guards had been sent back to
Alexandria and the Battalion took its place in the Guards
Brigade. It had lost all its anti-tank guns, most of its
mortars, and there was no troop-carrying transport.
Nevertheless the approximate strength stood at just over
500 all ranks and morale ran high. The 15th and 16th
June were spent in re-equipping, a "counter-attack"
role being allotted from a reserve position near Fort
Pilastrino in the heart of the Tobruk area. After a quick
reconnaissance company areas were allotted and defences
prepared.

A determined enemy attack now opened on the outer
defences, and by the afternoon of 20th June the enemy
were well inside the perimeter away to the east and had
overrun the Coldstream Guards and Sherwood Foresters.
Within the Battalion sector, in spite of a "counter-attack"
role, no chances had been taken and in three days as much
was done to prepare the position for defence as was
humanly possible. Where compressors were available
good progress was made. But work had to start from
scratch and much of it was on solid rock.

Information was again very meagre, but on the morning
of 20th June it became clear that the enemy were staging

1942 a full-scale attack with the object of breaking into Tobruk.
As the morning progressed it was known that a concen-
trated enemy attack on a narrow front in the Mahratta
Regiment's area away to the east on the Bardia road had
penetrated the defences, and at midday a tank counter-
attack, supported by two companies of the Coldstream
Guards, was unsuccessful. The fog of war now descended
completely and by 1800 hours communications with
Brigade H.Q. were cut. Later an officer sent to locate
Brigade found that it had been overrun. Since no contact could be made with any formation, the Commanding
Officer decided to stand on his ground and hold the position with all available troops. Throughout the night
the position was therefore strengthened, and it will be
readily understood with what dismay in the early hours
of the morning orders were received from an officer
from Divisional H.Q. that all guns and stores were to
be destroyed. The battle was over and the implication
was that at Force H.Q. a decision to capitulate had been
taken. If this decision could have been communicated
at the time it was made, undoubtedly many more could
have finally found their way out. In the meanwhile a
South African Colonel with twenty-four field guns and
part of a company of the Coldstream Guards had joined
the Battalion to strengthen the defence, and it was indeed
a black moment when, in the words of the Commanding
Officer,[2] a unit "in good heart and with their tails well
up" was ordered to destroy its guns and cease fighting.

All efforts to contact higher formations having failed,
the Commanding Officer determined to make at least a
bid for escape. Alas, the few vehicles the Battalion had
had with it had been sent off the day before to take cover
from bombing in valleys running down to the sea. Had
these been available a certain number might have found
their way out of Tobruk.

Previously, on the evening of 20th June, the Second-
in-Command, O.C. H.Q. Company and Carrier Platoon
Commander[8] had been sent to try and find a gap through
which the Battalion might break out and take its chance.

---

[8] Major R. E. L. Tuckey. Captain C. G. Burke. Captain R. H.
Keith-James.

Eventually a point was found a few hundred yards from   1942
"White Rock," which was a small feature on the edge
of the perimeter to the south. But their luck was out.
The enemy were too thick on the ground and the small
party was eventually captured.

In a last effort to escape on 21st June, Company Columns attempted to make their way independently to
White Rock. But by then the net had closed. The transport had found it impossible to reach White Rock from
the sea and so Company Columns arrived to find no
transport. Major Tuckey and some of the Carrier Platoon had cleared a path through the mine-field, but the
issue was placed beyond doubt by the appearance of
Mark IV tanks. Eventually the Adjutant and 29 men
from Tobruk managed to escape with superlative skill.
In addition, two officers and 36 men from the Acroma
box were collected later at the Infantry Base Depot at
Geneifa. From among these a small nucleus, which
included Captain Dray and some of his men, was selected
to return to England and formed the hard core round
which the Battalion was once again to take shape.

The subsequent fate of all other officers and men as
prisoners should be briefly recorded if only to indicate
that at this stage the fickle Italian enemy was by no
means a lamb of innocence as compared with his German
ally, as sometimes the tolerant historian would have us
believe. Officers were separated from other ranks and
were flown over to Italy. Only the Commanding Officer,
in the courageous hope that he might be able to alleviate
hardship and later organize a break-out, disposed of his
badges of rank and was able for a time to remain with his
men.

A p.o.w. cage of about 30,000 men was formed in
Tobruk, and our men had the humiliating experience of
seeing plenty of good food and ammunition in undestroyed
dumps pass to the enemy. There would therefore seem
little excuse for the "starvation" level of rations which all
ranks received as prisoners. Corporal Hughes[9] records

---

[9] For a vivid and refreshing account of life with the 1st Battalion
throughout its North African campaign there is available the "Adventures of Corporal M. B. Hughes, M.M.," in *Firm* of April, 1946.

1942 that his ration after Tobruk was salt water to drink and three ounces of bully with a biscuit a day, a statement which others have claimed as a generous over-estimation. Nor is it easy to forget the conditions under which our men were subsequently evacuated to Italy; conditions which well merited the analogy of treatment like cattle. In Tobruk one or two attempts were made to escape from the "cage," and of these none was more stirring than that of a small party under Lieutenant Ian Bain who managed to reach the boundary wire before they were all wounded and recaptured.

Later a few, including Lieutenant Bain, were to make their way to England ; and Major Keith-James, who successfully tunnelled his way out of Chieti camp and rejoined the Eighth Army on 4th November, 1943, has a story to tell which deserves a permanent record. Thus another chapter in the history of Farrington's Regiment of Foot closed in a manner which would have won the approval of the veterans of Neuve Chapelle and which was subsequently marked with the award of three Military Crosses and four Distinguished Conduct Medals.

CHAPTER THREE

THE FIRST BATTALION, 1943–1944

Normandy

It was a proud day for the Regiment when, on 1st January, 1943, the 1st Battalion once again paraded at Harrow to carry on the task which for six months had reluctantly been laid aside.   **1943**

The disbanded 11th Battalion formed the basis of the reconstituted unit, but shared the honours of the occasion in a joint Ceremonial Parade.[1] A Special Order of the Day was read out by Brigadier-General Grogan and both Field-Marshal Sir Claud Jacob and Lieut.-General Sir A. Smith, Commanding London District, were present. On 5th January, 1943, the Battalion Colours were laid up in Worcester Cathedral, where they were to remain until received again three years later on 20th February, 1946.

By 1st February the Battalion had assumed the new Establishment.[2] Headquarters were in Roxborough Avenue, Harrow, with the Support Company in the Drill Hall and other companies scattered around at Eastcote, Northolt and Ruislip. This was to remain the Battalion locality until August. In March equipment in profusion started to arrive, and it was good to receive 6-pounder anti-tank guns in place of the 2-pounders with which the Battalion had had to fight their desert battles.

In April the Carrier, Anti-Tank and Mortar Platoons were down to hard training at Ashdown. The Battalion

---

[1] Only a cadre of two officers and ten N.C.Os. from Tobruk were present with the reconstituted Battalion on 1st January, 1943. Their names appear in Major D. Y. Watson's "First Battalion the Worcestershire Regiment in N.W. Europe."

[2] Throughout the war the normal establishment remained, Battalion H.Q., H.Q. Company, "A," "B," "C" and "D" Companies, and the Support Company, consisting of Carrier Platoon (12 carriers in four sections), Mortar Platoon (3-inch), Anti-Tank Platoon (6-pounder), Pioneer Platoon.

1943   remained at Harrow until August, when it moved in turn
to Wanstead, Maresfield and finally to Hythe. Throughout this period it formed part of the 33rd Guards Brigade
Group. In September a move was made to Maresfield in
Sussex, where it joined the 214th Infantry Brigade.[3]
This Brigade had previously entered the 43rd (Wessex)
Division,[4] replacing an Army Tank Brigade, the Division
having changed from armoured status to that of
infantry.

By the middle of November the Battalion had arrived
at Hythe. Of those who had served in Tobruk only
Captain Dray, the former Adjutant, and some fifteen
other ranks were present to represent the unit which
had fought in Eritrea and North Africa.

For the next six months all ranks were absorbed in the
preparation for the great task ahead. Not only was it a
matter of working up to a high standard of physical
fitness, of perfecting men in the use of their weapons and
studying co-operation with tanks, but the duplication of
specialists had to be ensured and a very high level of
administration attained, so that if necessary each battalion
could fight its own battle from its own resources when
over the other side.

1944   In February, 1944, the Battalion put in a short spell
in billets at Worthing, where the South Downs offered
excellent opportunities for firing off an enormous amount
of ammunition with all weapons. They returned to Hythe
and were eventually rewarded for so much concentrated
effort by 75 per cent. of the strength qualifying as First
Class shots and by every man being able to handle the
6-pounder and 3-inch mortar. Accordingly the red
lanyard for First Class shots was inaugurated.

There followed in quick succession an inspection of the
Brigade by Field-Marshal Montgomery, coupled with a
few friendly words in an informal address, and the
250th anniversary of the founding of the Regiment.
Brigadier-General Grogan inspected the Battalion and
his subsequent address reflected the dramatic nature of

---

[3] Other units of the Brigade were 5th D.C.L.I. and 7th Somerset L.I.
[4] Commander, Major-General G. I. Thomas, C.B., D.S.O., M.C.
Throughout the campaign the Battalion fought in 43 Division.

the unknown future. Today a plaque in the Parish
Church at Hythe commemorates the ceremony.

By the end of March all ranks were fully keyed up and
training became more specialized. On 15th April a
move was made to Heathfield Park, which proved to be
the concentration area for operation "Overlord," the
mighty project which was to launch the Invasion Army
for the coast of Normandy. Loading trials, waterproofing,
rope climbing and swimming in the Park were the order
of the day. Loading had to receive particular care since
it became clear that transport and kit were to be pared
down to the minimum. This was due to the fact that no
space was provided for the Divisional Recce Regiment.
So keen was the Divisional Commander on taking this
precious unit with him that battalions had to sacrifice
space to allow it to be included.

May came, and there was time to spare for a little
cricket. French maps and detailed Guide Books arrived,
while at Corps Headquarters a top secret conference put
heart into all ranks, for in a manner which had now
become familiar the gist of Field-Marshal Montgomery's
estimate of the approaching operation was handed down
to the private soldier. With a shortage of officers the
Canadian Army was drawn on to lend officers to the
British Army, and the Battalion therefore welcomed the
arrival of three Canadian Officers—Lieutenants Hunt,
Bennett and Brigider. With them came Major A. A.
Grubb, who was later to play an important part in directing the interests of the Battalion. At the same time over
one hundred officers and men had reluctantly to be sent
away as first reinforcements. It was soon evident that
D Day might well interfere with the "Glorious First of
June"! Nevertheless, when the annual regimental occasion arrived no move had been made and permission was
given to celebrate on a modest scale. In the afternoon the
fun fair on the cricket ground at Heathfield Park, to
which each platoon contributed a side-show, was a
tremendous success. At one stage two Generals were
competing vigorously to "Wet the Worcestershire
Wench" for three shots a penny.

At last the great day came. The Battalion was to move

1944   in three parties, a small advanced party on D+7, the M.T.
on D+10, and the marching party on D+12, the under-
standing being that the M.T. would join up at sea with
the marching party, while the advanced party would be
ready on the other side. Such are the chances of war that
none of these calculations worked according to plan. It
was at 0730 hours on 16th June that the main party under
Lieut.-Colonel A. R. Harrison marched out of a well-
camouflaged tented camp in the marshalling area at
Filham Park, some twenty miles from Heathfield, and
embarked for Newhaven. Water-sterilizing tablets and
"Mae Wests" had been issued with a final supply of
chocolate and cigarettes. The M.T. in the meanwhile
had made for Tilbury. Having embarked successfully in
"Landing Craft Infantry" they were taken ashore to
stretch their legs due to a delay, only to re-embark in a
great hurry on the *Canterbury*, which in peace time was
familiar to passengers to the Continent in the service of
the old Southern Railway.

Not the least of the initiations which arose from order
and counter-order was a matter of transferring some 130
bicycles of "D" Company from the L.C.Ts., into which
with great difficulty they had been put away, to the
Canterbury.

When darkness came the ship moved out and a diversion was enjoyed when one of the ship's anti-aircraft
gunners, against all orders, successfully shot down a
flying bomb. It was thought that flying bombs, when
hit, might land in Newhaven. Nevertheless, the disregard
of orders on this occasion was not unpopular with the
mass of passengers on the *Canterbury*. Only a short move
out to sea was made that evening and it was not until the
following afternoon that the ship sailed. By dusk the
Isle of Wight was sighted, where a vast amount of
shipping lay at anchor. With a tot of rum in the cocoa
all ranks slept soundly, and on 18th June the *Canterbury*
with four other ships made the crossing without any close
escort.

At 1700 hours the coast of Normandy could be seen
with an even greater array of ships lying off the beaches.
On the left H.M.S. *Rodney* was blazing away in the

direction of Caen, where enemy planes and our own
aircraft were playing about in the patches of anti-aircraft
fire.

The sea was choppy, for the small convoy was the first
to make the crossing after the recent heavy gale. At one
moment it seemed as if disembarkation might be
delayed. But finally orders came through. Four Assault
Landing Craft were filled and made for the shore, the
first one touching down at 1920 hours at a map reference
918869, some three miles east of Arromanches.

Once ashore the Battalion moved up to the marshalling
area just west of Crepon and dug into shallow slits,
awaiting further orders. At about 2000 hours orders
arrived to concentrate south of Manvieux and eventually,
after trusting a subaltern who led the column to a point
just north of Bayeux and then disappeared, the Battalion
and 5th D.C.L.I. found its way to the new area just before
dawn. As yet there were no signs of Brigade H.Q., the
advanced party or the M.T., and the day passed digging
in and enjoying the first meal off the 24-hour pack. Ahead,
a line running east from Caumont through Cheux and
thence turning back north-west was held by 50 Division
on the right, the Canadians in the centre opposite Cheux,
and 3 Division on the left, north of Caen. Away to the
north 6 Airborne Division kept the left flank secure on
the east side of the River Orne.

At this point the Division was transferred to 8 Corps,
which was to carry the responsibility for an attack staged
with the object of seizing the crossings of the River Odon
and the high ground at Point 112, west of Caen.[5] In the
operation to be known as "Epsom" 43 Division were to
take over from 15th (Scottish) Division at Cheux and
St. Mauvieu and 214 Brigade were to lead the Division.

On a hot afternoon on 25th June the Battalion moved
to its concentration area west of Brecey through clouds
of dust and still without its vehicles ! Eventually after
much searching by the staffs of higher formations the
M.T. was traced. For five days it had lain off the beach,
having been sent over as part of 12 Corps which had

---

[5] 8 Corps included 15th (Scottish) Division and 11th Armoured
Division.

1944 lowest disembarkation priority, and in the meanwhile no
one concerned had been told of the change over to 8
Corps ! Great credit was due to the M.T. personnel who
after five days of thorough sea-sickness turned up complete in men and vehicles. De-waterproofing of vehicles
and the sorting out of M.T. personnel with the rifle
companies continued into the night, and by the following
morning the Battalion was set to face the task ahead.

So far as 1st Worcestershire Regiment was concerned
its introduction to the grim reality of modern war in
Europe was undoubtedly concentrated in the next two or
three days round the shattered village of Cheux. The
road forward to Cheux had been obliterated. Unsus-
pected minefields had taken their toll of our Sherman
tanks, and numbers of tanks and other vehicles were in
some bewilderment trying to grope their way forward
between the tapes. It was clear that the Scottish Division,
and before them the Canadians, had had some grim
fighting with the Hitler Jugend Division, which was
known to constitute the immediate opposition.

The immediate task was to take over from the Glasgow
Highlanders in Cheux, with 5 D.C.L.I. holding Haut-
du-Bosq just to the right of Cheux down to and including
Cheux Church. Eventually the village take-over was
completed in the early morning, "A" and "B" Companies
forward of the village and "C" and "D" in the rear.
The village itself was regarded as a death-trap and was
left unoccupied. But already there was grievous loss, a
mortar bomb having accounted for all the officers of "A"
Company, who had been holding a short co-ordinating
conference. The C.S.M. having been left out of battle,
the senior sergeant (Sergeant Dalloway) immediately
assumed command and completed the consolidation with
a confidence which betokened a high sense of leadership.
The Divisional policy of leaving numbers of officers and
men out of battle was frequently to be justified, and it was
unfortunate that on this particular occasion, heavy opposition not being anticipated, Battalions had taken all officers
with them for the sake of battle experience.

Throughout the day Cheux was subjected to heavy
mortar fire, while within the village snipers who had

stayed behind proved of constant nuisance value. Fortunately their accuracy was hardly compatible with their
undoubted courage. The Hitler Jugend, however, were
up to all sorts of tricks, some of which were hardly of a
nature calculated to encourage respect, and consequently
few prisoners were taken.

By the following day the Battalion had dug in effectively, two men in a slit, together with tinned food, tea
and chocolate, being capable of fending for themselves.
But it was clear that elsewhere the plan as a whole had
not been fulfilled and the crossings of the River Odon
were still obviously held by the enemy. Meanwhile 7
Somerset Light Infantry moved through Cheux and was
holding the rising ground in front. On the right 5
D.C.L.I. still held Le Haut-du-Bosq. In this situation
the Brigade received orders to attack and capture Mouen
village, which lay about one and a half miles beyond
Cheux.

At first the details of the enemy's strength or positions
in Mouen had been impossible to obtain and the Brigadier
was not for committing the Battalion to a task with only
the vaguest information available. Two battalions of
another Division had already attacked the village and
failed to take it. Nevertheless at 0330 hours in the morning the Commanding Officer was summoned to Brigade
H.Q. and told that, notwithstanding meagre information,
orders had been received that Mouen must be taken and
the Battalion was to be entrusted with the task.

The subsequent attack on Mouen and its successful
capture was certainly as happy an example of the reward
of months of sound training as a commander could wish
for. There was no time to link up a detailed reconnaissance with an artillery fire plan, and so the former was
dispensed with and the artillery plan was formulated
from the map with such knowledge applied to the general
intention as could be gleaned from a rapid glance at the
Mouen horizon the evening before. For about half a mile
up to the Villers Bocage–Caen railway the country lay
flat. But the other side of the railway was close country
intersected with high hedges and small orchards. In the
midst of this lay Mouen, into which ran two or three

1944   lanes typical of Devonshire. Beyond in enclosed country
lay the main Villers–Caen road and the River Odon with
Point 112 behind. On the right was open country for
half a mile which then gave way to orchards and farms,
while on the left the ground sloped away with open
cornfields up to Carpiquet aerodrome.

It was decided to avoid an attack with a right hook
through the more enclosed country, which was the more
obvious decision, and hope for surprise by accepting the
dangerous and open advance on the straight axis Cheux–
Mouen. In the event this proved a wise decision which
must have spared many lives. The artillery plan allowed
first for a bombardment of H.E. with smoke on the
railway line, to be followed by a barrage lifting 100 yards
in four minutes to the main Caen road. The leading
troops were calculated to be on the edge of the barrage
just before the first lift; 4.2 mortars were to fire smoke
and H.E. to cover the obvious line of counter-attack from
Carpiquet and Caen, while medium machine guns were
to fire on Carpiquet aerodrome. It so happened that the
axis of advance lay exactly on a line of pylons running
across the cornfields. Based on this convenient axis, a
simple deployment was ordered with two companies up,
right and left, one in support and one in reserve. Battle
drill procedure worked according to the text-books and
the Battalion moved forward with a precision worthy of
an Aldershot demonstration, covering a depth of about
half a mile with men in open formation at eight yards
interval. Once in the close country progress was slow.
Enemy tanks, dug into the narrow lanes, made effective
pill-boxes and the orchards harboured many active
Germans who had escaped the barrage. Nevertheless,
eventually all objectives were secured and casualties were
not heavy. Here and there opportunities for distinction
and leadership were presented in the course of the
fighting, and thus it was that Major A. J. Gutch won his
M.C. refusing to leave his company after a shrapnel
wound in the back, that "B" Company lost their gallant
Canadian, Lieutenant Brigider, that Sergeant Stupple, a
veteran of Tobruk, won his M.M. and that R.S.M. Hurd
brought in a Company flag of the Jugend Division,

which now hangs in the museum. It had perhaps been a
Company Commander's battle in which much of the
subsequent success was due to initial surprise. But high
leadership and months of sound training were the basic
elements of an initiation which gave confidence to the
Battalion throughout the subsequent months of the
campaign.

The Battalion dug in as quickly as possible, and indeed
the need was urgent, for that night (29/30 June) the
enemy brought down a rain of fire on Mouen and casualties mounted. As usual, mortar fire was responsible for
most of the damage and methods were hurriedly evolved
to pin-point enemy positions by taking bearings on the
sound of discharge and co-ordinating results. Plotted
positions were given to the gunners and counter-mortar
fire could eventually be brought down swiftly by a code
system which proved effective against the enemy's highly
mobile mortars, which were mounted on tracked vehicles.
It is perhaps appropriate here to pay a tribute to 179
Field Regiment, which supported the Battalion. In
particular, 172 Field Battery under Major Alexander
became their close friends and no call for assistance went
unanswered.

The Brigade was now in a salient, the Somersets having
passed through and dug in astride the main Caen road,
with the D.C.L.I. on the right and 1st Worcestershire on
the left facing Carpiquet aerodrome. There followed
several days of active reconnaissance which only just
stopped short of a full-scale attack, the Mortar Platoon
giving and taking more than its share of the exchanges.
Fortunately Captain J. Bannister, the Mortar commander,
had trained his 100 per cent. reserves in the rifle companies and these were available to draw on. To add to the
normal discomfort and initiations of war in this particular
situation, scattered platoons had to contend with the
stench of dead cattle, which in the heat was unbearable.
It had its practical side in that some of the live cows
which remained became friendly enough to be able to be
milked close up to the slit trenches !

In the heat of the Mouen battle "C" Company found
time to bury a little French girl killed by shell fire in a

1944   farmhouse. They dug her grave in the adjoining churchyard and gave her a cross, and were rewarded later by a
message from a deeply grateful mother who somehow
came to know of their care and thoughtfulness.

In the days to follow the Battalion was to experience
perhaps the most intense fighting of this phase of the
campaign. If progress was disappointing it was some
compensation to know that all ranks were successful
actors in the drama as a whole, for the role of the British
Second Army was to draw attention to the Caen area in
order to give the Americans away on the right their
opportunity to break out. Into this general picture the
immediate task of 43 Division became the capture of Hill
112, a feature which dominated the whole Caen position
based on the Rivers Odon and Orne, while 214 Brigade
was allotted the task of securing a position round about
Chateau de Fontaine, which lay in open corn country on
the left shoulder and a few hundred yards short of the
crest of Hill 112.

On 10th July at 0500 hours the battle opened. The
other two Brigades involved (129 and 130) gained most
of their objectives to the east and west of Hill 112, only
to be beaten back almost to their start lines. Thus when
the Battalion came into position late in the afternoon
just south-west of Chateau de Fontaine and dug in they
found themselves exposed, with no evidence of any
support near at hand. There followed a night of confusion in which much of our own armour seemed lost,
the crews having difficulty in seeing where they were
going. Late in the afternoon of 11th July it was known
that the D.C.L.I. were to attack Point 112 with tanks.
Their subsequent gallant attempt took very heavy toll of
their numbers. They were fiercely counter-attacked, the
heavier enemy tanks proving too powerful for our armour
in a straightforward trial of opposing armour. Thus it
was that the D.C.L.I. ceased to exist for all practical
purposes, and two battalions of 214 Brigade were holding
the Divisional front. In these circumstances orders were
received that 1st Worcestershire were to hang on at all
costs, a reminder which seemed redundant and came over
the wireless in "clear." At the same time the Second-

in-Command, Major G. Taylor, took over the difficult
command of the depleted ranks of the D.C.L.I., an
appointment which proved the beginning of a very happy
partnership.

The Battalion was certainly holding its ground; but in
an exposed position only 150 yards from the crest of
Point 112, with every movement under observation, it
could do little more than lie low and dig into trench slits
in company localities. Forward companies under the nose
of the enemy could not be supplied and they accordingly
held their positions by night, coming out just before dawn
and leaving standing patrols in forward positions. Over
the other side of the crest there were reports of enemy
movements and his armour could be heard on the move.
But a code system could call down fire on likely forming-
up localities and these shoots undoubtedly saved the
Battalion from counter-attack. Throughout these tense
hours it was difficult not to be conscious of isolation
within a salient seemingly in the heart of the enemy's
position. The 1st Worcestershire were certainly mindful
cf their motto, and it will have been with the events of
24th July in mind that the Corps Commander paid his
tribute to all ranks in his Foreword to Major D. Y.
Watson's history of the Normandy campaign.[6]

On 25th July welcome orders came in to fall back to
Mouen. There had been no break in the fighting since
Cheux, and fifteen days of life in slit trenches was as
much as was healthy for the most hardened unit. The
hand-over was carried through successfully in spite of
the enemy being only a stone's throw from the forward
slits, and in spite also of the unquestioned prowess of the
Germans at bold sniping and infiltration. There is a
story of an enemy mortar which one day hit a haystack
well within the Battalion area and set it alight. Out of
the haystack there then appeared a bedraggled German
rifleman who had lain up for five days and was apparently
prepared to continue to do so indefinitely !

---

[6] "With that Battalion [1st Worcestershire] in the thick of it, and on
more than one occasion reported as surrounded, neither I myself nor
anyone else ever worried or had the slightest fears as to what the results
would be."

1944   Hopes that a few days' rest in Mouen would be enjoyed were soon shattered, for within twenty-four hours orders came in to return to Point 112 to a hamlet called Baron, well to the right of the position just vacated. Yet another order quickly followed which amounted to a plan to capture the ground in front of the Battalion's previous position in a night attack to be carried out in silence. The order was accompanied by instructions to return again to Mouen previous to the attack, presumably with the object of affording all ranks a short rest, and some rather fruitless movement and counter-movement resulted in spite of representations that such a move could constitute no relaxation.

On the afternoon of 21st July once again a move forward was made. Companies got away well from the start line, guided towards the objective by two red lights put out by the "I" Section. But careful as had been the plan and its preparation, the difficulties of movement in the pitch dark through high-standing corn had hardly been appreciated. In the event casualties were heavy and, alas, included a very gallant officer, Major P. T. Weston, in command of "D" Company. Although companies reached their objectives, individual platoons did not arrive together, with the result that heavy counter-attacks forced our men back. On 22nd July the Battalion returned to Mouen for the last time and moved with the Division for a rest too long postponed to an area some twelve kilometres to the north-west at Jerusalem, thus saying goodbye to the small corner of Normandy which had been the scene of such swift and cruel loss and so much good comradeship in tribulation. In one way or another no less than twenty officers had been lost and rifle companies were at half strength. In these conditions it was certainly miraculous that the Battalion maintained its pristine spirit under those who had to accept heavy new responsibilities. A curious feature of the fighting had been that the most efficient Anti-Tank Platoon had hauled its guns round Cheux, Mouen and Hill 112 without ever firing a shot, the enemy using his tanks always in a defensive role lying well back behind the crests and engaging targets at 1,000 yards range.

At Jerusalem, while administrative problems of reconstruction took precedence, there was time for welcome relaxation and the lighter side of life. George Formby's show turned up. There were cinema evenings ; local Camembert cheeses supplemented the ration and went down well with a gift of a bottle of beer per man from Messrs. Mitchell and Butler. Mild preparations for parties were in hand when at the end of the fourth day of rest the warning came. This time the break-out was to come in the night, and on 27th July the Battalion came under command of 30 Corps, in which it was to serve until the end of the war, moving to its concentration area on 29th July at La Paumerie, a few kilometres north-east of Caumont.

After the destruction of the Caen area the quiet untouched landscape round La Paumerie hardly seemed normal. 50 Division had originally made a dash forward from Bayeux and the countryside had escaped the hand of war. In the concentration area the Battalion were joined by 4/7 Dragoon Guards in Sherman tanks, with whom it was destined to be linked in close partnership for a long time. Troops of tanks were detailed to companies, and very soon sub-units came to know each other and were busy evolving methods of dealing with resistance in the enclosed orchards which had again to be faced.

In their new locality 43 Division were more concerned with a full-scale break-out to the south with 15 (Scottish) Division on the right and 50 Division on the left. It fell to the Battalion to be the leading unit of the Division down the road Caumont–Cahagnes. Everywhere were minefields and booby traps and the enclosed country imposed great difficulties in inter-communication and co-operation generally. The orders were to push on and exploit success irrespective of the fate of units on the right and left. In these circumstances at one stage our men found themselves on 1st August in isolation. Nevertheless the objective, the Cantaloup cross-roads, was made good without heavy casualties and with an imposing display of captured equipment, arms and vehicles. By the morning 2nd August the Battalion was well consolidated with all-round defence and 7th Armoured Division

1944   were up and passing through. But opposition now
stiffened and throughout the day units of both sides were
intermingled in some confusion, the D.C.L.I. in particular running into pockets of resistance outside Jurques
which considerably confused the local issue.

Beyond Jurques the country ranged away in a sweep of
low hills with their crests thickly covered in forests.
Behind the first crest as it appeared from Jurques rose a
secondary feature, Point 361, with little to define it except
its height which gave it a silhouette on the horizon.
The D.C.L.I. were held up and it seemed that movement
round by the right flank in rear of the opposition would
open the way for them. Once Point 361 was cleared the
way would be opened to Mt. Pincon, eight miles away
across the River Odon.

On 4th August 1st Worcestershire received orders to
undertake this delicate operation. The advance up
through thick woods precluded the possibility of vehicles
accompanying the Battalion, and a bold plan was adopted
by which "B" Company were first to infiltrate up through
the woods to make good some portion of the objective
and then guide the remainder of the Battalion through to
complete the job. In the event, this met with the success
it deserved though there were some anxious moments
when for hours in the night no news came through of
"B" Company's progress. Wireless sets failed to keep
touch and "C" Company were sent off on a wider route
to the right with the same objective. At last news arrived
from "B" Company that they were through and the
remainder of the Battalion set out in single file, to arrive
on Point 361 at dawn. An officer of "B" Company,
Lieutenant A. J. Booth, certainly deserves much credit
for the successful direction of a very difficult movement
by night. He seemed to have an uncanny sense of
direction in the dark and was chosen to go back by
Major Grubb from "B" Company for his particular
facility in scout-craft. "A" Company were pushed on to
exploit, and sure enough found the Germans scurrying
away towards Mt. Pincon. The D.C.L.I. had kept up
the pressure, and between their efforts and the enemy's
astonishment at finding a battalion at his rear, he had

decided that discretion was the better part of valour. **1944**
That indefatigable pillar of strength, R.S.M. Hurd, was at the head of the hunt leading a patrol well forward into a village in the valley on the right, from which he returned without prisoners but with many eggs.

On 6th August, Lieut.-Colonel Harrison had perforce to leave through sickness and for a few days command devolved on Major A. A. Benn, who in turn handed over to Lieut.-Colonel R. E. Osborne-Smith from 4th Wiltshires on 7th August. The 4th Wiltshires of 129 Brigade, after a hard day, were precariously established around the foot of Mt. Pincon and the Battalion were now to relieve them as soon as possible. The manner in which that relief was carried through constitutes in itself a story meriting many pages. The efforts, finally successful, of the Commanding Officer and R Group to trace their opposite numbers through a night of chaos are elsewhere graphically described.[7] Here it must suffice to record that the relief was carried through with only light casualties, and on 8th August the Battalion sat on the summit of Mt. Pincon with men dug in all around in slits like ants, and the country on all sides obscured only by the heat haze in the far distance. That night the Battalion was withdrawn to take up positions round the cross-roads at La Variniere, leaving 5th D.C.L.I. to make history in capturing the first Royal Tiger tank of the war in their attack on Le Plessir Greinoult.

The D.C.L.I. attack had left the country to the south of the road which runs due east from La Variniere untouched, and this had now to be cleared before a start line for further operations could be fixed. "C" Company under Major H. R. Matthews were detailed for the task and it proved a most difficult commitment. Orchards, hedgerows and sunken lanes were once again interlaced to provide the enemy with enfilade positions, and his artillery took heavy toll, so much so that the attack had to be called off.

In the meanwhile "A" Company patrols had established that to the south the hamlet of Le Quesnee was held,

---

[7] See "The First Battalion the Worcestershire Regiment in N.W. Europe," by Major D. Y. Watson, p. 44.

1944   and early in the morning on 10th August they set about
the task of its capture. Again it proved an operation
calling for much individual initiative. Negotiation with
an unreliable deserter would have had the Company
Commander believe that the village was unoccupied.
But a couple of prisoners caused some doubt on the
matter, and patrols finally established that Le Quesnee
was in fact held in strength. A day of blazing heat and
foul smells passed unpleasantly with "A" Company and
their opponents playing at the opening moves until a
deadlock was reached. Amid the stench of death, human
and animal, ducks, chickens, and geese continued to roam
about completely unconcerned with the battle for life
which waged around them.

    In a position of stalemate, the Commanding Officer,
after a short visit, decided that "A" Company were due
for a short rest before a planned attack could be put in.
Accordingly the Company withdrew, enjoyed a hot meal
and returned to stage a full-scale attack in conjunction
with the Mortar Platoon. From the top storey of a house
overlooking the objective, Major Watson and Captain
Bannister watched a heavy rain of bombs fall on the
village for thirty minutes. At 1430 hours the attack went
in on a conventional plan with a platoon working round
either flank and Company H.Q. and a third platoon going
through the centre. On the right the objective was
reached, but the left and centre platoons met stiff opposition. The centre platoon had also to deal with a curious
situation outside the scope of the text-books when a
party of Germans appeared to wish to surrender. The
Second-in-Command, Captain K. R. H. James, with a
few men accordingly walked out to receive them. They
were, however, met by a German officer covered by two
men with sub-machine-guns, who proceeded to argue that
he was there to accept the surrender of our men. This
ridiculous situation could hardly be sustained for long and
very soon the opposing parties were back under cover
hitting at each other. Thus the situation remained
throughout the night, and in the morning a patrol was
about to investigate forward when once again R.S.M.
Hurd and two snipers turned up with a generous prize of

eggs to confirm that the enemy had disappeared and 1944
Le Quesnee was free to be entered. This small engagement of a sub-unit could not normally receive detailed
recognition in a short history which must cover so much
ground. But since it is but typical of the many similar
episodes throughout the campaign, there is perhaps
justification in its elaboration.

CHAPTER FOUR

THE FIRST BATTALION, 1944–1945

Normandy, Belgium, Holland, Germany

1944 THE net was fast closing on the German armies in Normandy. To the south the American sweep was within twenty miles of the Canadians north of Falaise. Conde-sur-Noireau lay at a junction covering one of their two escape roads and it was to Conde that 43 Division now advanced. General Eisenhower's message to his armies ensured that all realized the significance of the situation and was high encouragement in the relentless pursuit. For the Battalion this meant crossing the River Noireau and the capture of Berjou. The Noireau was crossed in the only way possible. It was twenty yards wide and about three feet deep, and without delay on the evening of 15th August, "A" Company in the lead waded through the water and under the lee of the hill on the far side found the re-entrant and track up which the Battalion was to follow. They crept up through the woods to the west and fixed the two white 2-inch mortar flares which were to indicate their success. By nightfall 214 Brigade were across the Noireau.

As dawn on 16th August broke the enemy came to life. His artillery opened up and nine good men of "A" Company's Headquarters were killed in a direct hit. Casualties mounted and it was a harassed unit which received its orders to capture Berjou. For this, the Commanding Officer gave his orders for a simple frontal attack from a well-defined hedgerow as a start-line. The usual powerful weight of artillery support was laid on and, as companies deployed to the roar of guns, with direct support from the Shermans in hull-down positions on the crest, all ranks sensed the stimulus of a knowledge of their own superior resources. It was the first set-piece since Mouen and it proved too much for the enemy. Those who stayed to fight were captured or wiped out

and by 1730 hours Berjou was ours. Alas, that gallant
servant of the Battalion, R.S.M. Hurd, M.M., met his
death from a chance long-range shell and with sixteen
officers of the Worcestershire Regiment lies buried
beneath the Calvary on Berjou Ridge.

Next morning, 17th August, 129 Brigade passed
through, leaving the Battalion to enjoy a much-needed
rest with the hospitable folk of Berjou.

From 17th to 22nd August the Battalion basked in the
sudden joy of idleness. Meanwhile great events were
shaping the fate of the remnants of the German 7th Army
which had escaped from the gap and were pressed against
the lower Seine. To the south the great American sweep
had reached the Seine from Fontainebleau north to
Vernon, and Paris was tottering.

On 23rd August the Battalion came under the command
of 129 Brigade, destined to cross the Seine at Vernon,
and at 1015 hours the Brigade column moved off on a
journey of triumph through villages and hamlets hysterical
in their wild desire to greet their liberators. It was an
experience of joy and emotion. There was time only for
the troops to bedeck themselves in the flowers showered
on them and drink down the odd bottle of wine. That
night in the village of Louge-sur-Maine the weather
broke, and the dusty lanes turned to squelching mud.
At 2000 hours on 24th August, Le Rue Bertrou was
reached, and at 1145 hours next morning the column was
racing on to Vernon. For once the familiar cautions
"15 v.t.m." and "25 m.i.h." were dispensed with and
vehicles sped on, keeping as close together as possible, in
as wild a drive as could ever have been undertaken by an
army trained to ordered and precise convoy movement.
It was a matter of making the Seine crossing before the
enemy could organize his defence.

The river by Vernon is 200 yards wide, and on the
north bank the village of Vernonnet seemed innocently
peaceful. Back in Vernon there was feverish activity as
battalions unloaded their storm boats to the chatter of
French civilians who excitedly offered advice and information. The subsequent crossing did not go through entirely
"according to plan." It was to have been an assault of

1944   two waves of two battalions each, 1st Worcestershire
being on the right in the second wave. But the air
photographs had hardly furnished an accurate picture of
the river-bed and the first wave were in trouble. The
Battalion had therefore to cross by a blown bridge which
was still passable for infantry. Dusk had fallen when
Sergeant Jennings with the leading platoon of "A" Company tumbled on some booby-trapped egg grenades just
as he was about to reach the northern end. He was
greeted with a hail of machine-gun bullets and with
difficulty crept back along the bridge to his platoon,
nursing a severe wound. The Commanding Officer[1] then
decided to run the gauntlet and rush the bridge, but just
as a bold plan was about to be put into effect orders from
Brigade called for a "stand fast." As dawn broke on
26th August once more a patrol of "A" Company crept
along the broken bridge. This time there was silence and
before long the men of 1st Worcestershire were hurrying
across in time to claim to be the first complete British
battalion to cross the Seine.

But if the crossing of the river had been unexpectedly
simple and economic, the enlargement of the bridgehead
on 27th August was to prove costly. Late in the evening
of 26th August the Battalion had returned to 124 Brigade,
and since the very close nature of the country had precluded distant patrolling in the night, the advance along
the road Vernonnet–Tilly was a step forward into the
unknown. An order of march of normal advance-to-
contact pattern was adopted, and in the event the forward
anti-tank section were by fine gunnery able to deal
effectively with a Tiger tank which at about 1000 hours
threatened to disrupt the advance. But by 1100 hours the
units on either flank were also in trouble and the Battalion
was ordered to stand fast. The enemy had skilfully been
holding the river line thinly, with the bulk of his troops
well to the rear ready for counter-attack at any point at
which we might cross. The advance lay up a road in a
valley with steep wooded sides and the Germans were able
to place their infantry on the heights of either side. In

---

[1] Lieut.-Colonel R. E. Osborne-Smith, D.S.O. (Northamptonshire
Regiment).

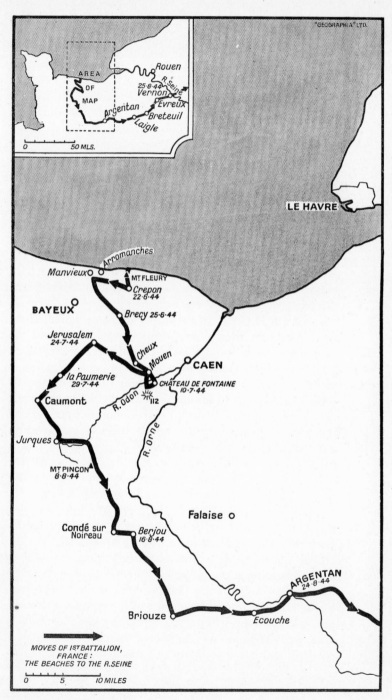

"GEOGRAPHIA" LTD.

AREA
OF
MAP

Rouen
R. Seine
25·8·44
Vernon
Evreux
Argentan
Breteuil
Laigle

0   50 MLS.

LE HAVRE

Arromanches
Manvieux○   Mt FLEURY
Crepon
22·6·44

BAYEUX ○
Brecy 25·6·44

Jerusalem
24·7·44
Cheux
Mouen
CAEN ○
la Paumerie
29·7·44
CHÂTEAU DE FONTAINE
10·7·44
Caumont
R. Odon   112
Jurques ○
R. Orne
Mt PINCON
8·8·44
Falaise ○
Condé sur
Noireau
Berjou
16·8·44
ARGENTAN
24·8·44
Briouze
Ecouche

MOVES OF 1ST BATTALION,
FRANCE :
THE BEACHES TO THE R.SEINE

0   5   10 MILES

F

1944 actual fact the enemy, advancing, had appreciated our own line of advance while we were still unaware of their presence. Thereupon a desultory and confused battle in the enclosed country developed in which 172 Battery R.A.—that same Battery which through the old 12th Battalion could claim such close relationship—were indefatigable in engaging targets of opportunity. By now the casualties had mounted. Major A. A. Benn, the Second-in-Command, had been killed and two other officers wounded, while the strength of companies had fallen to 45. It was a weary and depleted unit which consolidated for the night, but fortunately the enemy were in far worse condition. With dawn on 28th August it was clear that once again the enemy had faded away, and throughout the morning the Battalion had the satisfaction after a hard battle of watching others pass through and on in the direction of the distant sound of guns. At noon they relieved 5th D.C.L.I. in Pressagny L'Orgueilleux. There for a fortnight they were to enjoy rest, peace and the overwhelming hospitality of the kind folk of Pressagny. The transport personnel were less fortunate, the battalion three-tonners with their drivers being borrowed to assist R.A.S.C. Supply Columns on tasks between the coast near Bayeux and the Seine. Two ceremonies were to mark the stay at Pressagny, the one a Brigade gathering at Panilleux where the citations of Major A. J. Gutch (M.C.) and Sergeant Stupple (M.M.) were read,[2] the other a short but moving little ceremony conducted at the request of M. le Maire at the village war memorial.

While the Battalion rested and received reinforcements, the British Second Army was sweeping across the battle-fields of 1918, Canadian and Polish troops were in the Pas de Calais, while to the south the Americans were at Aschen tapping at the Siegfried Line. The drive therefore forward into Belgium on 14th September was uneventful, for by now the frenzied welcome of the countryside was a normal experience. On 18th September a concentration area near Hechtol on the north Belgian frontier was reached, and here the plan which was thought might bring

---

[2] Neither was present since Major Gutch had been wounded at Mouen and Sergeant Stupple at Mt. Pincon.

about the final collapse of the enemy was elaborated.
Within the massive movement of the Second British
Army, 30 Corps were to break out of the bridgehead
across the Escaut canal and drive for Eindhoven, Arnhem
and the sea, 43 Division linking up with 1st Airborne
Division a few miles north of Arnhem.   Over a sand-
model detailed objectives could be worked out down to
companies, and at 1630 hours on 20th September the
Battalion formed up to take its place in the long column
making for Eindhoven. Eindhoven was left behind in the
early morning and the first Dutch town to welcome our
troops was Graves. Perhaps because the Dutch had had
harsher experience of German occupation than French or
Belgians, the demonstrations were even more overwhelming.

On the morning 22nd September orders for a limited
operation were received involving the capture of the
village Oosterhout, beyond Nijmegen, where a bridgehead
over the Waal had been secured. The plan was in hand
when late in the evening, Oosterhout having been taken
by the Somersets, counter-orders were received to make
quickly for Valburg. Without lights along a narrow road,
with Dutch dykes waiting for the sleepy driver on either
side, the drive through a dark night in a drizzle of rain
was a test of nerves and temper. Somehow in the dark
companies and their vehicles sorted themselves out around
the Valburg cross-roads, and as day dawned the Dutch
emerged from their houses, curious to inspect the new
arrivals. Alas, their peaceful village was soon to have
shells crashing through their roofs and only the cellars
were safe.

The unhealthy climate of Valburg was to lead to a yet
more desperate situation at Elst, some ten miles to the
north-east. At 1200 hours orders were received to attack
the town four hours later. The country was open and a
long, straight road led to Elst. After artillery preparation,
"D" Company, with tank support, deployed and advanced
across the flat fields. "C" and "A" Companies followed
and, with darkness descending and Panther tanks prowling
around, it was only possible to cling to the edge of the
town. The times demanded much local initiative and

1944   quick decisions, and the fight for Elst on the following
day, 24th September, was therefore an isolated battle, the
enemy hitting back in fierce street fighting with a tenacity
which damped the optimism of many who a few days
earlier had looked to the beginning of the end. Every
house seemed to shelter a German automatic weapon,
and before the end of the day two fine Company Commanders, Majors Souper and Gibbons,[3] were to lose their
lives. By daybreak on 25th September Elst was in our
hands.

The clearing of the town itself had been left to "B" and
"D" Companies. The leading section of "D" Company
came in for intense automatic fire. Major Souper dashed
forward in an effort to rally his men and for a few minutes
the section, dashing from cover to cover, attacked the
open windows with grenades. But the odds were against
them, and in running across an open space a burst of fire
struck Major Souper and he fell mortally wounded. He
had commanded his company since the early days of
Normandy, a leader of courage and ability and a friend of
great personal charm.

On 27th September the Battalion was given a much-
needed rest back at Andelst, seven miles west of Nijmegen,
but the following day they moved forward to Randwijk,
overlooking the Neder Rijn, where they relieved the
Somersets. It was at Randwijk that two more good
officers were killed when a stray shell fell on the house
where "B" Company Headquarters was established.[4]
Thus in one week four senior officers were lost, and it was
not easy for brother officers who remained to face the
day's work with that indifference to adversity which
modern war demands.

By now it was evident that the drive through Holland
would not effect the final collapse of the enemy and a
winter campaign against the Siegfried Line had to be
faced. 30 Corps were the centre of a triangular wedge
with its apex thrust towards Arnhem and its right and left
wings back on the River Maas and the Belgian coast

---

[3] Major M. A. Gibbons, "A" Company. Major M. M. Souper,
"D" Company.
[4] Major W. H. Broom, Company Commander ; Captain N. Watkins, Second-in-Command.

respectively. Within this spearhead 43 Division were
committed to a sandy, wooded stretch of hills south-east
of Nijmegen, and early in October the Division took over
this area from 3 Division, with its north and south flanks
on Groesbeck and Middelar respectively. For the next
month the situation was stabilized and a war of nerves
developed within sight of the pine trees of the Reichswald
forest and the outposts of the Siegfried Line. At one
stage the Battalion found itself holding the village
de Klop, with sixty feet of the main road only separating
it from the enemy, a situation which at night lent itself to
many adventures. It was in these circumstances that the
Brigade Commander initiated the "mad minute," and
accordingly at 1915 hours on 21st October, rifles, Brens,
Stens, mortars and the artillery blazed off in a festival
spirit and in due course received the obvious retaliation.
It was without regret that on 15th November the Brigade
handed over to the Canadians and took the road south
towards Aachen.

While in central Holland 43 Division had been comparatively static, elsewhere the situation was rapidly
changing. In the south the Americans were feeling
forward towards Cologne and already the Siegfried
Line was breached. At the base of the wedge the
Canadians were busy opening the Scheldt estuary for
further seaborne landings. In this general picture of high
hope, the battle for Tripsrath is a landmark for the 1st
Worcestershire which is elsewhere set out in all its
exciting detail.[5] Before the battle the Battalion had tasted
the overwhelming generosity of the population of the
village of Pulth in southern Holland. Americans had
already passed that way, but it seemed that there was a
special welcome saved for the British soldier. Amid the
sordid impositions of occupation and war, Dutch homes,
spotlessly clean, were opened to our men in a manner
incongruous, which moved the more sensitive to long for
the day when the cheerful courage of these great people
would be rewarded.

On 13th November the Battalion arrived at the mining
town of Brunsum, and during the next few days the

---

[5] See Major D. Y. Watson's account, pp. 76—78.

1944 orders for operation "Clipper" were elaborated. The
Americans were launching east from Aachen and 43
Division was to secure their left flank, cutting the escape
routes from Geilenkirchen. 214 Brigade were to seize an
area north of the town, with villages allotted to battalions
as objectives, and in the luck of the draw Tripsrath fell to
the Battalion.

As compared with previous operations, perhaps even
more careful preparation was lavished on the plan for
Tripsrath. The operation fell into two stages, and it is an
over-simplification to state that the first phase went
according to plan while the second was a costly business
and nearly a glorious failure. First "B" and "C" Companies were to take the intermediate village, Rischden,
and a strip of wood. When these were secured "A" and
"D" Companies were to pass through and take Tripsrath
itself. In support were a squadron of tanks and an intense
fire plan was to pave the way.

The 18th November was a clear, bright day and,
according to plan, companies moved forward to the
assembly area in M.T. along tracks through the woods
cut by the Sappers. Debussing in the pinewoods to the
east of Niederbusch, they found that "A" Echelon had
beaten them to it in the race to be first on German soil
and a hot meal was ready. Rightly the cooks merited the
congratulations of all ranks as, fortified with tea and rum,
they awaited the order to move up to the forming-up point.
Then, reinforced by a party of the Press armed with
cameras, the Battalion threaded its way forward through
the battle-scarred village of Gillrath to the starting
line.

At 1400 hours the leading companies advanced, keeping
direction by compass and chosen landmarks and heartened
by the din of a full-scale barrage. The rain had helpfully
washed away the top soil, leaving the enemy's mines
exposed, and the troops were able to step between them
while the Sappers were busy lifting them and clearing
lanes for the tanks. Thus the first objective was cleared
without serious opposition, and the second phase was
launched with high hopes. But such luck could not last.
Between the wood on the left and Rischden was a small

copse which the Carrier Platoon was ordered to capture. 1944
It proved a death-trap and in less than twenty minutes
31 casualties were suffered. At the same time the
Commanding Officer was wounded. The Second-in-
Command, Major R. C. Thompson, was at the time back
with "A" Echelon. Accordingly the Adjutant, Captain
W. L. Leadbeater, hatless and regardless of danger, set
out for the forward positions to find Major J. D. Ricketts,
commanding "B" Company, to take over command. It
was some time before he could locate him, and meanwhile
the battle hung in the balance. With the tanks bogged
down in the mud and the artillery switched on to the
objectives of other battalions, Major Ricketts decided to
proceed with the original plan. He had, however, secured
a concentration of Medium Artillery on the objective
itself. For once our gunners were at fault and shells
falling 600 yards short caused casualties to "D" Company. Nevertheless, as the Mediums closed down, the
advance continued and three companies entered Tripsrath
simultaneously in the dark and dug in for the night. Of
many intense subsidiary dramas, not the least which
merits a reference was the enemy's luck in dropping a
shell on to Battalion H.Q. and setting it alight. Major
R. C. Thompson (York and Lancaster Regiment), who
had now taken over from Major Ricketts, continued to
direct from the cellar of the house until literally matters
became too hot. Thus was the stern assignment at
Tripsrath brought to a close, and it was a very weary,
unwashed and unshaven unit which was relieved on
23rd November and found its way back in M.T. to the
kind hospitality awaiting it in Schinveld over the Dutch
frontier. All too soon three days passed and never were
hot baths more welcome.

On 27th November orders to relieve 4th Dorsets in a
wood west of Tripsrath were received, and once more the
Battalion, now under command of Lieut.-Colonel A. W.
Vickers (K.O.Y.L.I.), set out in M.T. along the Geilenkirchen road to Bauchem. Back again at Rischden, they
moved across country in silence and apprehension into the
wood. The Dorsets had tasted the full weight of the
Siegfried Line artillery and casualties had been heavy.

1944 Fortunately, the relief went through without interference and the Battalion went to earth in shelters actually prepared by the enemy which well served their purpose though designed to face the opposite direction. But Dorsets Wood was an unpleasant home with a sinister atmosphere which clung to it, to fray sensitive nerves and test quick tempers; and it was a relief to hand over to the Cornwalls on 30th November and make for Niederbusch, close to the point where only a few days previously the Battalion had concentrated for the Tripsrath attack.

On 2nd December the order was received to relieve 12th K.R.R.C. in the village of Birgden, an operation which will be remembered for the particular measures which were taken to deal with enterprising enemy patrols who were using the night to lay traps for sleepy drivers and unguarded vehicles. It was perhaps as well to be kept up to the mark through ambiguous periods when operations were not governed by staged attacks. Birgden will be remembered for the excellent use the signallers were able to make of the very comprehensive German signal system. In spite of heavy casualties, the Signal Platoon under Captain P. E. Gray had recently surpassed itself in efforts to maintain communications, so that Birgden proved a welcome reward. Battalion H.Q. was able not only to establish its own exchange, but a forward exchange under Sergeant J. Norton was a link with the companies in Birgden. Late in the night of 6th December the Battalion arrived once more in the friendly environment of Brunsum, where it was to spend a surprisingly long period out of contact with the enemy. Until 16th December much thought and time was given to plans for an operation "Shears" which in the event never materialized. But in any case all speculation on a final assault on the Siegfried Line had to be set aside when on 19th December it was clear that von Rundstedt was making his last desperate bid in the Ardennes to rescue Nazi Germany from its irrevocable doom : and so when the Battalion moved to occupy billets in Tilburg it found itself suddenly diverted to concentrate hastily in the Belgian town, Bilsen. Incredibly, while the German armies were driving forward with Tiger tanks in use for the first time in

quantity and last reserves of men and planes thrown into 1944
the scales, 30 Corps was comparatively idle in reserve
with orders to deny the line of the Meuse to the enemy :
and so it was that the 1st Worcestershire came to spend a
normal, even exuberant Christmas at Bilsen with tinned
turkey, pork and Christmas pudding, and many trim-
mings which the resourceful Quartermaster and P.R.I. had
managed somehow to accumulate. There were warnings
against the wood alcohol which the local cafe passed off as
"brandy"; warnings not necessarily heeded, and several
adventurers spent their Christmas in the guard-room.

On 27th November a move back to Bunde in Holland
was made again in the vicinity of Brunsum, and the next
few days were spent in defensive digging all over the area,
much to the bewilderment of the Dutch, for whom the
prospect of a return of the German armies was too
hideous to contemplate.

But von Rundstedt was at last held, and as the New 1945
Year wore on tension relaxed. There was even a sense of
resentment when on 10th January it looked as if the
officers' dance staged in a cafe in Meerssen might have
to be abandoned to conform with orders to return to the
Tripsrath area.

In Tripsrath other formations with other habits had
apparently used the neighbourhood in the interim, for
the enemy seemed surprisingly carefree and aggressive.
However, so far as the Battalion was concerned, the
Commanding Officer[6] quickly set about re-educating the
other side to a more humble attitude in co-operation with
American gunners who were for the time attached. The
actual role of the Battalion for the next fortnight was the
unusual privilege of acting as spectators to operation
"Black-cock," which was to clear the area known as the
Sittard–Roermond Triangle. The days passed with
various activities in which the Pioneer Platoon were the
chief actors. Their ingenuity in staging a bogus patrol at
night to draw enemy fire and their herculean efforts to
lift over one thousand enemy mines in the snow to enable
our tanks to pass through deserve a fuller record than can
be attempted here.[7]

[6] Lieut.-Colonel A. W. Vickers.
[7] See Major D. Y. Watson's account, page 87.

1945   By 25th January the Tripsrath area had ceased to be of significance within the scope of operation "Black-cock" and the enemy had melted away. On 26th January once more the Battalion concentrated at Tripsrath and Rischden and motored next day to Hulsberg, before taking the road on 31st January for Beersse near Turnhout in Belgium, there to await orders for the final phase of the war in Europe.

On 8th February Lieut.-Colonel Vickers, whose superhuman energy had been an inspiration to all, was admitted to hospital for an operation, and Lieut.-Colonel M. R. J. Hope-Thomson, M.C., arrived to take command. The same day the Battalion moved and in the early hours of 9th February was back at Nijmegen. Here it was obvious that big plans were brewing and the place was congested with troops. To the north the Canadians had started their drive for the Rhine. The immediate task of 43 Division in the opening stages of operation "Veritable" was to follow through a gap made by two other divisions which were directed on to Cleve and the Reichswald forest. 214 Brigade were in the lead, with one squadron of tanks of 8 Armoured Brigade to each battalion. For the Battalion the move on the evening of 9th February proved one of the most exhausting night expeditions yet experienced. It was wet and cold. The road was congested and traffic control had broken down. It was indeed lucky that the Luftwaffe had little to spare to pay the area a visit. More by good luck than by good management, on 10th February some order came of chaos and that night the Battalion halted about four miles from Cleve. It was another three days before the objectives around Cleve were secured in desultory fighting, much of which was tip-and-run warfare among buildings and through streets with tanks and infantry helping each other along in small house-to-house encounters. Delay was imposed by the necessity to capture the Materborn feature in the vicinity of Cleve which was firmly held by the enemy. On 10th February the Somersets had taken the village of Hau, and the Battalion was ordered to seize and hold the line of the ridge on their left. In describing the operation, Major Watson quotes Lieutenant D. J. Pullen, whose vivid impressions of house clearing deserve a record.

"It was my first experience of house clearing and seemed to consist mainly of firing the contents of a Bren gun magazine through the windows, battering the front door with a pick-axe and wandering through the house firing an occasional round just to lend colour to the situation."

A few days later, on 16th February, the same officer was to win a Military Cross leading his platoon gallantly in a frontal assault on some farm buildings which were captured at the point of the bayonet. Previously, on 12th and 13th February two more officers had won their Military Crosses in the spasmodic fighting which constituted operation "Veritable," Major B. R. N. Elder, M.B.E., for his untiring leadership of "D" Company through ten weary days and nights, and Lieutenant R. N. Fellows for the handling of his platoon in capturing his objective under heavy Spandau fire without the loss of a single man.

On 15th and 16th February operations had developed into co-operation between 214 Brigade and 130 Brigade in the alternative seizure of objectives. The fighting was close and intense, but there was compensation in the large number of prisoners which were now offering themselves, no less than 210 being taken in two days. From 17th to 20th February Battalion Headquarters were at Imigshof. Heavy shelling and mortaring were exchanged and patrols were active on both sides. On 21st February a Brigade of 15 (Scottish) Division attacked through and pushed on south, after which the Brigade was withdrawn two miles. Though the nights 21st and 22nd February were spent in shattered buildings in the area of the gun lines, the Battalion slept their first sleep out of contact with the enemy for many a night; and not even the roar of artillery could disturb their slumber.

On 23rd February they embussed back to a very battered Cleve; no light and no water, but also no enemy; and for two days mobile baths and a mobile cinema seemed luxuries.

On 26th February a take-over from 4th Wiltshire[8]

---

[8] On 27th February for a few days the Battalion assisted a Canadian formation and took over from the 1/2nd South Saskatchewan Regiment.

1945   astride the Cleve–Calcar road led on 4th March to orders to seize and hold the villages of Vynen and Wardt on the banks of the Rhine.   Already the great river had been seen in the distance, and now on 5th March the Battalion could claim to be the first British troops to establish the "Watch on the Rhine."

For several days our men could watch with intense interest the preparations for the Rhine crossing. Sappers reconnoitred bridging sites, traffic control points were established and counter-battery and counter-mortar spotters worked for hours from the tops of buildings. To cloak this feverish activity the Pioneer Corps laid their smoke-screen on the east bank from huge generators.

On 12th March the Battalion was relieved and moved back to a so-called rest area at Afferden in Holland. It was then that there was opportunity to note at leisure the nature of the hand of modern war laid over lands of developed civilization.

Afferden, to everyone's disgust, could only offer bivouacs in the open fields. But there were cinema and E.N.S.A. shows and the weather was kind.

In the great Rhine operation 30 Corps were destined to cross in the area of Rees. After several cancellations final orders confirmed the move at 0545 hours on 26th March. Already on 23rd March the Sappers after artillery preparations had thrown a Class 9 bridge over the river half a mile down-stream from Rees. The task of passing over break-out formations called for the highest degree of detailed staff preparation. Units and their vehicles were allotted blocks of serial numbers. Assembly areas were well signed and policed ; and routes were named and lighted. Eventually "Bank Control" called up the 1st Worcestershire, and by 0530 hours on 27th March the whole Battalion found itself crowded into a field in the area of Esserden on the west bank.

As daylight broke a mighty concentration of men and vehicles in the small bridgehead area offered the answer to the dreams of pilots and gunners. But at this stage of the war the enemy's resources were not equal to the golden opportunity. It was, however, obvious that such congestion was unhealthy, and 214 Brigade were given

the task of attacking through 129 Brigade and enlarging
the bridgehead. It was to be a two-battalion assault with
1st Worcestershire on the right and 7th Somersets on the
left, the objective being a feature which appeared to be
the preparations for completion of an autobahn.

Major G. C. Reinhold, M.C., who had now assumed
command, gave out brief orders, for speed was more
essential than detail. The approaches to the objective
were open and dominated by wooded positions and the
prospect was not attractive. The text-book reconnaissance had to be ignored, and even so the two assaulting
companies were fifteen minutes late across the start-line.
Tanks in close support were early bogged down, while
from woods, hedgerows and isolated farmhouses a spate
of fire greeted the deployment and casualties were heavy.
It was perhaps one of those occasions when months of
tiresome training were repaid rather than success won
through any circumstances on the ground. Not until the
evening was it known that elsewhere 51 Division, which
was to have timed its attack simultaneously, failed to get
away until 1700 hours and throughout the afternoon our
men had battled alone. On 28th March the Brigade
advanced to the line of the River Issel west of Arnholt.
Our patrols seized several small bridges, the enemy having
withdrawn. On the same day Lieut.-Colonel Hope-
Thomson returned to assume command after having been
married in England.

When on 30th March Brigade Orders were issued for
operation "Forrard-on," it needed little perception to
know that the vast accumulation of supporting arms of
every variety and design heralded the end.

Early on 31st March harbours were broken and the
long column set out, 214 Brigade following behind 129
Brigade. Craters cut up the broken roads and progress
was slow, 214 Brigade having at one point to by-pass the
leading formation. On 1st April the enemy managed to
pull off an "April fool" trick by blowing a bridge over the
Zutphen–Hengelo Canal under the nose of "B" Company,
who were then leading the Brigade, the Battalion then
closing up with Headquarters in Diepenheim. Eventually
the canal line was turned farther afield at Enschede by

1945   130 Brigade, and on 5th April the advance continued in
the wake of 51 (Highland) Division. That night at 1800
hours again the Battalion passed into Germany. Noord-
horn, where a night's rest was called, was untouched ;
and indeed the complete and unseemly breakdown of
traffic control on 6th April outside the town was a greater
limitation than enemy action. Thus it continued, so that
when minor opposition around Haselunne developed on
8th April a full-stage attack by the Battalion and the
Somersets under cover of smoke evaporated into thin air,
for the enemy had gone. For three hours all was quiet and
companies took stock of a prize won without a fight. But
alas, success was marred by the gallant Medical Officer,
Captain R. Duff-Chalmers, being put out of action by a
wound in the leg from a splinter from the shelling which
came down at about 1430 hours. He had been with the
Battalion since the previous autumn and had proved a
devoted servant of sick and suffering.

For two days the Battalion enjoyed Haselunne. The
advance had taken on a festive air. There was plenty to
eat and drink and the mobile bath unit and mobile cinema
added a flavour of comfort and well being. Early on
13th April the advance continued on through Herselake,
Lorringen and Oldendorf with little else but craters and
road-blocks to check our crowded columns. When on
14th April Cloppenburg had fallen to 130 Brigade, the
enemy communications between Holland and Bremen
were cut.

On 15th April 43 Division was to experience the last
serious opposition in its concentrated campaign. It
opened when "D" Company in the lead found a bridge
over the River Lethe blown 2,000 yards short of Ahlhorn.
They managed to cross and fanned out to form a bridgehead, while 400 yards to the south "A" Company found
a bridge and were able to join them. Early the next
morning the enemy put in a determined counter-attack
with tanks and infantry. The main thrust fell on "A"
Company, and Major P. G. Hall had his cooks in action
before the enemy were beaten off. On the following day
the Somersets, moving round the north flank, cleared the
Ahlhorn cross-roads, and the Battalion then moved back

to probe the wooded area of Forst Cloppenburg which lay
centred on the hamlet Baumeweg a mile to the north of
the axis of advance. Thus was rounded off the last formal
engagement, not without casualties and the loss of three
carriers from mines.

The final stages do but constitute a series of moves
through areas already cleared and are related only for the
satisfaction of leaving historical fact on record.

The move from Forst Cloppenburg on 18th April was
to occupy Steinloge, four miles farther east, to protect the
left flank of the divisional axis. On 19th April a Canadian
unit relieved the Battalion, and three days' rest were
taken four miles to the south of the axis in the villages
Rechterfeld and Bonrechten. Here the Commanding
Officer had at last to surrender to a leg wound received
in the Lethe battle, and command passed to Major A. A.
Grubb, M.C., who happened to be up from the Divisional
Battle School.

On 23rd April a move was made to Schwarme, thirty
miles away, and on the following day the Battalion found
itself deployed along the River Weser two miles from the
bank, with Headquarters south of Donnerstedt. On
25th April the river was crossed by a Bailey bridge and
the Somersets were relieved at Stellenfelde. The situation
was changing hourly so that the efforts of Brigade to
frame orders for an attack on nebulous objectives were
out of date as soon as they were issued, a process which
successfully irritated Commanding Officers and Adjutants. Eventually, however, firm orders to clear an area
west of Burger Park in Bremen were received with relief,
and Bremen was entered in the early hours of 27th April.
Here the full significance of modern war for a defeated
nation was evident. Piles of rubble, open stinking sewers,
yawning craters and a dazed, disillusioned population
sobered and sickened British troops in the flush of victory.
There was no opposition and liberated slave labour, who
as "Displaced Persons" were destined to become a great
international problem, were now more trouble than the
enemy. They knew where the wine stocks lay and made
reckless use of their knowledge. The removal of a road-
block in the northern suburbs of the town resulted in a

1945 wound for the Commanding Officer, and Major Ricketts took command once again but later handed over to Major Reinhold, who returned from a staff attachment on 28th April. 43 Division now left Bremen to others and on 29th April moved out east in a wide encircling move which, with the Guards Armoured Division, 53 (Welch) and 51 (Highland) Divisions, was to comb through the Cuxhaven Peninsula. Such operations as were necessary amounted only to clearing up marsh-land which lay off the axis of advance. The roads and culverts were heavily mined and there were many good lives lost in the seemingly capricious and cruel play of fate in these last hours long after the German capitulation had become inevitable. That night the Battalion lay up in the area of Wilhelmshausen, and by 1900 hours the next day had collected in 105 dazed bedraggled prisoners.

The Cornwalls had made a bridgehead over the River Worpe at Grasberg, and the Battalion was passed through with little rest in the morning of 1st May. On the evening of 30th April Lieut.-Colonel Hope-Thomson had rejoined from hospital. The command had changed hands several times within weeks, and it was certainly a matter for congratulation and a tribute to basic training that its effective striking power in no way suffered from many changes.

The daily role had by now become a simple business of probing territory on either side of the axis of advance, and it was in this capacity that the Battalion operated on a stretch of country to the north for the last time under Major Reinhold on 2nd May. The day will be remembered for Major Reinhold's amazingly lucky escape from death as his jeep was destroyed in running over a mine. He escaped with a perforated ear-drum, his driver breaking a leg.

That evening the Battalion was relieved by 4th King's Own Scottish Borderers and moved back to the village of Westertimke. There, surrounded by hilarious prisoners of war of all nations who at last knew freedom, news of the close of the greatest drama of history was breathlessly awaited. On 4th May it came.

CHAPTER FIVE

THE FIRST BATTALION, 1945–1950

Trieste, Berlin, Göttingen, Chester

THE scattered farmhouses of Westertimke will always be   1945
remembered by those who served with the 1st Worcestershire at the time as the background against which the end
of World War II was announced by the Intelligence
Officer to a party of officers who were enjoying a good
dinner in a farmhouse on the evening of 4th May.
Throughout Western Germany in a hundred similar
situations the incomprehensible message was spreading,
and when the first wild jubilation had subsided the
unspoken thought of many may well have been of those
who had fallen in guarding so loyally the motto of their
Regiment, not only in the orchards round Caen and along
the Siegfried Line but across the sands of North Africa
and on the heights of Keren.

So unexpected has been the picture of ever-changing
international relations since May, 1945, that the soldier
who is the servant of policy may be forgiven if some of
the burdens which he has had to carry in the past five
years have taken him by surprise. The modern demands
of policing a world caught in the frustrations and
entanglements of a cold war have created situations which
none could have foreseen who fought the last battles
in North-West Europe. Thereafter many minor dramas
were to be enacted in which Germans, Poles, Italians,
Yugoslavs, and—last but not least—Russians were to tax
the tempers and diplomacy of the men of the 1st
Worcestershire Regiment. It is but a symptom of the age
that this story closes with a fresh call on the services of
the Battalion from the jungles of Malaya.

From 5th May for three days the Battalion cleaned up,
reorganized and relaxed. Appropriately on 8th May
(VE Day) they transferred to the German occupation area

1945   which was flanked on the east by the River Elbe and
extended to the west of Lüneburg. There they were
dispersed in three villages with Headquarters at Rosen-
thal. Almost immediately the task of scouring the country
for the scattered German Army, their weapons,
equipment and supply dumps, began.

The 20th May found the whole Battalion posted at a
small village, Neetze, near Lüneburg, where it was
destined to remain until early in October. The great
German machine had disintegrated and the autobahns
and highways were littered with the soldiers of the
Wehrmacht, lost and bewildered. These had gradually
to be rounded up and sorted into prisoner-of-war camps.
Simultaneously two companies of the Battalion were busy
patrolling a stretch of the River Elbe near by. Gradually
as the work of concentrating a mass of prisoners and
dealing with adventurous Polish marauders progressed,
so there was opportunity to return to the dull, unspectacular yet essential side of soldiering : drill and weapon
training. Though Poles were prominent among the
great roving community of displaced persons, there were
also French, Belgians, Dutch, and Russians, and all these
had to be sorted into their separate enclaves. But the
lighter side of life could at least be accepted now without
interruption from enemy action, and so the Battalion
found time to stage "This is It," a flourishing music-hall
show which successfully toured the whole Divisional
Area.

In October the Battalion moved to Goslar and at the
same time said farewell to 214 Infantry Brigade and
43 Wessex Division, entering the 5th Division as a unit
in 13 Infantry Brigade. A week or so later Brigadier
R. W. M. de Winton handed over the Brigade to Brigadier
D. C. Bullen-Smith, M.C.

Goslar is an attractive medieval town of old stone and
semi-timbered buildings. It stands at the entrance to the
Harz mountains and in happier circumstances is of
interest for the tourist who seeks a holiday off the beaten
track. But in an intensely cold winter in post-war
Germany its attractions were hardly noticed. "D"
Company were detached fifteen miles to the north in

Liebenburg and the Support Company were at Oker 1945
some five miles away, but the rest of the Battalion were
in scattered billets spread through the town. Few of the
German houses had fireplaces, while timber which was
readily available was not suitable for use with central
heating. Goslar is therefore remembered for a very cold
winter.

A detached platoon was permanently posted on the
border by the Russian zone just outside Bad Harzburg,
its work being to prevent movement either from or to the
Russian Zone. It was not an unpopular duty and was
regarded in the nature of a holiday camp. Little contact
was ever made with the corresponding Russian post ; but
the Russian commander on several occasions tried to
exchange Leica cameras for gallons of British petrol.
This seemed a mystery, until it transpired that he had
recently commandeered a German motor-cycle and was in
difficulties over procuring petrol from his own official
sources !

The duties of arrest were unpleasant but not exacting.
Arrested civilians were passed on to Goslar for interro-
gation by the Field Security personnel, and occasionally
they included a poor wretch who had stopped a Russian
bullet in his escape. Apart from work at the border post,
some ten miles of the zonal frontier had also to be
patrolled.

After the stern reality of war, it was perhaps not easy
to return to a necessary enthusiasm for day-to-day
training. The emphasis was on patrolling and map
reading, and it was gratifying that "D" Company was
able to win the Inter-Brigade treasure hunt in company
with teams from the Manchesters, Wiltshires and
Cameronians.

At this time memories of war were too vivid to permit
of any close association with the inhabitants. Yet, even
so, a mild liaison with some of the young ladies of the
town was beginning ; and the end has been that the
Battalion returned to Chester in 1950 with a dozen or so
wives from Germany, to whom we wish all good fortune
in their share of the unknown hazards of "following the
drum." The officers of the detachment of Liebenburg

1945   were grateful for the hospitality of the local Baron who was glad enough to find guns ready to shoot his hares.

But while much of the daily routine at Goslar calls for no particular comment, there was one commitment which proved definitely unpleasant. A local Board of British and Russian representatives, which included Major D. Y. Watson of the Battalion, sat under an officer of the Control Commission to arrange the repatriation of local Russian prisoners of war in Germany. The greater number of them protested at their classification as Russians and refused the privilege of return, whereupon it was the unpleasant duty of two companies of the Battalion to have to deal with them by force. At one period they had forcibly to be carried into their vehicles. Yet the performance of this highly disagreeable task only resulted in a protest from the Russian officer concerned, who complained that bayonets had not been used in the execution of the hand-over ! This rather profitless work continued for five weeks, and it was a treat to escape to 30 Corps leave centre which had opened up at Bad Harzburg near by and which proved a paradise of freedom. Apart from this, seven days' leave in the United Kingdom was now available and served to remind the fortunate ones that ultimately there was no place like home.

1946   On 5th March, 1946, a move was made to Gandersheim on the way to Einbech. Here, modern barracks in some disrepair housed the Headquarter Company and two rifle companies, the other two companies being billeted in the town. The Support Company was some four kilometres away at Kreiensen. One platoon stood by always for internal security purposes, but otherwise normal training proceeded. On the recreational side, Gandersheim will be remembered as an opportunity for everyone to learn to ride. Fourteen good horses had been collected off the Wehrmacht the previous summer and were available for the purposes of an organized riding school. The success of the riding school was due to the efforts of Captain T. J. Bowen, M.C., who not only collected horses and the saddlery, but converted an old barn into excellent stables. He also commissioned the

construction of a pony trap by a local German coachman   1946
which travelled with the Battalion until sold two years
later in Berlin. Not only could all ranks become horse-
masters, but they could shoot pig on a scale usually
associated with a partridge drive. In co-operation with
the willing forest masters, any number of German
ex-Wehrmacht beaters were always available, and two or
three packets of cigarettes made payment ! A percentage
of the meat went back for the beaters and the remaining
portions were eaten and enjoyed by all.

Organized sport had by now developed to absorb all
spare time and Brigade and Divisional soccer, boxing,
swimming and athletic meetings were making their
demands.

On 3rd June the Battalion lost their Commanding
Officer, Lieut.-Colonel C. P. G. Wills, on promotion to
Brigadier, and the Second-in-Command, Major A. H.
Nott, took temporary command until the arrival of
Lieut.-Colonel R. E. L. Tuckey, who was to hold
command for the next two and a half years.

At the end of August the Brigade were perhaps lucky
to set out on a temporary adventure which constituted a
complete change from the prevailing conditions in
Germany, and as the 13th Independent Infantry Brigade
they made their way down to the blue Mediterranean
coastline by Trieste. A train journey of four days took
the Battalion to Calais, thence by the "Medloc" route
through Nancy, Karlsruhe and Salzburg to the Austrian
southern frontier at Villach. Here a change of trains was
made, and Trieste was reached on 10th September after
a final lap of six hours. It was an attractive but uneventful
journey, to be remembered only for the spasmodic meals
which were snatched at the food halts. Had the train
always arrived on schedule there could have been no
complaints. But with the midday meal possibly consumed
at 2 a.m. in the morning, it was difficult to absorb the
sudden change to a new and happier environment.

As an independent formation, 13 Brigade were now
attached to 1st Armoured Division with its headquarters
at Miramare Castle outside Trieste. The town itself and
its security, however, was the sole responsibility of the

1946 Brigade. In addition, a subsidiary commitment was to share the duties of guarding the frontier between the allied and Yugoslav zones with the other Brigade in the Division. In theory this involved a preparation to support the Venezia-Giulia, which was the local mixed police force of Italians and Slavs officered by British and Americans. But in practice, so far as the Battalion was concerned, it amounted to one platoon being posted at a railway station by the frontier on the Trieste–Equile–Lipizzano road. The association with the Venezia-Giulia Police will be remembered chiefly for the efforts of the British to dress up the Italians and Slavs in uniforms of the London Police. Somehow the familiar dark blue helmet never looked happy on an Italian head! The platoon on isolated duty lived in Nissen huts and never made contact with its Yugoslav counterpart, and could hardly have discovered much compensation for an uneventful two months' tour of duty. Moreover, life in Trieste and the surrounding country in the winter is governed by the "bora," an ice-cold wind which blows down off the mountains at ninety miles an hour from December to February. It found no difficulty in penetrating the corridors and living rooms of Rossetti Barracks, and barrack life was a matter of dodging the draughts! After the big storms of January, 1947, snow piled up high on the barrack-room verandas. It is even related that on one occasion an officer who had dined well after a guest night awoke to find an accumulation of four inches of snow on his camp bed!

Nevertheless, after Germany, Trieste presented a striking contrast. Officers were able to welcome their families from England. The restaurants were full of good food and wine, the shop windows displayed a variety of goods and the people were friendly. Rossetti Barracks, which formerly had housed Italian Cavalry units, were shared with the 1st Battalion Oxford and Bucks Light Infantry, since before leaving Gandersheim the Brigade had been reconstituted on a three-battalion basis to include 1st Battalion Oxford and Bucks Light Infantry and 2nd Battalion The Essex Regiment. It was the latter who remained mainly responsible for the

frontier, while the Worcestershire and Oxford and Bucks   1946
Light Infantry policed Trieste itself.

The British soldier took some time to appreciate the
novelty of macaroni and "pasta-ascinta," but he was
grateful enough for Italian company, and some half a
dozen wives who deserted Trieste to share the fortunes
of the Worcestershire Regiment are testimony to a mild
social relationship with the inhabitants.

Throughout the period in Trieste there was the
implication of a general responsibility to act as a reserve
of force in an emergency. But in practice the only occasion
on which the garrison was called on to operate in its
collective capacity was when a search was made of the
dockers' living quarters to trace the suspected smuggling
of arms. In December early one morning at 3 a.m. the
two Battalions surrounded the area and spent the next
twelve hours in a fruitless search.

On 7th and 8th November a Brigade Rifle Meeting,
held on an old Austrian Army range at Villa Opicina, a
village to the north of Trieste, produced a close contest
with the Oxf. and Bucks in which the Battalion defeated
their opponents.

It would be overstatement to say that the Trieste
experience was accepted with unqualified appreciation by
all ; for a couple of cigarettes could hardly command the
services with which they could be associated in Germany !
Nor, apart from the excellent restaurants, was there much
gay night life. But by and large there was satisfaction for
many interests, from the local Opera House to duck
shooting in the marshes by Monfalcone, fifteen kilometres to the west of the town. For those who rode a
horse there were days with the draghounds of the 4th
Hussars, who had exploited the famous Lipizzano stables.

On 31st January, 1947, a move was made south to Pola   1947
in the Yugoslav zone, more familiar to students of the
current international problem as "Zone B." The situation
in Berlin had its analogy in Pola. Only one main road led
in through the Yugoslav zone to a city which was administered as part of the Allied zone. A small party with the
carriers, anti-tank guns and heavy baggage made the
journey by sea so that their introduction to Pola was by

1947   its excellent natural harbour, formerly an Austrian naval
base protected by a ring of forts. The main body, however,
moved by road along the only permitted road to Pola,
which twisted and turned over hills, giving drivers
anxious moments on account of its incredibly bad surface.

The short stay in Pola was, however, marred by
tragedy, for on 10th February Brigadier de Winton, a
much respected and popular leader, was assassinated
while inspecting the Brigade H.Q. Guard, which on that
morning was provided by the Battalion. He fell to the
bullets of a crazy Italian woman, named Maria Pasquin-
elli, a fanatic who produced a statement to say that she
had no personal enmity for the Brigadier but that she
took action in protest to a policy which handed over
Italian soil to Yugoslavia. The manner of assassination
was curious in that when the Brigadier fell forward with
three bullets in his body the guard facing him did not
immediately realize what had happened. Thinking he had
fainted, the Guard Commander ran forward to pick him
up. Only then was it realized what had happened and the
woman, who made no effort to escape, was arrested. She
was later tried by an Allied Court, the immediate effect in
Pola being the imposition of a 24-hour curfew.[1]

In Pola companies were separated in scattered barracks,
"A" Company forming a detachment in a fort at the
eastern point of the harbour. Harbour protection was a
somewhat nebulous role and was perhaps a matter more
of appearances than of problematical action. By the
middle of March the weather had settled to a cloudless
Mediterranean spring and Pola had its compensations.
A wonderful beach provided bathing and the opportunity was taken to train men to become sea-minded. A
fishing boat was acquired from the Navy and was
appropriately christened H.M.S. *Brunswick*. The boat
boasted a small auxiliary engine in addition to its sails,
and crews of about twenty at a time were encouraged to
try their fortunes at sea over the week-ends.

In the sphere of training the Battalion concentrated on
weapons and a chance to fire the 3-inch mortars was

---

[1] Captain St. J. C. Brooke-Johnson of the Battalion, acting as Brigade
Intelligence Officer, took charge of the assailant.

welcome ; for though the Battalion still had much of its **1947**
war-time personnel, there had been little opportunity for
field firing. Training was marred by one serious accident
when, due to faulty mortar bombs, a bomb blew up inside
a mortar and killed two good men.

As incitement to concentrated weapon training,
Brigadier de Winton's successor[2] introduced the "Pola
Marathon." At the time it was not very popular, but the
1st Worcestershire successfully accepted the terms of
competition, their teams winning the officers' competition
and taking second and third places in the corporals' and
sergeants' races. The tests were exacting with results
based on both a time and scoring element. It was curious
to find that an American team from the U.S. Independent Company at Pola, which volunteered to compete,
were well at the tail of competitors, only three of their
team of eight finishing the course. Since they came with
a reputation as tough fighters from Okinawa in the
Pacific war, they presumably entered the Pola marathon
in confidence of success.

At the end of April, Brigade Headquarters and the
Oxf. and Bucks left for Germany via Trieste, leaving the
Battalion alone in Pola. The month of comparative
isolation in a small town presented the opportunity for a
closer liaison with the Yugoslavs, many of the Italians
having now left. Thus on at least two occasions the Corps
of Drums beat Retreat in the main square, and if the rank
and file found no particular reason to wish to prolong their
stay, at least the inhabitants showed some interest in the
Battalion when the day came to leave.

When that day came, the Battalion marched through
the town and on to their ship behind the band, and the
entire population turned out. But it was a silent, unre-
sponsive crowd with no particular affection for the
British soldier. The Italian element had some cause for
gratitude, for men of the Battalion had guarded an
Italian flour-mill which the owners had decided to
remove to Italy rather than risk it falling into the hands
of the Yugoslavs.

On 17th May, having handed over to 2nd Battalion The

---

[2] Brigadier J. Scott-Elliot, C.B.E., D.S.O.

1947   Cameron Highlanders, the Battalion embarked by L.S.T. and retraced the journey back to Trieste. Thence only a short halt was called before entraining once again for Germany. The Mediterranean experience had been of rare interest and provided a chance to take a look at a corner of Europe to which little attention was ever given in the far-off days of normal peace and sanity.

The journey north lay through Karlsruhe and Göttingen to Lüneburg, about sixty kilometres to the south of Hamburg. Life in Lüneburg in the early summer was pleasant enough. Once again the Brigade was back with its old formation, 5 Division, and the opportunity was taken at last to attempt training on a higher level than that of a battalion. In June the Brigade Weapon Training Meeting was won, and in the Divisional Meeting later at Sennelager the Battalion only just yielded first place to 1st Manchesters. For three weeks the Brigade went into camp at Sennelager and a start was made with serious field training. Near by Sennelager is a patch of country not unlike the heath outside Camberley. Fir plantations interrupt the rolling bracken-covered landscape and there was opportunity to try out the full cycle of operations from the approach march to the attack and a withdrawal. In a Brigade Exercise ("Hotfoot") carried out from Lüneburg in the Amelinghansen area the Battalion discovered that it had certainly not forgotten the lessons learnt two years previously.

In August the Battalion had a welcome visit from Brigadier Clarke, the Colonel of the Regiment. From 7th to 9th September the Battalion was involved in operation "Oasis," which was one of those variations within the scope of police duties that have become frequent in the uncertainties of the international situation. Three shiploads of Jewish refugees who had attempted to run the blockade of Palestine had to be taken ashore, an operation which was completed in face of resistance from those on board the s.s. *Runnymede Park.*

At the end of September all training ceased and an entirely new role was temporarily imposed. This time all ranks became lumber men. Operation "Woodpecker," as it was known, proved to be a test of temper and

endurance. The Battalion worked in all weathers, **1947**
including snow. The necessary "target figures" *had* to
be produced, and in a not very popular role the Battalion
managed to produce the greatest tonnage over the four
months in the Brigade group. Previously in July one
company under Major D. B. Haslehurst had made a good
start. It involved an early morning start for the woods
near Lüneburg, the whole day on the job, and a return to
barracks late in the evening. Sunday, indeed, was a day
of rest well earned. The timber was destined for England
and was, it was hoped, a contribution to help solve the
housing problem.

Work in the forests kept the Battalion occupied until
Christmas. It was then that 5 Division and its brigades
went into "suspended animation," and the Battalion set
out for Berlin.

Whatever may have been the limitations of life in **1948**
Berlin, the experience could hardly have failed to leave
lasting memories in the minds of officers and men who
served with the Battalion throughout 1948. The sense
that great international issues were in the melting-pot in
the capital city of Germany must have lain in vague
subconscious recess even among the least imaginative of
those who formed the Berlin garrison. The journey up
was uneventful. The entire Battalion, except the
transport, packed into one train and arrived at one o'clock
in the morning on 31st January, whereupon a take-over
from 1st Battalion the Northamptonshire Regiment was
effected in the record time of three hours !

The Montgomery Barracks near Gatow airport lie some
eight miles from the city, right on the border between the
British sector of Berlin and the Russian Zone. Life was,
therefore, obviously destined to be full of minor incidents
and mild excitement. British Troops, Berlin, constituting
in effect a separate independent command, had first to
furnish innumerable guards all over the city, while
secondly they were a reserve of force which if necessary
would be called upon to preserve the peace, even to the
point of representing the Western will against the Soviet.

Guard duties which absorbed the entire strength of the
Battalion varied from guarding the High Commissioner's

1948 house to watching petrol dumps and food depots.

Barely a month had gone by when the first encounter with the Russians occurred. The Russian Zone ran round the west and southern sides of Gatow aerodrome, with opposing Russian and British posts facing each other in the south-west corner. Quite suddenly and without warning the Russians moved their check post into our sector, claiming that the move represented the correct delimitation of the frontier. In effect this manœuvre cut across a road running round the aerodrome and a number of Battalion vehicles were detained, including a party of wives returning from a shopping expedition. Accordingly, acting under direct orders from the G.O.C., Berlin,[3] the Commanding Officer, Lieut.-Colonel R. E. L. Tuckey, took out two companies and surrounded the Russians. After twenty-four hours they withdrew as suddenly as they had arrived. The incident had served as a useful introduction to the unexpected tactics of our former Allies, and it effectively warned all ranks of the type of contact to watch for in the future.

Amid much human misery it was perhaps difficult to appreciate the fact that the Battalion was probably better housed than ever before in the past or may be likely in the future. The Luftwaffe had a reputation of living well and the ex-Luftwaffe barracks were almost luxurious. In addition, married families began to arrive and were housed in quarters on the edge of the Warnsee Lake such as could never be available in the garrison stations of the United Kingdom. The Officers' Mess in particular will seldom find a more comfortable home.

April and May, 1948, passed without incident save that a representative detachment furnished a guard of honour for the C.I.G.S., Lord Montgomery, and "D" Company took over for a month's tour of duty at Spandau gaol, guarding the former celebrities, Hess, Raeder, Doenitz, Funck, and Neurath. It was then the practice for representatives of the four Allied Powers to assume duty at Spandau for a month in turn. It was hardly a task with a popular appeal and held nothing more stimulating than an occasional glimpse of former Nazi leadership at

[3] Major-General E. O. Herbert, C.B.E., D.S.O.

exercise or employed in innocuous gardening, Herr Hess 1948
being particularly occupied with tomatoes.

In June "D" Company moved from Spandau to assume
duties which promised more varied chances of incident,
and accordingly that central area of controversy, the
Tiergarten, where the Russian War Memorial gazes
gloomily across at the Brandenburg Gate, was occupied as
a permanent commitment for which the Battalion had to
furnish one company on detachment. "D" Company
under Captain Brooke-Johnson took over from a company
of the Norfolks and found themselves living in a rather
rickety old house of former glory, but now converted to
flats. It had had a thorough shaking from our bombs and
altogether did not appear too secure.

The company at the Tiergarten subsequently came in
for its share of mild excitement, and one incident at
least might well have initiated a major international crisis.
It deserves record if only to indicate how exasperatingly
provocative the Soviet Berlin command could be and the
lengths to which they were prepared to go in execution
of an unfathomable policy of studied hostility.

The Moltke bridge crosses the River Spree in the
Tiergarten. Near by within the British sector was a
scrap-metal dump. Quite suddenly on a night late in
June Russian lorries appeared over the bridge and their
men started to load the scrap in an attempt to remove it.
Major A. B. de Quincey, then commanding "D" Company, acted promptly, surrounding the dump and refusing
to let the Russians leave. Later in the following morning,
Major de Quincey's command was reinforced by "A"
Company, under Major D. J. Patrickson. The Russians
brought up troops on the far bank of the river and both
sides dug in! At this stage there were all the elements
of a serious crisis. After twelve hours the Russian
Deputy Military Governor arrived on the bridge and
demanded that his troops and lorries be released. Equally
firmly he was told that they could leave provided the
lorries were first emptied. There was thus a deadlock.
The Russian Commander commented that though we
might display machine guns he could and would display
tanks ! Rather naturally this caused some consternation

1948   and our troops were accordingly reinforced by a squadron
of 11th Hussars and a troop of R.E., with orders to mine
the bridge and if necessary cover it by fire. The
following night Russian tanks were heard, but by day they
fortunately kept out of sight. True to form, on the third
night the lorries were duly unloaded and by the following
morning both sides had melted away. It is easy to speak
lightly of such an affair after the event ; yet, in truth, it
seems difficult to contemplate circumstances in which the
chances of the shooting war could have been more
definite.

On another occasion a warning was received for a secret
operation of some delicacy which, however, finally
demanded no action. Near by the Moltke bridge the
Lehrte civil gaol housed German prisoners convicted of
the despicable crime of trying to abduct Germans from
the Western sector and hand them over to the Russians.
Information was received that an attempt would be made
to storm the prison and release the prisoners. Fortunately or unfortunately, it came to nothing. In such ways
the company at the Tiergarten had their hands full until
the end of August, when the 1st Royal Norfolks relieved
the Battalion of these duties.

Against the background of such ominous events "The
Glorious First of June" was remembered with a parade
at which Long Service and Good Conduct Medals were
awarded to five W.Os. and N.C.Os. ; while on 10th June
the King's Birthday was celebrated with a fine parade of
the British garrison in the Olympic Stadium, the salute
being taken by Major-General Herbert, who throughout
troublesome times in Berlin was to prove a tower of
strength to the British element of occupation. It was
perhaps some tribute to the temper and behaviour of the
British garrison that the Berlin public turned out in vast
numbers to witness the parade.

Yet again in July, "A" Company paraded with an
available strength of one weak platoon of cooks, clerks,
and batmen, to greet some Russian troops who had
wandered several hundred yards into our sector in the
Potsdamer Platz. They said they had come in by mistake
in pursuit of black marketeers, and for once there was

some logic to their excuse. Early in August the whole 1948
Battalion turned out to man various corners of Berlin for
two days while the new local currency rate was being
introduced. But there were no incidents.

Throughout this period, while "A" and "D" Companies had been exchanging the duties of Spandau and
the Tiergarten, "C" and "B" Companies had been
taking in and training the first National Service men
who had started to arrive in June. Training was necessarily restricted and could only be at platoon level, the
available ground being either the barracks themselves
or around the pleasant Grunewald wooded area
surrounding the lake. For musketry purposes a range in
the Stadium was available, and there was also a 300 yards
range at the barracks. In spite of the varied and constant
demands on personnel, the Battalion was able to produce
weapon teams which could fully maintain the fine record
which has come to be associated over many years with
the Regiment. Thus all events were won at the rifle
meeting in Berlin in 1948, including the capture of the
Company Shield by "A" Company in the A.R.A. non-
central series, while Captain J. D. Reynolds, M.C., was
awarded a shield as the best individual shot of the
meeting. Since 1946 the Battalion had entered for the
A.R.A. non-central matches with increasing skill each
year, and the winning of the Company Shield represented an achievement never before accomplished in the
Home Series in the last thirty years. In the same year
the Battalion was also third in the Queen Victoria Trophy.
Full teams were sent to Bisley in 1948 and 1949 and did
well.

The winter of 1948 will ever be remembered for that
phenomenon of civic life in Berlin, the Berlin air lift.
The Russian blockade brought untold and useless misery
to Western Berlin, the repercussions of which were
evident to our troops in the form of severe lighting and
fuel restrictions and dehydrated food. To cope with
blockade conditions, the French constructed Tegel aerodrome within their sector, and in a thick fog on a morning
in December, with visibility little more than ten yards
distance, the Battalion turned out for the inaugural

1948 ceremonial parade. It proved as cold a ceremonial ordeal
as had ever been experienced.

Sufficient has been said to indicate the precarious
nature of the work of policing Berlin. Yet in spite of living
on a potential political volcano, social and recreational
facilities were perhaps more readily to hand than in any
other station of the post-war era. The lake in itself with
its Yacht Club provided the troops with canoes, sailing
and rowing. The finest sports stadium in the world was
available to cater for every form of physical exercise
together with excellent expert German instruction. The
Church of England and Salvation Army provided Clubs,
while until the blockade there were regular race meetings.
The three Western Allies staged Show jumping competi-
tions in their sectors. Military missions came and went
and were entertained in a continuous round of social
hospitality. Innumerable liaisons with frauleins in the
city resulted in some twenty bi-national marriages. Life
indeed was one of contrasts, and just as Shanghai in the
spacious nineteen-thirties might well have corrupted a
1949 good Battalion if enjoyed for too long, so in May, 1949,
the Battalion was ready to say farewell to Berlin and make
for one of the most attractive of German University
towns, Göttingen, by the River Leine, in a country of
long, rolling hills on the boundary of the British, American
and Russian Zones.

In the return to post-war conditions the 1st Battalion
experienced those many difficulties of the transition stage
which are a feature of a system by which a large short-
term national army is entirely dependent on a small
efficient Regular nucleus. The release scheme hit the
Battalion hardest in the period 1945-1947. But the
gradual return of Regular officers, senior Warrant officers,
and N.C.Os. had a steadying effect. The period saw the
arrival of the Band, the Colours, the Regimental silver,
the overhaul of the whole administration, and the
production of post-war Standing Orders.

In June, 1948, successive batches of National Service
men began to arrive. At first the drafts came in at
regular intervals and rifle companies in turn were
cleared to receive them. But as time wore on and the

effects of the air lift became apparent the system developed **1949**
irregularities and training inevitably suffered. Throughout
the Army, responsibility for the many by the few has
presented a constant and frustrating problem, and for
the 1st Worcestershire these difficulties were not
diminished by the particular conditions of Germany in
general and Berlin in particular.

The move to Göttingen on 16th May covered four days
and represented a particularly smooth and successful
piece of administration. Although the Berlin blockade
had been raised three days previously it was decided to
carry on with the first stage by air to Lübeck. The
relieving unit, 1st Battalion the Gordon Highlanders,
were flown in by small parties, and as they arrived so
parties of the Battalion left. It was good flying weather
and generally all went "according to plan." After a night
in the rest camp at Hamburg the journey was completed
by train in time for a parade in barracks in celebration of
"The Glorious First of June," when the Brigade Commander took the salute. After the varied commitments
of Berlin, the role of the Battalion in its new formation at
Göttingen seemed clear enough and more in accordance
with the normal expectations of a modern infantry
battalion. Nevertheless the need for some intensive
retraining was obvious, since the Battalion now entered
the 31st Lorried Infantry Brigade,[4] which was the lorried
formation opposite to the Armoured Brigade, the two
Brigades together composing 7th Armoured Division.
Previous to the move from Berlin, Lieut.-Colonel A. H.
Gillmore, O.B.E., had assumed command on 3rd March,
and it was under this officer that the Battalion later
sailed for the Far East.

Göttingen was certainly a pleasant base from which to
set to and study the new demands of higher training.
Any number of partridge, pheasants, duck, and hares
were shot. But though there were pig in the forests, a
number of organized pig shoots failed to produce results.
However, with roebuck waiting to be shot in the summer
there could be no complaints and all ranks were able to

---

[4] Commander, Brigadier C. E. H. Dolphin, C.B.E.

H

1949   shoot. Through the Regimental Shooting Club licences[5]
could be obtained from the Kreis Resident Officer.
Contact with the local population was therefore usually
through the medium of shooting, and some of the small
land owners and forest masters became good friends. In
Göttingen itself occasionally a German family would turn
up to a small sherry party, but the demands of training
under an energetic Brigadier did not allow much time
over for social engagements. In later years, however,
officers of the Battalion may remember with interest one
particular evening when the members of a German
ex-officers' institution dined them well. After a few short
appropriate speeches, the Germans suddenly produced a
collection of papers and cuttings which recorded every-
thing that had ever been said by any responsible statesman
in England on the subject of German rearmament!
What were the views of the guests ? The question was
applied tactfully but with persistence. In watching the
shape of events to come it will be of interest to have
placed this occasion on record.

The Göttingen barracks had previously housed a
German regiment of Hussars so that they were equipped
with four excellent riding schools and fine stables, which,
however, had been wrecked for their timber by wild gangs
of displaced persons. The place was therefore ideal for
those who liked their "huntin', shootin', fishin'," while
for others with time and inclination there was a small
Opera House with singers of that high quality invariably
associated with all German towns. After the quarters in
Berlin, the married families found they had to forgo a
few luxuries. Even so they were housed in greater
comfort than was ever available at home, and there will
be not a few housewives in Chester who must miss some
of the domestic facilities of Germany.

But since the emphasis was now on solid training, some
mention must be made of the stages by which the
Battalion was seeking to fit itself for its new role. While
the Brigade of four battalions of lorried infantry had to
regard themselves as the element of exploitation to the

---

[5] £2 for all game ; £1 for small game only.

armoured attack, they yet had also to be inter-changeable   1949
with the armoured Brigade, the Division as a whole
regarding itself as a highly flexible formation, capable of
adaptation to many situations. Training therefore resolved
into four distinct stages. In July the Battalion was back
at Sennelager for Company and Battalion training. From
the middle of August to 7th September the Brigade
concentrated at Soltau for Brigade training, subsequently
extending the period to work with 7th Armoured Brigade.

From mid-October, Exercise "Agility 1" was intended
to test out 7 Armoured Division as a complete formation.
Finally Exercise "Agility 2," in which 31 Brigade assumed
the role of enemy to 2 Division, was intended to test staffs
and the Higher Command and bring light to bear on the
many problems on inter-allied co-operation in a modern
war in Europe, which at present remained unanswered.
Every phase was thus to be studied, the advance to
contact, the attack, withdrawal and defence.

But the practical demands of policing were not quite   1950
over, for on 6th March, 1950, the whole Battalion, less
two platoons, suddenly had to turn out at the vast
Hermann Göring works at Immendorf, south-west of
Brunswick, to assist in the destruction of certain plant.
At one stage a large smelting furnace had to be surrounded
to prevent some 4,000 German workers hindering the
party responsible for laying the charge. Two platoons had
in the meanwhile been left behind on the frontier near
Friedland to deal with anticipated trouble of a different
nature. In this case the Russians were busy pushing
through German refugees, only some of whom could be
accepted by the British and American authorities. But
neither at Immendorf nor at Friedland were any serious
measures eventually necessary.

Late in October, 1949, the news had arrived that the
Battalion was due for the Far East in the New Year, and
accordingly the Commanding Officer started thinking of
the new role. But nothing could be usefully carried out
for the practical reason that very few of the men with the
Battalion in Germany were destined to serve with it in
Malaya. Such is the effective application of a system of
National Service that two-thirds of those destined to sail

1950 for Malaya at the end of May, 1950, will have served but
one week with their unit. It is a situation which throws
tremendous responsibilities on that hard core of Regular
officers and N.C.Os. who have to see to it that in the
jungles of Malaya the motto "Firm" is never in jeopardy ;
yet even though it seems that they are only to enjoy a
period of three weeks' intensive preparation in jungle
warfare the other end, we may be certain that somehow
there will be no doubt as to the safety of their motto and
the manner in which those responsibilities will be
discharged.

On 10th March a parade in Göttingen, when the salute
was taken by the General Officer Commanding, 7th
Armoured Division,[6] was the Battalion's farewell to
Germany. Crowds had gathered in the streets and it
seemed that the unattractive task of "occupation" had at
least been accomplished without ill will to the men of the
Worcestershire Regiment.

After an uneventful journey through Hanover, Hook
of Holland, and Harwich, Chester was reached on
30th March. At Chester the Officers' Mess of the
Depot, The Cheshire Regiment was at the disposal of
the officers, and generally that regiment, as part of the
Mercian Brigade Group, was most hospitable. On
24th May the Battalion sailed from Liverpool for Singapore. The local Embarkation Staff hardly offered that
cordial co-operation which would have been welcome on
such an occasion and unwelcome restrictions were
imposed. There we must leave them as they set out for
the very different life which lies ahead. Wherever they
may be, hundreds of their comrades in Worcestershire
and farther afield will follow their fortunes with that
solicitude which comes of pride of ownership.

---

[6] Major-General H. R. B. Arkwright, C.B., D.S.O.

CHAPTER SIX

THE SECOND BATTALION, 1922–1944

Dublin, Dover, The Rhine, Plymouth, Malta,
Shanghai, Tientsin, Sialkot, Waziristan,
Wellington, Madras

THE story of the 2nd Battalion opens in Ireland. It is **1922**
incidental that we take up its record with the first issue of
The Green 'Un, which was to tell of the life of the Battalion for the next few years. If the records of *The Green
'Un* are studied at this time, it would seem that life in
Dublin was governed by inter-unit sport. Cricket, football, hockey and athletics are faithfully recorded in detail.
The Dublin Garrison was a large one and there were
opportunities for battle on the Phœnix Park ground with
the Border Regiment, the Wiltshires, Lancashire Fusiliers,
the K.S.L.I., and others. Even so, the Battalion were
apparently not satisfied with their organization for games,
for in April, 1923, at Dover a Central Sports Committee
was formed and we read that "it has already accomplished
much and gives promise of a long life of genuine
usefulness."

The Battalion moved under the command of Lieut.- **1923**
Colonel G. M. G. Davidge, D.S.O., from Dublin to
Dover in January, 1923. It left an unhappy country
with little regret. The task of policing a people so
near to us in associations of blood and sentiment yet so
bitterly hostile in national relationship had not been
pleasant. The last days in Dublin were confused not only
by the age-old feud of British and Irish, but also by rivalry
between the Free Staters, who represented the official
Irish new administration, and the rebel Republicans.
The British Garrison had withdrawn into camps and were
waiting orders to be gone, only retained to see if the new
Free State had its roots deep enough to govern. In the

1922   case of the 2nd Battalion this situation meant a move from
        Portobello Barracks to Kilmainham Camp in the spring
        of 1922. The barracks were handed over to the Free
        State Forces not without some mild friction which
        prompted an Irish newspaper to speak of the "exceedingly
        terse" manner of the Second-in-Command.[1] In actual
        fact this officer had merely insisted on the production of
        an Official Pass by the Irish representative, which on a
        first encounter was not forthcoming. There was also a
        legitimate objection to an attempt to hoist the Free State
        flag before our men were clear of the barracks. All this,
        however, did not prevent the Dublin crowds from turning
        out in overwhelming numbers when the day came to take
        leave of Ireland ; and the troops left paradoxically to
        chants of "Auld Lang Syne" and an astonishing display
        of warm-hearted sentiment.

            At Dover the familiar cycle of English garrison life was
        resumed. There was a lot of ground to make up, for
        whatever else life in Ireland represented, there was
        certainly little opportunity to train soldiers for normal
        warfare. The Connaught Barracks above the Castle were
        good. As one of four battalions in the 8th Infantry
        Brigade, the 2nd Worcestershire were up against healthy
        competition and more than held their own in athletics and
        football. Under the direction of Lieutenant J. J. Abbott,
        an Army champion who might have been an Olympic
        runner if the exigencies of the service had permitted, the
        Battalion led in cross-country running, while at football
        three players were provided for the Army soccer team in
        1924 and 1925. One ceremonial parade will be well
        remembered by old members of the 2nd Worcestershire.
        On 31st October, 1924, that fine old soldier, Field-
        Marshal the Earl of Ypres, took the salute at a parade
        held to commemorate the Battle of Gheluvelt.

1926   In January, 1926, the Battalion joined the Army of the
        Rhine in Germany and was posted to Biebrich, a suburb
        of Wiesbaden on the Rhine. Excellent German barracks
        were taken over and were promptly renamed "Ghelu-
        velt Barracks." But they needed considerable spring

---

[1] Major B. C. S. Clarke. Later, Colonel of the Regiment.

cleaning, as the French unit which vacated had different
ideas as to what constituted clean accommodation.

In 1927 the Battalion moved on to Bingen, near
Coblenz, where the time seemed to pass all too quickly
before returning to Plymouth in 1928. This is no reflection on life in a happy English garrison town, but it truly
represents the reactions of officers and men to occupied
Germany after World War I : and it is of interest to note
those reactions in the light of very similar views which
have been expressed by the 1st Battalion in their recent
experience twenty years later. At both Biebrich and
Bingen the reception was peaceful and friendly. Just as
today Berlin and Göttingen has held its compensations
for married families, so in those days the wives from
England enjoyed willing and friendly service from the
local Rhinelanders. Moreover, in 1927 there was none of
the new shyness for military display which today charac-
terizes the Germany emerging from the rubble heaps of
her shattered towns. In those days a military band and a
ceremonial parade were festive institutions to be enjoyed,
and it mattered little that they were staged by a British
battalion. Indeed, the uncased Regimental Colours
frequently received more public respect in Bingen than
has subsequently been paid them on their native soil.
Certainly the 2nd Worcestershire were in a position to
provide display where it was appreciated. They had
accumulated the trophies, silver and equipment of the old
4th Battalion from Ireland, and they made the most of the
comfortable accommodation in Germany.

For much of the time at Bingen two companies were on
detachment at Scherstein. Formation training—both of
Brigade and Division—went ahead and Rhine Army
manœuvres were held. But for the Battalion perhaps the
significance of training in Germany lay in the fact that it
enabled the foundations of a great musketry tradition to
be rebuilt. Competition shooting began. Teams were
sent to Bisley which won the Roupell Cup and tied for
the Small Arms Trophy, while in Germany itself a tie also
resulted for the Rhine Army Championship with a
battalion of the Royal Fusiliers.

When at the close of 1928 the time came to say farewell

1928   to the Rhineland, the Germans turned out in the streets
        of Bingen to shower parting presents on the Battalion and
        give them a true and hearty send-off.   Once again the
        British soldier had proved a worthy ambassador of his
        country, and a small party of German wives who set out
        for Plymouth testified to his success.

1929   Early in 1929 the 2nd Battalion renewed an old regi-
        mental association with Plymouth when they marched
        into Crownhill Barracks to relieve a battalion of the
        Hampshire Regiment.

           Plymouth was essentially a station of Naval co-opera-
        tion and friendship.   There were full facilities for hard
        training, and Willsworthy Camp on the edge of Dartmoor
        provided the training ground for both the Battalion and
        the Plymouth Brigade.   The march up to Wilsworthy
        was never accepted with any enthusiasm.   It was a steady
        uphill climb for sixteen miles, and it always seemed to
        rain for most of the time in camp.   For Divisional
        training once a year the long journey to Tidworth had to
        be made, which meant an absence of about a month from
        home.   The units which completed the Brigade were for
        much of the time the 2nd Devons and the Duke of
        Wellington's at Raglan Barracks, the 2nd Wiltshire being
        close companions in hutments at Crownhill.

           It is of interest to note the comparative simplicity of the
        organization and equipment as compared with the em-
        barrassing wealth of weapons of all types today.   There
        were no mortars, no anti-tank rifles or Brens and no
        armoured vehicles.   Horse-limbered wagons provided the
        transport for a H.Q. wing, three rifle companies and a
        Machine Gun Company.   The rifle, the Lewis gun and
        the .303 machine gun were the only means of fire power ;
        yet such conditions invited a very high standard of
        musketry.   This was no new exactment for a regiment
        which has laid claim consistently to a high standard of
        shooting.   At Plymouth companies in turn undertook their
        weapon training at Fort Tregantle.

           On 1st November, 1929, Lieut.-Colonel B. C. S. Clarke
        assumed command from Lieut.-Colonel F. P. Dunlop,
        D.S.O.   Colonel Dunlop had been commissioned into the
        Regiment from the ranks of the Royal Welch Fusiliers in

Presentation of new Colours to the 2nd Battalion, under command of Lieut.-Colonel B. C. S. Clarke, D.S.O., by His Royal Highness The Duke of Gloucester at the Royal Naval Barracks, Devonport, on 1st June, 1930.

1900. He served on the staff in the 1914-1918 War and   1929
he now passed on to be A.A. and Q.M.G. of Baluchistan
District. Plymouth for Colonel Clarke represented something of a homecoming, for under his father many years
before the 1st Battalion had been the first unit of the
Army to occupy the new barracks. In 1929 the Commanding Officer therefore stepped into the house he had
known as a boy, and the place must have held many vivid
memories for him of the Worcestershire Regiment of
another generation. In those days the keep at Fort
Tregantle had been the officers' quarters. But thirty
years had added or subtracted little to the sturdy façade
of the main entrance. The place is certainly now of
permanent interest for the Worcestershire Regiment
since it was the home of the 5th (Reserve) Battalion
throughout a large portion of World War I.

The more historic ceremonial parades in the life of a
unit are landmarks by which the men of the future may
judge the standards of their forefathers : for in the
British Army at least, a battalion that drills as one on
parade is also firm in war. Thus there is a very legitimate
sense of pride among men of the 2nd Battalion in recalling
the ceremonial which marked "the Glorious First of June"
in 1930, when new Colours were presented by H.R.H.
the Duke of Gloucester on the parade ground of the
Royal Naval Barracks at Devonport.[2] Very appropriately,
it was also a Naval occasion, for rarely can 140 sailors have
come under the direct orders on parade of the Officer
Commanding an Infantry Battalion. Yet that was exactly
what happened when the Naval detachment lining three
sides of a square on their parade ground conformed to
the drill of the Battalion under the orders of Lieut.-
Colonel Clarke. Yet another symbol of association with
the Royal Navy was in rare evidence when, after the
ceremony, two soldiers and two sailors stood guard over
the Colours in the square.

Of all the foreign stations in which over the years the   1930
Worcestershire Regiment has served, none perhaps has
been more popular than Malta, which the 2nd Battalion

---

[2] The new Regimental Colour reverted to the old green, in place of
the Red Cross of St. George on a white field.

1930   were able to enjoy from September, 1930, to 1933. From a strictly professional viewpoint there was the limitation that collective training on any basis higher than that of a unit was impossible. On the other hand, individual training could and did reach a high standard of efficiency. The actual role was that of "coast defence," but there were many opportunities for combined exercises with the Navy at sea ; and indeed liaison with the Navy was not limited to professional training, but was continued closely into the spheres of social relationship and sport. Combined operations invariably took the form of defending the island from the land or landing and attacking from the sea. Whatever the form, it was all good fun, though it involved an immense amount of careful staff preparation. Apart from these stimulating exercises with the Navy, the Battalion lived and worked under the permanent obligation of being at six hours' notice to move as first reinforcements to the Near East. The implication was that the situation in Palestine might demand a sudden intervention. But the need never arose and for three years the value of Malta was thoroughly exploited at work or play.

Previously the laying of the foundations of a fine musketry reputation has been referred to. There was nothing very new about this, but after World War I the old reputation had to be recaptured. In Germany and at Plymouth this process was in development, and it perhaps reached its climax at Malta when the 2nd Worcestershire captured the Queen Victoria Trophy. The three divisions of this great prize were keenly contested at home, in India, and in the foreign stations other than India ; and it was indeed a satisfaction to have such striking evidence of the continued excellence of the Battalion in this vital aspect of competitive training. Not only was the Battalion in the lead in competition with all units of the Army, but in consistent successes in the United Services Small Arms meeting, the Royal Navy were also challenged and well met on their own terms.

The island certainly offered more opportunity for a variety of concentrated sport than most stations. There was polo, not perhaps of the Indian standard but friendly

and to be taken seriously without being too expensive. **1930**
The Battalion football team, led by Sergeant Dalloway, a
former Army full-back, never played better, winning the
United Services Cup three years in succession and the
Malta Army Cup in 1931. Apart from the normal interest
of football, hockey and cricket, there were exceptional
facilities for yachting, rowing and swimming. Every man
learnt to swim, and the Life Saving Society made their
certificates available. For the rank and file the opportunities to learn to row were appreciated perhaps on many
subsequent holiday occasions in an English summer.

All this could be enjoyed from St. Andrew's Barracks,
which happily overlooked the sea ; and it will be readily
appreciated that to overlook the sea at Malta is a different
experience to the vistas to which we are accustomed "who
only England know." Such were the compensations for
being confined to the shores of a tiny island, though
officers could escape for short leave to Italy.

The brief but happy reunion with the 1st Battalion has **1931**
been recorded elsewhere. For the 2nd Battalion its
significance afterwards lay in the fact that some 250 men
were dropped by the 1st Battalion and remained in Malta
to complete the establishment to "Colonial strength,"
ready once again for the Far East. Their arrival brought
the total up to "war strength" with first reinforcements,
which was the recognized status of "Colonial strength."
There is one other feature of life in Malta which distinguished it from the daily round elsewhere. This was
the constant demand for the various guards which had to
be furnished. The island is given to a healthy tradition of
ceremonial occasions. One company was permanently on
duty in Valetta finding the main guard on the Palace,
which also housed the Secretariat. Strict orders covered
the duties in connection with the Archbishop of Malta,
who was entitled to receive recognition from a guard on
all occasions except when taking part in religious pro-
cessions.

Of social life in Malta it can only be said that the
general hospitality given and taken was on a lavish scale,
yet without the less healthy associations which seemed to
attach to the parties and to club life later in Shanghai.

1933   At least two distinguished visitors were persuaded to
come up to the barracks, and both H.R.H. the Prince of
Wales and King Alfonso of Spain spent a morning
looking round the Battalion and exchanging a few happy
informalities in the Officers' Mess. Such visits were
gratifying if only to break down a tradition that the
Royal Navy held the monopoly of interest ! It was with
many regrets that in October, 1933, the Battalion once
again embarked on the old *Neuralia* for Shanghai,
receiving a tremendous send-off from many friends in
Malta and a parting message from the Fleet. Previous to
sailing they marched past their Commanding Officer for
the last time, for Lieut.-Colonel Clarke was destined for
a brigade at home, and Major J. H. Pelly took the
Battalion on to China. As the men of the Battalion swung
away through Sliema to Valetta they took leave not only
of Lieut.-Colonel Clarke the son but also of the father,
now an old man of eighty-six years of age. Both were
together to take a last salute, and a swift—almost im-
promptu—occasion held for a moment a more profound
significance.

The journey to the Far East has so often been told in
history and fiction that it needs little embellishment here.
Port Said held all its usual menaces and attractions, and
the Red Sea was so hot that once or twice the Captain
circled the ship to get some fresh air aboard. At Colombo
the Battalion managed to stretch its legs ashore with a
route march. The days following in the Indian Ocean
were again hot and airless, and an inclination to surrender
to the intense heat was only defeated by the organization
of every conceivable form of deck exercise. Collecting
potatoes from buckets, tugging at a rope and competitive
movement of every variation kept all ranks busy. The
Band and Drums lent encouragement from opposite ends
of the ship sometimes in simultaneous competition !

Singapore came and the Battalion said farewell to
Captain S. W. Jones, who was bound for staff employment. At Hong Kong our "cousins," 1st Battalion The
Lincolnshire Regiment, were there to offer their prover-
bial hospitality. Efforts to keep fit on deck proved not
wasted, for the Battalion football team won the match

ashore with their "cousins" comfortably by three goals to 1933
one. The journey continued on through the Formosa
Straits, and as the East China Sea was entered the
weather became colder—too cold, in fact, for "khaki
drill !"

On 31st October the *Neuralia* slipped into its wharf on
the Bund at Shanghai, and on 1st November the Battalion
landed and marched up to Kiaochow Road Camp, led by
the pipes of the Argyll and Sutherland Highlanders.
Later they moved to Great Western Road Camp, with a
detachment at Jessfield Park.

The same conditions at Shanghai which had previously
governed the life of the 1st Battalion naturally applied to
the 2nd Battalion. The latter were even able to repeat the
achievements of their brothers in winning the Shanghai
Cross-country Championship. Lieutenant J. J. Abbott,
though no longer running as he had done in 1921,
effectively passed on his great powers of endurance to
others and managed to train a magnificent team. Private
Wallace won the Shanghai Individual Championship.

Of several ceremonial occasions, the Trooping of the 1934
Colour on Empire Day, 24th May, 1934, merits a record.
A huge crowd of spectators of all nationalities had
gathered on the race-course in the evening. The Russian
Company of the Shanghai Volunteer Corps offered to line
the parade ground and their smart appearance and fine
physique certainly lent colour to the occasion. The
Commander-in-Chief of the China Station, Admiral Sir
Frederick Dreyer, K.C.B., C.B., took the salute and later
addressed the Battalion in a speech in which he paid a
tribute to the past and present achievements of the
Regiment. A fine parade was executed with the customary
precision of movement.

As with the 1st Battalion, the joys and terrors of
Shanghai were sometimes obviated by the demands of
Shipping Lines for protection and by welcome cruises
with the Royal Navy. Visits to Weihaiwei, the summer
health resort, with accommodation provided on H.M. ships,
were particularly appreciated, and one party on H.M.S.
Eagle were lucky enough to come in for a brief but
exciting encounter with pirates who had raided and taken

1934   command of a British trading ship at the mouth of the
       Yellow River.

       Late in 1934 the Battalion packed up and moved north
       to Tientsin. Life in Tientsin held all those features of
       variety and colour associated with Shanghai, but there
       was a greater sense of freedom. Tientsin was just a large
       prosperous commercial city of imposing modern stone
       buildings and was concerned mainly with foreign trade.
       One company was permanently on detachment eighty
       miles away at Peking, where there was a very different
       atmosphere. For Peking was and always will be the heart
       of China, and there were few symbols of the modern
       world of the West. The Peking company furnished the
       British Legation Guard and passed many pleasant un-
       eventful days in comparative isolation.

1935   Just as in Shanghai the city divided into various Inter-
       national enclaves, so in Tientsin the British, French,
       Italians and Japanese had their respective settlements.
       The Americans, without a settlement of their own, shared
       the British area. As was to be expected, our men made
       good friends of No. 15 U.S. Infantry Regiment, and were
       on better terms with the French than in Shanghai. There
       was continual trouble with the Japanese, who were out to
       insult us, and there was at least one open encounter with
       the Italians. The scuffle with the Italians in the Christmas
       of 1935 was certainly not started by the men of the
       Battalion. Italian sailors and marines came into the
       British Cabaret Quarter bent on making trouble, and they
       received back better than they gave. Moreover, once
       officers appeared on the scene our men responded to
       orders with admirable discipline in face of great provo-
       cation.

1936   But the Tientsin routine was not all social frivolity :
       and a measure of the keen spirit which was very much
       alive in comparative military isolation is indicated in
       noting that in 1936 the machine gunners won the A.R.A.
       Non-central Machine Gun Cup for units abroad.
       Throughout the period in Tientsin the greatest co-
       operation was forthcoming from the British Municipal
       Council in the British Concession. The Tientsin volun-
       teers proved a close link with the British civilians, for the

Battalion trained them and lent them an Adjutant. They   1936
were a cheerful, efficient body of men and included
infantry, armoured cars and artillery armed with 12-
pounders. They also included a curious party of "White"
Russians, a legacy from World War I.

Those were the days indeed ! Officers could enjoy the
finest snipe and duck shooting. The British, French and
American community played polo and raced on the
astonishingly tough little Chinese ponies. If there were
no fences to jump, there were many open ditches sufficient to test the staunchest rider.

In regard to training, the obvious limitation was the
lack of the competitive element and, with no other unit
near by, Company and Battalion training were the only
forms which could be exploited. Even this was vaguely
directed from a distance of 3,000 miles away in Hong
Kong!

The extraordinary climate of Tientsin and Peking
demanded particular measures, for in the summer a
temperature of 105° F. was not unusual, while the winters
were intensely cold and dry. It is on record that thirty
miles down the river at Taku on one occasion the sea
froze up to a distance of twelve miles out from the shore,
and an invitation was actually extended to a few officers
to man the ice-breakers which were freeing the fishing
vessels held in the ice ! In such circumstances sheep-skin
coats and gloves were adopted for sentries, and a fur hat
with the Regimental badge was worn in the winter
months.

In the summer the Indian routine was followed and a
move was made to a pleasanter climate to Shanhaikuan,
which was a twelve-hour journey down the coast. Details
were, of course, left behind in Tientsin, and the company
in Peking had to remain on its ground. It was at Shanhaikuan that companies could feel they were sub-units
with a spirit of their own, for Company training took the
form of marches into the country over three or four days,
which included the usual exercises—advanced, rear and
flank guards—*en route*. The going was hard. The so-
called roads were mere tracks and thick maize fields,
bamboo jungle and sandy river-beds had to be negotiated.

1936   But though the usual oaths accompanied these struggles
over the Chinese countryside, there will be many who
look back to those tough company marches with happy
memories of days spent in good fellowship away from the
madding crowd.

In November, 1936, the Battalion embarked on the
Dilwara from Chingwanto. Except for a football match
with the British battalion at Hong Kong the journey was
uneventful. The port of Chingwanto lay north of Tientsin
and was experiencing a typical Chinese winter, with the
troops breaking icicles on the ship's deck. Disembarking
at Bombay, they were in time to celebrate Christmas at
Sialkot in Northern India, Lieut.-Colonel C. Deakin,
O.B.E., taking over from Lieut.-Colonel Pelly soon after
arrival. There they relieved the 2nd Dorsetshire and
settled down to the normal cycle of life in an Indian
Cantonment. Colonel Pelly handed over the Battalion of
which he had been Adjutant and in which he had spent
many years of his soldiering. He had a fine athletic record
and, with little stimulating competition in China, his
enthusiasm kept sport at a high level. His happy tem-
perament and imperturbability had often steered the
Battalion through stormy seas of international incidents
and jealousies. As compared with the colour and variety
of China, Sialkot was drab and dull. It was the home of
a Cavalry Brigade, and the 3rd Carabiniers, a battery of
Horse Artillery and an Indian Cavalry Regiment were
perhaps inclined to regard the station somewhat as a
cavalry preserve. The barracks were of that good solid
Victorian variety, built to resist the heat, but not luxurious.
Though the Kashmir mountains are close at hand, the
country around is flat and uninviting, while in their
leisure hours the troops quite naturally missed the
constant allure of the towns in China.

In the summer there was an exodus to the Simla hills,
and the Battalion less two companies were stationed in
Solon and Jutogh. The men could enjoy week-end leave
in Simla, while many took their fortnight's annual leave
and trekked over the hills. Throughout the Sialkot period
the Battalion formed part of the Jhelum Infantry Brigade,
and consequently there were annual battles in the cold

season in the Pabbi hills and that forbidding patch of **1936**
country on either side of the Grand Trunk road between
Jhelum and Rawalpindi.

In January, 1939, for a few months the Battalion re- **1939**
lieved the Royal Ulster Rifles in Rawalpindi, who were
bound for Waziristan, and it was there that first news of
the declaration of war was heard and all ranks knew that
the days of Indian cantonment routine were numbered.

From Rawalpindi the Battalion put in one month's
training near Jhelum under the 3rd (Jhelum) Infantry
Brigade, and returned to Sialkot in October, 1940, direct
from the Jhelum area. Individual training continued and
a start was made with the training of M.T. drivers.

In February, 1940, the Battalion was moved to Wazi- **1940**
ristan to take part in operations which never really
materialized. From Bannu in April they moved on to a
perimeter camp at Razani, on the Bannu–Razmak road,
for road protection duties. A few minor skirmishes with
tribesmen resulted in some twenty casualties, and in
September the Battalion returned to Sialkot, where once
again M.T. training was resumed. On 21st November
Lieut.-Colonel P. W. Hargreaves took over command
from Lieut.-Colonel Deakin. Colonel Deakin had assumed command at a difficult time. The Battalion came
straight from the fleshpots of the Far East to a Cavalry
station in Northern India, with the promise of early
service on the Indian frontier and with the threat of a
second world war. He had wrestled with his problems,
never sparing himself, demanding application to duty,
integrity and loyalty. But his austerity was often relieved
by unorthodox method and a mischievous sense of
humour which had endeared him to officers and men
alike.

In January and February, 1941, once again the Bat- **1941**
talion trained under the Jhelum Brigade in the Jhelum
area, and there was now some emphasis on open warfare
to supplement the continuous concentration on Frontier
training which had been almost an obsession for some
time past. In April Battalion Headquarters and two
companies went up to the Murree hills ; but such was the
hectic atmosphere governing strategic considerations in

I

1941   India that in July the whole Battalion suddenly removed
to Manduri, in the Kurram valley, to place that area in
some state of defence as a precaution against a possible
German invasion through Afghanistan. Indeed, at one
period in the war the authorities hardly knew which way
to face the defences of the Indian Frontier ! The move
was effected in a manner which would have delighted the
veterans of former campaigns, with mules, camels and, as
a concession, five lorries. In this so-called "operational
area" the Battalion entered a composite brigade with
Gurkhas, Jats and a Nepalese Army battalion. A lot of
hard digging and rock blasting was undertaken, when
again a surprise was sprung and a move to the very
different climate of Wellington was ordered. Only three
days were allowed to pack up the entire paraphernalia at
Sialkot and entrain, complete with families and followers,
for Mettapullyam, whence the journey to Wellington was
completed by road. After seven days in the train and a
hazardous drive by road it was comforting to arrive
without mishap. Previously at a time when drivers might
have trained at Sialkot all personnel had perforce to
accompany the Battalion to Manduri. Therefore, when
on arrival at Mettapullyam an embarrassment of M.T.
greeted the Commanding Officer, he was slightly apprehensive of the drive ahead, and several officers were
detailed to take charge of lorries.

At Wellington some of the younger members of the
Officers' Mess had ambitious ideas of setting up their new
home in somewhat elaborate comfort. But the Commanding Officer gave the movement no encouragement,
since there was obviously a sterner role than that of
internal security not very far ahead. From Wellington in
November Battalion and Brigade training was carried out
in camp near Bangalore, a composite brigade being
formed for the purpose under Bangalore District. Back at
Wellington, an unexacting role was relieved only by the
need to furnish a permanent guard over the large cordite
factory outside the station.

1942   In February, 1942, Singapore fell, and immediately the
Battalion was ordered to Madras to join the Madras
garrison. The families remained in Wellington, and in a

search for some security the Colours and all mess silver
were lodged with the Imperial Bank of India in Ootaca-
mund. If the Japanese landed, "Ooty" appeared to be as
remote an immediate hide-out as was available ! Later,
when the Battalion were to enter 19th Indian Division,
one solitary private soldier was left to keep an eye on the
bulk of Battalion property left in Wellington.

For the first three weeks in Madras the Battalion was
housed in the spacious barracks at St. Thomas's Mount.
Camp equipment hardly did justice to the enormous
Officers' Mess. Later, various schools and large buildings
were occupied in the town.

It was indeed fortunate that the threatened Japanese
landing never materialized, for so far as the Madras
coast was implicated, by sea, air or land there was nothing
to stand in their way. In the local defence plan the
Battalion was ordered to construct defences along the line
of the Adyar river on the southern boundary of the river.
With few stores available, the gardens round the bungalows of Madras merchants were exploited for wire and
timber. Later, when the owners returned, the Commanding Officer received an official protest and demand
for compensation ! An appropriate reply was given.

It was an anxious period. To meet a force which was
estimated at three divisions, two British battalions, two
Indian Garrison battalions and the Madras Guards, an
auxiliary unit, were available. The Indian battalions had
no automatic weapons ; while the officers of 2nd Worcestershire, though in possession of revolvers, were
without any ammunition and consequently armed themselves with rifles. Bren carriers were issued, but no
drivers had yet ever driven them. It was therefore in the
belief that the Japanese would invade the Peninsula across
the Bay of Bengal that in April, 1942, the new 19th
Indian Division was hurried south to the defence of the
Madras coast. But the grave threat gradually evaporated
and the Division was then free to set about training for a
more aggressive role.

Indian brigades were now to be organized with one
British battalion and two Indian battalions, and it was to
complete the 64th Indian Infantry Brigade in its new

1942 composition that 2nd Worcestershire joined the Brigade under canvas some twenty miles west of Madras in August, replacing the 3/6th Rajputana Rifles. Two other units, the 5/10th Baluch Regiment and 1/6th Gurkha Rifles, completed the Brigade under Brigadier H. M. Chambers, which was destined to keep its three battalions throughout the Burma war and was thus able to develop a very real sense of brotherhood.

At this stage the training of higher formations had become impossible, and under Major-General G. A. P. Scoones, 19 Division were busy trying out their subtleties on another new formation, the 25th Indian Division.

1943 Early in 1943 the usual general post of units and formations took place, as a result of which 64 Brigade found itself in the area of Betamangala, near the Kolar goldfields. But by May units were back again outside Madras, and in July the Brigade entered a new area near Trichinopoly. Meanwhile Lieut.-Colonel Hargreaves had relinquished command and Lieut.-Colonel B. C. Wilkinson of the K.S.L.I. took his place. He in turn handed over to Lieut.-Colonel B. G. Symes[3] in November. In the higher command there had been several changes and the Division was now led by Major-General T. W. Rees, the Brigade being commanded by Brigadier G. A. Bain of the 2nd Gurkha Rifles.

From Trichinopoly the whole Division moved on into the Travancore forests near Nilambur in the heart of the Moplah country. Conditions were ideal for training in jungle warfare, and the onset of the monsoon was an incentive to the men to build their bamboo "bashas" well and strong. Jungle navigation, map reading and movement by river on rough bamboo rafts were all matters which could be studied, and by November the troops were ready for Exercise "Malabar," a full-scale war of ten days against the 25th Indian Division under operational conditions. The Brigade then moved to Thondebhavi, some miles north of Bangalore, where it remained until February, 1944.

---

[3] Lieut.-Colonel B. G. Symes, D.S.O., O.B.E., was to see the Battalion through the subsequent twenty months, including most of the Burma campaign.

The next stage in the new education began when the Division moved up to Nasik for preliminary or "dryshod" training in combined operations. The Battalion was under canvas and put in much time embarking and disembarking from dummy landing-craft and scaling rope nets down the sides of phantom ships. Finally, in May the Nasik experience was put to the test with the Royal Indian Navy at Marve, near Madh island outside Bombay. The tricky business of putting vehicles on to pitching landing-craft at sea was tackled with the enthusiasm which comes of high hope for future events. The concluding exercise at sea needed some improvisation since the vast Bombay dock explosion of an ammunition ship had knocked out several ships earmarked for the exercise.

Back at Nasik in July, the Battalion put in a second bout of jungle training in the reserved forests at Igatpuri. Memories were refreshed and the 19th Indian Division were ready for war.

CHAPTER SEVEN

THE SECOND BATTALION, 1944–1945

The Chindwin, The Irrawaddy, Ngapyin, Kule, Nyaungwun

1944 IT was with a sense of intense relief that the 19th Division —which had sometimes come to be spoken of as "the best trained Division in India"—received its orders to concentrate on the Assam–Burma border, in the neighbourhood of Imphal, in readiness for action. Vehicles moved under their own power across India, personnel going by train to Manipur Road, thence by M.T. to a camp in the scrub jungle near milestone 113 on the Kohima–Imphal road. Everyone had now taken to the inelegant but effective jungle-green battledress. Anti-malarial and anti-scrub typhus measures were adopted and training in jungle warfare continued. The opportunity was taken to make full use of the knowledge of hardened troops on the spot with instruction from 89 (Indian) Infantry Brigade (7 Indian Division), while senior officers were attached to 11 (East African) Division and toured the Kohima battlefield.

Early in November it was known that soon the Division would be in action and a forward move towards the Chindwin river was made. Of the two roads which led to the river the southern route from Tamu to Sittaung was given to 64 Brigade. East of the river the known opposition on the Shwebo Plain amounted to eleven battalions of the defeated 15th and 31st Japanese Divisions. Still farther to the east the 36th British Division was advancing down the railway corridor from Myitkyina, driving the Japanese 53rd Division before it, and by 9th November they had reached a point ten miles north of Naba.

Work on the Tamu–Sittaung road proceeded apace, all units competing to finish the job in time for the Chindwin

to be crossed before the end of the month. The plan was
for 62 Brigade to cross first and head east for Paungbyin,
to be followed by 64 Brigade who, having reached
Paungbyin, would turn north and make for the Japanese-
constructed road running from the Chindwin through
Leu to Banmauk. Having reached the road, they too were
to turn east and move along it. To effect these moves
some redistribution of units between the two Brigades
was necessary, but this in no way affected the 2nd
Worcestershire. First, reinforcements having been concentrated under divisional arrangements, kit was reduced
to a minimum, surplus stores and personal baggage being
returned to Imphal where most of it was successfully
looted ! The transport was cut down to six jeeps and
trailers and 54 mules, while attached transport amounted
to another six jeeps with 40 mules. Early on 27th November the Brigade started to cross the Chindwin, and by
the afternoon 28th November the 2nd Worcestershire
under Lieut.-Colonel B. G. Symes, O.B.E., were all across
and were concentrated at Mogaung in the Sittaung loop
of the river.

On 30th November a monotonous march began in
search of the enemy, which was to last for twenty-two
days, during which time some two hundred miles were
covered.[1] Fortunately, the villagers in the Sittaung area
were friendly once they had grasped the fact that the
British had come to stay. Salt passed as effective barter
for information, but the individual local guide was
frequently to prove unreliable.

On 1st December the night was spent at Nanpan on
the track to Paungbyin. It was here that the first day's
air supply was dropped, inaugurating a method of
maintenance which had previously been perfected on the
experience of the Wingate expedition and without which
operations in Burma on the scale envisaged could never
have been undertaken.

From Nanpan the two Brigades separated, 62 Brigade
moving south-east on Pinlebu while 64 Brigade moved

---

[1] In the first thirty-one days across the Chindwin, so far as the
Battalion were concerned, twenty-six days were spent marching,
companies covering about 400 miles.

1944 through Paungbyin on Len, some twenty miles to the north. Leu had been reported clear of the enemy by 4/4 Gurkhas, who had crossed the Chindwin opposite the road from Settaw to Leu, so that the column could press on without having to be delayed by the need to patrol. Accordingly the Brigadier went ahead with an escort of "A" and "C" Companies of the Battalion, the remainder of the Brigade reaching Leu on 8th December. From Leu the uneventful march to the east was continued with 2nd Worcestershire still in the van. The immediate task was to improve the track to make it fit for 3-ton lorries up to Wetkauk, thence onwards to restore it at least for the use of jeeps.

On 12th December Sinlamaung was reached, 5/10 Baluch, who had been left behind on the Chindwin, rejoining and 4/4 Gurkhas remaining at Sinlamaung to await further orders from the Division. Thus the Brigade was once again complete with its normal units and the advance continued with 1/6 Gurkhas in the lead, followed by the Battalion, with 5/10 Baluch in the rear.

The country now became more difficult with tracks winding over the hills, traversing deep gorges and penetrating the dense jungle. Luckily the Jap had previously worked hard on the road and omitted to blow the bridges, so the pace was maintained.

On 13th December an air-drop which landed on the tops of tall trees on a ridge was mostly lost, though the agile Gurkhas managed to rescue some of the loads. The advance continued over the route previously taken by Ferguson's Chindit Column on the first Wingate expedition, and Naungkon was reached on 14th December without event.

From Naungkon the Battalion was ordered to furnish two patrols, and these accordingly set out on 15th December under Lieutenant D. R. C. Bailey[2] and Lieutenant D. A. Wright. Wright, who took the route to the south from Naungkon, discovered that his track petered out in a quagmire after only sixteen miles. He accordingly rejoined on 16th December at Pinbon, having heard

---

[2] Later Major D. R. C. Bailey, M.C.

nothing of the enemy. Bailey, who took the track to the east, reached Aunggon at 1400 hours on 15th December to find that the enemy had left the village six hours previously. Bailey's patrol also rejoined on 16th December, but returned to Aunggon the next day. Shortly afterwards the Divisional Commander arrived and the whole party moved on to Pinlebu, contacting 62 Brigade which had just captured the town. Bailey and his patrol then rejoined the Battalion which had reached Banmauk.

In Banmauk news was received that the enemy were to the south in the vicinity of Nankan on the Myitkyina–Shwebo railway.

In the meanwhile 36 Division away to the east were moving down the railway corridor, and 1/6 Gurkhas were dispatched to effect a link between the two Divisions. 19 Division now swung south, and on the night of 18th December it fell to 2nd Worcestershire to lead the Brigade in the advance from Banmauk towards Nankan. Pemnegon was reached on 20th December and the information indicated that the Japs were retreating some twenty-four hours ahead of the column. Plans were made to continue the advance on 21st December, but the Commanding Officer requested permission for his men to push on that evening by forced march. Tired as they were, the troops were in high spirits at the prospect of coming to grips with the enemy and were anxious to make the extra effort.

Permission having been given to push on, the Battalion set out at 2300 hours with the object of encircling Nankan, some seven miles away, before light and cutting off the Japs in the village. The local guide, however, lost his nerve and bolted into the jungle. With doubt as to the way forward, hopes of a night attack had to be abandoned. By 0630 hours on 21st December a halt was made one mile from the Nankan railway station. It was then decided that "A" Company should advance direct on the village and stage a diversion while the remainder of the Battalion, with "C" Company in the lead, moved in a sweep round to the west with the object of attacking the village from the less exposed flank.

At 0730 hours "A" Company with the Defence Platoon

1944 were ambushed. By this time "C" Company, having attacked and cleared some huts, were half a mile from Nankan before they were fired on. "C" Company continued to advance to a point south of the railway line astride the main road some 500 yards south of the station. The remainder of the Battalion meanwhile cleared the area north of the station and consolidated. A platoon sent down the road to the south from "C" Company was ambushed after it had covered 200 yards, the commander, his runner and platoon sergeant being killed. Spasmodic fire was exchanged and at 1300 hours "C" Company were able to retaliate and ambush a Japanese patrol. At 1600 hours the Brigadier was on the scene to congratulate the Battalion on its success. A welcome diversion occurred when some Dakotas effected an unexpected air-drop. Without the necessary air strips, the Brigadier's maps had hastily to be put to use to form the code recognition letters, and with much frantic waving a successful air-drop was effected. At dusk the Battalion dug in and the night 21/22 December was uneventful. The following morning innumerable flags, weapons and documents were collected. The administrative elements of the Battalion moved up and the advance continued. Such was the first encounter. The initial success of two ambushes effected by the enemy brought home a lesson which was not forgotten. Nevertheless all realized that they were on the winning side and morale was high.

The enemy in front of 64 Brigade appeared to be the 51st Regiment, with responsibility for the whole area between the Myitkyina railway and the Irrawaddy, with the 31st Japanese Division in reserve round Shwebo. The enemy were obviously retreating faster than ever, and with 2nd Worcestershire still in the lead the Brigade reached Padonma on 22nd December. Information was then received that the Japs were holding some hills west of a village, Thitseingon, about three and a half miles to the south-west on a road running east and west from Kawlin to Tawma. Elaborate plans were accordingly made for the attack on 23rd December after a night approach, when just in time information was received that the supposed enemy were our own 62 Brigade ; while similarly

2nd Worcestershire had also been mistaken for the Japan-   **1944**
ese, and the guns of 115 Field Regiment, R.A., were at one
moment ready to greet our men in their enthusiasm to
close with an elusive enemy ! Once again the local guide
proved ineffective and lost his way, luckily, through the
particular circumstances, without prejudice to any final
issue. As no rest was anticipated on Christmas Day,
24th December was observed as a day of rest and Church
services were held.

Christmas Day of 1944 proved a curious and memorable
experience. The Battalion once again led the column with
Brigade Headquarters and 5/10 Baluch following behind.
It was intended to reach Taungbon. A detachment of the
Battalion had previously been dispatched to escort 25
Mountain Battery across country from Kyaukpyintha, and
the detachment and Battery were due to join the column.
The detachment with its charge duly joined its position
at about 1100 hours at Kokkogon. In the meanwhile the
Battalion in the lead had taken the wrong track south of
Kokkogon, and a liaison officer sent forward from Brigade
Headquarters discovered that the column was being led
confidently only by the Battalion mules ! Having discovered the mistake they retraced their steps, but were
unable to make Taungbon by the evening.³ Having
established contact with Brigade through an officer sent
for the purpose, the Battalion halted for the night by a
small stream on the main track a few miles to the north of
the Brigade, where, having covered many miles by day,
all ranks slept soundly. The march was continued on
26th December, the Battalion catching up in rear of the
column and reaching Letpanda in the evening. On
27th December a further advance brought the column to
the outskirts of Baw, where the Baluch in the lead ran into
a typical Japanese ambush. By the time Baw was cleared
the Battalion had arrived and a supply drop had been
started. The advance continued on 28th December, the
Baluch encountering minor opposition. That evening the
Baluch and Brigade Headquarters settled into Sabenatha,
the Gurkhas moving on to Ngapyawdaing and the

---

³ This account is reconstructed from 64 Indian Infantry Brigade
War History.

1944 Battalion reaching Hlwezeik. There they remained for two days, and on 31st December they moved on to relieve the Baluch in Sabenatha, the latter having been sent off to co-operate in the drive south that 62 Brigade were exploiting away to the west.

1945 New Year's Day passed quietly at Sabenatha, and on 2nd January the Battalion with Brigade Headquarters moved on to Myemun. On 3rd January reconnaissances in force were ordered in the area round Thabeikkyin, a steamer station on the Irrawaddy some eighteen miles to the north-east of Kongyi. Information was needed about suitable crossings, conditions of tracks and sites for light aircraft landing strips. Accordingly "A" and "C" Companies were dispatched, thus having the distinction of being the first troops in Fourteenth Army to view the Irrawaddy. A large rice dump was discovered and its guard were successfully dealt with, the documents taken including an excellent set of photographs of Nipponese "pin-up" girls ! On 5th January two companies from the 2nd Welch Regiment relieved "A" and "C" Companies, which were ordered to rejoin the Battalion at Kongyi, whither it had moved in the meanwhile.

Their efforts to return were, however, destined to prove a desperate adventure. The track to Kongyi was found to be so bad that the company vehicles had to turn back and rejoin the 2nd Welch Regiment, the two companies plodding on in a pitch-black night. After two hours' rest at 0130 hours on 6th January the detachment had reached a "T" junction nine miles from Kongyi. Here the leading Company ("C") and the first two platoons of "A" Company swung west and moved on to Kongyi. But the rear platoon under Lieutenant Bailey, just as it was about to take the bend leading west, was challenged by a Japanese sentry. Simultaneously rifles and L.M.Gs. opened on the party from only a few yards across the path. There was nothing for it but to lie up dead still and hope for assistance from the remainder of the detachment. Control was almost impossible and the necessity for silence added to the difficulties. By 0445 hours the platoon commander, realizing that he could expect no help, decided to make a dash for freedom before daylight exposed his position. It was a bitter decision **1945** for it entailed the abandonment of his wounded in the hope of rescue later. With great skill sixteen men were withdrawn in three parties. Hand grenades were flung across the track and group by group they scattered for the safety of the jungle. Lieutenant Bailey managed to contact his detachment, and at 0630 hours both companies attacked the track junction, recovering the two wounded men. The two companies then. returned to Kongyi, where they were subsequently joined by their transport from Thabeikkyin. Later they rejoined the Battalion at Bodawtaw after being helped out by transport lent by the Gurkhas.

In the meanwhile the Brigade had closed up, arriving at Kongyi on 6th January and at Bodawtaw on 7th January. Shwebo, the goal, was now in sight. In the next phase of movement to the south the Battalion took over Myothit from the Gurkhas, who pushed on leaving one company under command of the Battalion. In the event, however, Shwebo was to fall to the 2nd British Division under Major-General Nicholson, who brought in his attack from the north-west. Only the Baluch were there to co-operate by blocking the eastern exits when the town finally fell on 11th January, and it so happened that an officer of The Worcestershire Regiment, Major Alan Rowley, commanded a Baluch company who were the first troops to enter Shwebo. Anticipating a hurried enemy withdrawal from Shwebo, 1/6 Gurkhas had been sent on a wide movement round the east flank to close the approaches from the south. The Battalion was in fact at this stage the Cinderella of events. It had moved to Minbe, where it remained until 11th January. "A" and "C" Companies having rejoined from their exploits, they remained at Minbe to guard the Brigade administrative area while the rest of the Battalion set out for Padaung, a village on the main road leading from Shwebo to Moksogyon. It was hoped that some Japs might still be in the area between Shwebo and the Gurkhas. But neither at Padaung or at Bonbwet on 12th January were any enemy seen. It so happened that the commander of 5 Brigade, 2 Division, had met Brigadier Bain at the Moksogyon cross-roads and had told him that the 7th Worcestershire from his Brigade was moving next day to Padaung. It was then arranged that the two battalions should meet in Padaung, and thus there was staged a memorable encounter which is described elsewhere.

On 14th January the Battalion moved to an area just north of Gyogya, the Brigade being disposed east of Shwebo. Then it was that preparations were made to cross the most formidable of obstacles, the great Irrawaddy river. The crossing was first effected by a patrol of 1/15 Punjab Regiment (the Divisional Reconnaissance Regiment) on the night 12/13 January without opposition about a mile to the north of the eventual bridgehead which was established opposite Kyaukmyaung. An unopposed crossing seemed too good to be true and it was quickly exploited ; so that by the evening of 17th January the Baluch and Gurkhas were enlarging the bridgehead and had had some severe fighting. During the night 17/18 January the Battalion, less one company, crossed with elements of Brigade Headquarters without interference. It was then decided to slide the bridgehead down to Ngapyin, which faced Kyaukmyaung on the opposite bank. For the next two days the Baluchis were in the lead, the Battalion taking over their positions as they moved south. On 20th January patrols entered Ngapyin and found the village empty, whereupon the bridgehead was established, the Battalion furnishing the northern face of a box of which the river constituted the western face with the Punjabis and Baluch completing the square. On the same day "D" Company was dropped off the main Brigade column as it moved along the river bank and furnished a fighting patrol in the area north and north-east of Ngapyin. It returned at 1500 hours, having contacted a strong Jap position which it had immediately attacked. A single company was in fact not strong enough to carry the enemy position, and there remained some doubt as to enemy strength and dispositions in the area.

The Japs now managed to bring an unpleasantly heavy weight of shelling on to the bridgehead, particularly at night.

Since 19th January 1/6 Gurkha Rifles had been estab-

lished at Minban Taung, a low broad spur which constituted the main feature on the horizon two miles to the east
of the bridgehead. On 21st January two companies of the
Battalion set out to contact the Gurkhas and they ran into
a Jap patrol of some thirty men when only 600 yards from
the perimeter. In the course of the battle which then
ensued amongst the thick scrub and thorn bushes of the
jungle, seventeen Japs were killed and one machine gun
captured, the Commanding Officer himself accounting
for three of the enemy. The delay imposed, however, was
sufficient to prevent contact with the Gurkhas that day,
and the force returned to find that in the meanwhile the
Battalion had received some heavy shelling, losing eight
mules but otherwise suffering comparatively light damage.

The next day once again an attempt was made under
the Second-in-Command, Major C. H. Hodder, to reach
the Gurkhas on Minban Taung, and once again after two
hours' hard fighting the action had to be broken off.
This time the force undoubtedly ran into a strong Jap
position, and to continue the effort would have involved
sending back a platoon to the bridgehead to evacuate the
wounded. That night the enemy made a determined
attack on the bridgehead, the main weight of his thrust
falling on 1/15 Punjabis. But the attack was held and on
23rd January the Battalion made its third and successful
effort to contact the Gurkhas. At 0700 hours the whole
Battalion moved, their sector of the perimeter being taken
over by other units. This time, with the exception of a
small patrol, the enemy were not encountered. Rations
were delivered, the wounded evacuated and the Battalion
returned, passing on its way an apparently extensive but
unoccupied enemy position. Next day the Intelligence
Officer confirmed that the same position remained
unmanned.

But the Japanese had by no means abandoned their
efforts to break up the bridgehead. For the next two days
their attacks continued, the brunt of the fighting now
falling on a company of the Baluch, who were holding
Pear Hill, a prominent feature which commanded the
countryside about two miles down the river on the east
bank. In the meanwhile 62 Brigade were to relieve 64

1945 Brigade, and the Battalion accordingly throughout
26th January were occupied handing over to 3/6 Rajputana Rifles and moving company by company back to
Yedaw on the western bank, the Brigade relief being
completed on 28th January. On the same day the
Battalion moved south from Yedaw to Shwedaik, with
one company detached farther south at Makauk. On
29th January rumours that a strong Japanese force were
at Madaw Taung, a hill feature four miles south of
Makauk, involved the dispatch of a company to investigate. They returned to report the area free, and the only
enemy interference came from some stray shells on
Shwedaik from enemy artillery who were still shelling
Pear Hill on the opposite bank of the river.

On 1st February the Baluch relieved the Battalion in
their area and a move back to Kyaukmyaung was made in
readiness to recross the river for the break-out at
Ngapyin.

Throughout this period, for security reasons, the
identity of the formation fighting the battle of the Irrawaddy bridgehead was kept a secret; and it was not until
12th February that the world was to know that the 19th
Indian Division had crossed the great river and held the
crossing against desperate endeavours to dislodge them.
Honour was satisfied and morale ran high.

The immediate plan of operations now necessitated
some reshuffling of units. The intention involved 64
Brigade eventually recrossing the Irrawaddy to capture the
villages of Ywathit and Singu, three miles to the south of
Pear Hill, while 62 Brigade enlarged the bridgehead. For
this purpose the Battalion passed temporarily under 62
Brigade and was ordered to seize Kule. To the east three
ridges known as Able, Baker, and Charlie were to be
captured by the Rajputana Rifles, who were to pass
through. Accordingly, on 4th February the Battalion
recrossed the river into 62 Brigade area at Ngapyin, and
the next day two companies relieved the Rajputana Rifles
on Pear Hill without incident. For the forthcoming attack
on Kule a squadron of 150 Regiment, R.A.C., was allotted
in support. On the morning of 8th February the Battalion
concentrated some 2,000 yards north of Kule village.

Reports were to the effect that one company of the enemy
held the village, but this proved an optimistic under-
estimate. At 1215 hours Hurribombers delivered a
fifteen-minute attack, to be followed by a heavy artillery
concentration by 4 Indian Field Regiment and a 3-inch
mortar battery of 33 Anti-Tank Regiment. Under this
cover the Battalion advanced on a two-company front
with "A" and "D" Companies leading, each supported
by a troop of tanks. On reaching the edge of the jungle,
with only 100 yards of open paddy fields to cross, "D"
Company on the left swung round to face east and protect
the flank, while "A" Company, under cover of a smoke-
screen, advanced at 1300 hours behind the tanks. Only
after the tanks had strafed the edge of the village with
their 75 mm. guns and Brownings was "A" Company able
to enter the village. Snipers were still active and the
casualties included Captain A. Maycock, the Company
Commander, who was wounded. There followed five and
a half hours of close fighting before Kule could be
considered to be clear of the enemy. By nightfall the
Battalion held a small precarious perimeter in the north-
west corner of the village. But they were eventually able
to consolidate a perimeter, with "A" and "B" Companies
south of the village, "D" to the east and "C" to the north,
the river protecting the western face. The night passed
with spasmodic attacks on "D" Company from grenade
dischargers, and early in the morning of 9th February a
counter-attack against the south face of the perimeter
appeared imminent. At 0500 hours this materialized with
full force on "A" and "B" Companies. Fanatical attempts
to overrun the position all failed, though for a short time
the situation on "A" Company's perimeter was critical.
At 1030 hours a company of 4/6 Gurkhas from 62
Brigade arrived to reinforce the position, but the issue
was now settled and they passed through to mop-up the
southern edge of the village. Thus at 1110 hours the
Rajputana Rifles were able to move out to capture Able,
Baker, and Charlie in the knowledge that their right flank
was secure. When the battle ended, among the many
enemy dead outside the perimeter was the body of the
Japanese Commander of the 119th Infantry Regiment, his

K

1945   1st Battalion having failed to retrieve their despairing
efforts to break the 2nd Worcestershire defence.

The Gurkhas now relieved the Battalion, which withdrew to an area just below Pear Hill, where a welcome rest
was taken that night and the following day (10th February). In the meanwhile the battle for Singu waged
furiously and eventually the Gurkhas fought their way
into the village.

During 11th February the Battalion moved out from
Pear Hill and occupied Able, Baker, and Charlie without
incident, again enjoying a comparatively peaceful night.
On 12th February Brigade Headquarters and the Baluch
moved into Singu, the Battalion moving down from the
three ridges and passing through the Baluch east along
the track to Myingyan, a mile and a half from Singu.

The Battalion set out and at 1400 hours made contact
with a Jap position well sited and approached across 200
yards of open ground. While the leading company
engaged the position, a second company moved round
the left flank. The latter put in two attacks which were
held, and it was evident that the position could not be
taken until the next day. Accordingly they withdrew
about 1,000 yards and harboured for the night. Orders
having been issued that Myingyan would be captured by
0900 hours on 13th February, the Battalion moved at
0700 hours the next morning and again contacted the
same position. In spite of the fact that two batteries of
115 Field Regiment engaged the enemy, this second attack
was again unsuccessful, and it was not until the Brigadier
had placed "C" Squadron, 7 Cavalry, at their disposal
that one company under cover of a smoke-screen occupied
the objective without resistance. The Battalion had
suffered twenty-four casualties which, alas, included the
Medical Officer, Captain A. M. Ogilvie,[4] who was killed
while trying to rescue a man who was covered by an enemy
automatic.

For the next few days the Battalion was not involved in
the heavy fighting which the Baluch and Gurkhas were
to experience in efforts to dislodge the enemy from

---

[4] Later, the award of the M.C. to this officer was announced.

Khanpa, a village two miles south-east of Myingyan. After 1945 dark on 16th February the Battalion moved into the Gurkhas' position at Singu, leaving one company behind at Myingyan. At Singu a well-earned rest was welcome and the opportunity to wash and bathe and generally clean up was taken.

On 17th February another company pushed out three-quarters of a mile to the south of Singu. But on 21st February the whole Battalion concentrated again at Myingyan, where it continued to patrol locally until 25th February, accounting for a dozen of the enemy.

The bridgehead was now centred round Kule, Divisional Headquarters having moved into Singu. Control at the Singu end of the Mandalay road was in our hands. But the enemy was undoubtedly in a determined mood and his declared intention was to wipe out 19 Indian Division and drive it into the river. Simultaneously the Division were with equal confidence planning a thrust in strength down the road to Mandalay. In this operation, the attack by 64 Brigade was planned in four phases, the last phase being the capture of the village Nyaungwun by the Battalion. The estimate to complete the operation in a day proved optimistic, and it was not until 2nd March that the Battalion finally occupied Nyaungwun.

The four phases divided into separate operations by each Battalion, 1/6 Gurkhas completing Phase 1 on 26th February. The Battalion passed through and made slow progress in the tall elephant grass and belts of bamboo. That night "B" and "D" Companies were astride the Mandalay road, but 500 yards short of the objective for Phase 2. On 27th February the Baluch passed through and again after severe fighting were short of the objective for Phase 2. At this stage the country presented yet more difficulties, for the Mandalay road now ran between a large lake on the west while on the east it was overlooked from steep banked hills covered in bamboo jungle. Nor was an air strip available to assist in country which denied the use of tanks.

On 28th February the Battalion came up through the Baluch with the object of capturing Ngwedaung, the objective for Phase 2. In face of strong opposition a

1945   hastily formed perimeter in the jungle a few hundred yards short of the village was occupied for the night. Mines held up vehicles on the only road available and there were anxious moments when the Battalion appeared isolated and cut off. But next morning patrols found to their surprise that the enemy had withdrawn from Ngwedaung and the Battalion, after putting down a screen to prevent the reoccupation of the village, remained on its ground for the day. Finally, Nyaungwun was occupied without opposition.

The advance down the Mandalay road continued, "A" and "D" Companies soon coming up against another enemy rear-guard position. Fighting developed and casualties amounted to three killed and sixteen wounded. A perimeter was formed for the night (2/3 March) and the attack was resumed the next day. But in face of continued opposition from well dug-in positions astride the road at Pyindaung, the Battalion by-passed the enemy by swinging south-west to the village of Shwepyi.

Shwepyi was indeed an oasis and the Battalion was able to enjoy its welcome shade and clean water supply until 6th March. The dry bamboo jungle through which the Brigade had fought was waterless, and the Japs had oiled the village wells. Every drop of water had therefore to be brought up in water-carts or in jeep trailers. Only surface water off the paddy fields some miles back was available and it was far from clean. But in the increasing heat our men drank it without complaint, leaving none over for washing.

While the Battalion were in Shwepyi the Baluch and Gurkhas fought the last real battle before resistance crumbled and the pursuit to Mandalay was begun. The action developed into a fight for several large hill features which dominated the road a mile beyond Shwepyi, and their capture was obviously facilitated by the rapid advance of the other two brigades across the more open country on the right flank. Apprehensive of being cut off in the Shwepyi area, the Japs retreated in some confusion, leaving large dumps of stores by the side of the road with transport bullocks exhausted and dying of thirst, and the dead unburied.

The Brigade was now in a position to continue the **1945** advance and the Battalion moved straight down the road to Pinle-in, which was found to be unoccupied. While Brigade Headquarters and the Baluch now made for Yenatha, where 62 Brigade had already arrived, the Battalion was ordered to strike south-west to the Marble Quarries some twenty-four miles from Mandalay. This move was carried out with only the loss of a jeep from a mine, Captain Lord suffering serious ear injury and having to be evacuated next day. Only a short halt was made at Marble Quarries, since a signal came in to rendezvous at Thayetchaung. Brigade Headquarters and the Gurkhas were now at Thayetchaung, and the Battalion passed on to Impetlet and was back again in the original axis of advance.

The Brigade thus faced the open cultivated plain of Mandalay, intersected with irrigation channels, and was ready for the final thrust.

Of the three possible lines of advance to Mandalay, 64 Brigade was allotted the route which lay down a motorable track along the line of one of the minor canals, the Dinga Chaung. An Armoured Column ("Stiletto" Force) took the west route along the mud flats of the Irrawaddy, while 98 Brigade operated in the centre along the axis of the main road from Madaya.

Orders were issued from the Brigade group to move at 0100 hours on 8th March, the Battalion in the lead with tactical Brigade Headquarters and the Gurkhas behind. A broken bridge imposed considerable delay so that the Dinga Chaung was not reached until dawn. A day of some confusion followed. Owing to the delay, the Baluch, who had come in from the west flank on to the Dinga Chaung, failed to contact the Brigade. Furthermore, owing to an error in picking up a code name on the air which bore a striking similarity to another code name, they attacked the wrong objective and made for Mandalay hill. The eventual task allotted the Battalion was a comparatively simple one. To the east of the axis of advance was a large hill feature, Payangokto Taung. It commanded the countryside and the Battalion was ordered to investigate it and discover if it was held. A platoon sent to recon-

1945   noitre was heavily fired on and it was obviously held in
force. Since it was too late to stage an attack that day, the
Battalion harboured for the night three-quarters of a mile
to the north of Payangokto Taung.

On 9th March east of Mandalay the Japs opened some
sluice gates connecting a local irrigation distributary with
the main Mandalay canal running north and south to the
east of Payangokto Taung, thereby flooding the countryside. This successfully excluded the participation of the
armour from "Stiletto" Force which had successfully
cleared the area round Mandalay hill from co-operation
with the Gurkhas who were busy clearing the ground near
Patheingyi, a village to the east of Mandalay. In the
meanwhile on the night 9/10 March the Battalion sent
out a patrol north to Ngamundaung on the Mandalay
canal. It saw no enemy movement and returned. Another
patrol from "A" Company which approached Payangokto
failed to make progress, although the following morning
the whole company occupied the feature and found the
enemy gone. The same night "C" Company, which were
detached at Dahattaw alongside the Mandalay canal, were
rushed, one man being killed and two wounded. They
were successful, however, in preventing the Japs from
crossing the canal. On 11th March the Battalion moved
from the northern end of Payangokto Taung to the
village of Tada-U, which lay to the west of the same hill.
The day was uneventful except for the capture of a Jap
prisoner by the Commanding Officer, while making his
reconnaissance.

On 12th March some men from the Battalion participated in a small operation of unusual interest. Recently
there had been evidence that elements of the civil population were actively engaged in a Burmese movement
against the Japanese. Two such agents, students of
Rangoon University, reported at Brigade Headquarters
with a story of secret orders arriving from India by
wireless instructing them to co-operate with the British.
Their claim needed verification and accordingly the
Divisional Liaison Officer, Major D. Price of the Burma
Intelligence Corps, set out with the two agents, protected
by a platoon from the Battalion, to find their hide-out.

The party made its way through the jungle by a most 1945 tortuous track, accounting for three Japs on the way, and were rewarded by arriving in time to receive an air message from India confirming the story. A fortnight later, on 27th March, the Burma National Army rose in open participation against the common enemy.

On 12th March the Battalion moved south to join Brigade Headquarters at Patheingale and the following day moved on to Yangindaung, an important feature four miles east of Mandalay. The stage was now set for the capture of the city itself, a prize which would have vital significance for the bewildered people of Burma.

CHAPTER EIGHT

THE SECOND BATTALION, 1945–1947

Mandalay, Kalaw, Rangoon, Maymyo

1945 IN the confused movements which led up to the capture of Mandalay, units of the two Brigades, 64 and 98, had to some extent become interlaced. It is unnecessary to trace the devious courses of each battalion. Suffice it to note that by the evening of 12th March 98 Brigade had cleared Mandalay hill, which dominated the city and Fort Dufferin from the north-east, and that at 0800 hours on 15th March operational command of the battle for Mandalay passed to 64 Brigade, now under the command of Brigadier J. G. Flewett, D.S.O.

A mile or so to the south-west of Mandalay hill the city itself, now an empty shell, lay nestling under the protection of the great Fort Dufferin. Though devised for the warfare of other days, Fort Dufferin was in fact as formidable an obstacle as 64 Brigade had yet been called upon to tackle. Its walls, about eighteen feet high, were surrounded by a moat forty yards in width.[1] Inside the banked-up earth gave immense thickness and enclosed a cantonment of about a mile square. King Mindon of Burma in 1859 had certainly intended that his splendour should be protected by a fortress worthy of his dynasty. On 15th March no less than six battalions under command of 64 Brigade surrounded the fort, with a Sikh M.M.G. battalion on Mandalay hill. The 2nd Worcestershire came in from Yangindaung Pagoda hill and occupied a small village, Ashebyin, facing the east wall of Fort Dufferin, with "C" Company detached some 500 yards to the south. The same day "B" Company moved south to the area of St. John's Leper Asylum in order to block the road which ran out east from the city

---

[1] The War History of 64 Brigade gives the width of the moat as 75 yards.

136

to the Mandalay canal. Inside the Asylum were a number
of priests, nuns and refugees. It was decided to evacuate
160 of these unfortunate people, and transport was
accordingly arranged. Our men were the first British
troops they had seen since 1942, and their joy was a
measure of their past suffering.

On the same day "A" Company advanced west to
occupy a walled enclosure, Taiktaw, which protected a
cluster of pagodas. A 6-inch howitzer breached the walls
to make an entry for tanks and was followed by an air-
strike and an artillery concentration. The company then
attacked with two troops of medium tanks in support
and completed a most successful small operation. On the
night of 16th March "D" Company undertook a delicate
commitment, their task being to patrol across the moat
and discover if the fort was in fact still occupied. The
object was, if possible, to see and hear without being seen
or heard, making use of one of the several breaches in
the wall which our artillery had effected. The information
was obtained without a shot being fired, and Japanese
occupation was confirmed. On the night 18/19 March
"B" Company, who were still detached at the Leper
Asylum, were heavily fired on, the Japs bringing grenade
dischargers and machine guns up very close and firing
into the perimeter all night. Several casualties were
sustained, and the next morning two platoons of "D"
Company reinforced the position. Later the same day a
company of 3/6 Rajputana Rifles (62 Brigade) relieved
them.

On the night 16/17 March a full-scale attempt to
take Fort Dufferin was made by 8/12 Frontier Force
Regiment and 1/15 Punjabis. Assault boats and scaling
ladders were issued, and the two battalions were allotted
the north-east and north-west corners respectively, the
plan being to effect surprise and gain a footing if possible
inside in silence. Though leading elements of both
battalions reached the slippery rubble within the crumbling walls, surprise was lost and a very gallant attempt
was called off.

For the next two days and nights units on all sides of
the fort continued to probe the defences and search for

1945 all possible opportunities of exploiting the havoc which
the artillery was creating, the intention now being to stage
a second assault on 22nd March. It was a bitter twist of
fate that 20th March, which was indeed a day of triumph
for our forces as a whole, was marred by a tragedy which
cost the Battalion six men killed and eighteen wounded,
including four good N.C.Os. who could ill be spared.
A heavy air strike by the American 10th Air Force had
been arranged for 1100 hours in the hope of smashing
down the north wall at the north-east corner of the fort.
The order to the Battalion to move back 1,000 yards to
be clear of danger arrived only a few minutes before the
strike began, and it was then too late to move. Even so
the bombs fell inexcusably wide of their mark and
straddled the battalion area. Promptly on time a squadron
of Mitchells appeared, flying west to east. They circled
the fort and came down with their misdirected destruction. It was thus a cruel blow to learn a couple of hours
later that a small party of civilians had emerged from the
fort with a Union Jack and a white flag to announce that
during the night the enemy had disappeared and Fort
Dufferin was undefended and awaiting occupation. A
stampede then ensued to be the first within the walls,
the race being won by 1/15 Punjabis. Within the Battalion
the Commanding Officer and a small party scaled the
wall near the east gate. Amid much enthusiasm, there
was an inevitable sense of anti-climax after the careful
preparation which was in hand for an attack on
22nd March.

Inside the fort was a scene of utter desolation. Neither
King Thibaw's Palace nor the pleasant European bungalows were recognizable. On 21st March the Union Jack
was hoisted over Government House, Mandalay, before
a parade representative of 64 Brigade and in the presence
of General Sir William Slim, Commander of the Fourteenth Army, and many others.[2] Major G. P. Tipler of
the Battalion commanded the guard of honour, representative of the battalions of 64 Brigade. Three cheers

---

[2] Lieut.-General Sir Montagu Stopford, K.B.E., C.B., D.S.O.,
M.C., Commander, 33 (Indian) Corps. Major-General T. W. Rees,
C.B., C.I.E., D.S.O., M.C., Commander, 19 (Indian) Division.

for His Majesty The King closed a short and impressive gathering.

By now 2 Division had closed up from the west and were busy dealing with many Japs who had hoped to escape southwards. Both on 21st and 22nd March brief meetings with the 7th Battalion took place, and parties were able to pay short visits to each other.

On 22nd March the Battalion moved to the area of Yedwet, on the Mandalay canal some four miles east of the city. At last there was time off for attention to the many little matters of repair and replacement so long overdue. On 28th March the Battalion moved up to the hill station of Maymyo by M.T. for a short but very welcome rest away from the scene of battle. For the first time since going into action the men were housed in proper buildings, and all ranks were left to enjoy a full week of complete leisure.

Elsewhere the Armoured Column had raced south to win the battle of Meiktila, the key centre of communications in central Burma. The main Japanese forces had no alternative but to retreat down the main Mandalay–Rangoon road. But splinter forces were moving in other directions, and it was with the pursuit of those portions which were retreating up east of the Shan States road that 64 Brigade were to be concerned. In addition, a Japanese counter-attack on Meiktila from the east was not improbable ; and thus 64 Brigade's orders were to concentrate at Wundwin, twenty miles to the north of Meiktila. The concentration was effected without opposition, and at the same time the Brigade came under command of 17 Division at Meiktila. By 4th April, the day on which the Battalion rejoined the Brigade, Brigade Headquarters and the Baluch had left Wundwin, and Brigade Headquarters with supporting troops had harboured close to Pyintha, the Gurkhas in the meanwhile having been dispatched on an independent role to Hlaingdet by another route. The next day the Battalion occupied Kyeikpale railway station, the Baluch pushing out farther east to Segyi, where they were joined by Brigade Headquarters.

The immediate objective was now Thazi, a town of

1945 some size ten miles to the east of Meiktila. On 7th April the Baluch captured two small villages, Kanzwe and Katke-in, on the outskirts of the town, after an artillery concentration. But they had had a very tough fight and were therefore withdrawn to Segyi, "A" and "B" Companies of the Battalion taking over their positions in the two villages. The 8th April passed quietly, and that night the Battalion pushed out a patrol from Kanzwe to investigate two pagodas to the north-east. They were unoccupied, but the area was heavily mined, whereupon orders were given for the remaining two companies to move from Kyeikpale and concentrate in the area of the twin pagodas.

On 9th April the Baluch entered Thazi. For the Battalion it was a sad day, for the Second-in-Command, Major C. W. Y. Pickett, while going to the pagodas, drove over a mine and was instantly killed. He had only arrived in February, and his loss was a tragedy. During the afternoon the Battalion moved east from Thazi to occupy a village, Ywamuntha, again repeating the process of relieving the Baluch. The next three days were spent in efforts to reach Hlaingdet, which lay about ten miles to the east of Thazi. Between the Brigade and its objective a dry water-course, the Samon Chaung, constituted an obstacle capable of imposing considerable delay. Running as it did north and south across the flat country between Thazi and the Shan states, it was an admirable main escape route for the Japanese from the north. Near Hlaingdet the main road crossing over the Samon Chaung was a point which might obviously be held by the enemy, and it was to make the line of the Samon Chaung that the Battalion now advanced from Ywamuntha. On 11th April the Battalion set out and moved four miles down the main road before "D" Company, in the lead, was held up by grenade and M.M.G. fire at the demolished bridge which formerly spanned the Samon Chaung. Immediately the leading platoon, followed by "A" Company, moved north along the banks of a subsidiary chaung in an attempt to cut the road 200 yards to the rear of the Japs. This platoon and "A" Company lost touch with each other in this process, and enemy sniping and

grenade fire continued. A grenade which killed Lieutenant Lund, when he was explaining the situation to the
Commanding Officer, miraculously left the latter untouched. Failing to make progress, the Battalion withdrew for the night to Kyabetkon, about a mile back down
the main road. They had had a day of hard fighting in
gruelling heat with the temperature at 107° in the shade,
and the thick scrub had added to the difficulties of
control. The next morning one platoon again approached
the bridge, this time from the south. Its approach was
covered by an artillery concentration, and it reported its
arrival without incident by wireless. "C" Company
immediately moved up to take over the area, and another
platoon patrol was sent farther east when it again contacted the enemy. The platoon commander was wounded,
and the patrol withdrew. "B" Company now joined
"C" Company, and patrolling continued. In pouring
rain, as night came on two more patrols went out, one
reaching the old ruined palace north of Hlaingdet and
the other to a pagoda by the entrance to the same village.
Both patrols reported their objectives free of the enemy.

On 12th April a troop of 8 Cavalry reported that
Hlaingdet was clear. Accordingly two companies of the
Battalion advanced from the Samon Chaung with a troop
of armoured cars in support. Their orders were to hold
the village only if it was unoccupied. The original report
proved inaccurate, for they were met by fire. They
therefore returned. That night, however, the Baluch
were luckier and early next morning they discovered the
village unoccupied. The process of encountering resistance the first time, to find the enemy gone on a second
investigation, was becoming familiar. It will be recalled
that 1/6 Gurkhas were making for Hlaingdet from the
north, and on the same day their arrival synchronized
with that of the Baluch.

No sooner was one objective dealt with than another
invited attention. Brigade Headquarters and the Battalion
now moved down to Zibindwin, a village five miles across
country to the south, coming in for some heavy shelling
as they entered the area. South-east of Zibindwin the
edge of the jungle-clad foothills which rise 4,000 feet up

1945   to the Shan plateau were pierced by the road running
south out of Hlaingdet in a defile by the village of
Payangazu, the road then bending east round the hill
features. This defile now became the next Brigade
objective. The hills dominating the road at the bend
were devoid of shade, precipitous and covered in low
thorny scrub. The various features were allotted code
names and plans for the assault went ahead.

On 14th April Lieutenant Overton set out on patrol
to discover if the small feature, Egg, to the south of
Payangazu was held. From the actual slopes of the
objective his patrol suffered casualties, two men being
killed and five others wounded. With much difficulty the
wounded were extricated and the patrol then rejoined.
On 15th April the Battalion was ordered to take the
Payangazu defile next morning. The other three features
to be captured went under the homely names of Tickle,
Pimple and Slap, and the plan was for two companies to
assault Slap and Pimple while a third company with two
troops of armoured cars in support moved to Shwedokkon, a mile and a half to the south of Zibindwin, before
following up the Thettaw Chaung to attack Egg and
Tickle.

Early in the morning of 16th April the Battalion
deployed. Without difficulty "A" Company occupied a
feature, Point 1175, which overlooked Slap. But efforts
to infiltrate on to the latter position were met by heavy
fire from a pagoda. A new enemy now intervened in the
form of the sun, whose overpowering rays rendered the
position critical. This, together with lack of water,
produced a total of no less than thirty casualties from
heat exhaustion, and it was clear that the operation could
not be completed that day. "D" Company now relieved
"A" Company and dug in for the night, the remainder
of the Battalion concentrating east of Payangazu, where
plans were laid to continue the operation the next day.

In the meanwhile 1/15 Punjabis with a squadron of
8 Cavalry had suddenly appeared from the south to
occupy a large feature, Orange, which dominated Egg,
and the situation took on a new complexion. The plan
for 17th April was that 2nd Worcestershire should only

take Slap and Pimple, while Egg and Tickle were to be
captured by the Gurkhas. Accordingly, on the night
16/17 April the Gurkhas joined the Battalion near
Payangazu. "C" Company now arrived on Point 1175
alongside "D" Company and, covered by a concentration
from 4 Indian Field Regiment, went in to the attack, the
Sikh machine gunners providing overhead fire from
Point 1175. Resistance on Slap crumpled, but the enemy
still fought stubbornly on Pimple. Yet a second attack
after an air strike and artillery concentration was held up.
It was not until a third company, "B" Company, was
called upon to operate across the open country parallel
to the axis of the road that with the extra display of force
Pimple finally fell. With Slap and Pimple cleared by
1130 hours, the Gurkhas assaulted Tickle, and by 1300
hours had effectively overcome opposition. Both engagements had had considerable assistance from a well-timed
air strike from B29's. The battle over, the Battalion was
relieved and moved to a harbour area at Shwedokkon,
some four miles west of Payangazu.[3]

Though the hill positions continued to receive hot
attention from the enemy artillery, they were not seriously
challenged in attack, and in these circumstances 64
Brigade handed over to 36 Division and concentrated by
the side of Meiktila lake for a week of unbroken rest.
On 29th April they moved into camp away to the south
into the grounds of the old remount depot at Pyawbwe,
where there was a more comfortable area. There they
came under direct command of Fourteenth Army
Headquarters.

But the welcome respite was not to be enjoyed for long,
and orders to be back in action arrived during the first
few days in May. To the south in front of Kalaw
29 Brigade, who were due for evacuation to India, were
still battling down the Kalaw road. 64 Brigade were now
to relieve them in the area and capture Kalaw. The
preliminary moves involved retracing the road back to
the scene of recent battles, and Hlaingdet and Payangazu

---

[3] In detail this account, taken from 64 Brigade History, differs
slightly from Capt. B. E. St. L. Stuart's account in *Firm*. In essentials
there is agreement.

1945   were both revisited. On 6th May the Battalion left
Pyawbwe in M.T. and spent the next night at Pyintha,
some way out along the road from Meiktila. On the
morning of 10th May the Brigade column reached
Nampandet, eighteen miles north of Kalaw, and 29
Brigade handed over operational control and went their
way.

Between the Brigade and its goal at Kalaw the road
climbed seven miles up through a massive hill system
known as the Staircase, the summit lying some 2,000 feet
above the level of the country below. It was known that
the hills were held in strength, and the first step was
obviously to discover the exact measure of the enemy's
position. Such a formidable task took time, and it was
not until 29th May, after three weeks of careful patrolling,
that the small force was considered ready to tackle the
assault. The Commanding Officer had previously spent
a day forward with 36 Division studying the local situation. It was hardly encouraging. At the foot of the
Staircase two British infantry battalions were held up
where the road wound up out of the valley of the Magwe
Chaung. Behind them long and thinly protected communications ran through thick teak forests and deep
gorges. The bridges had been destroyed and the chaungs
would soon be impassable through heavy rain. Various
moves and reliefs had resulted in only two battalions,
2nd Worcestershire and the Baluch, being available, a
third battalion, 2nd East Lancashires, having to be held
at Pyinyaung to prevent an enemy encircling movement
up the railway line from Kalaw, and the Gurkhas being
down the Rangoon road. The necessity to hold a battalion
back on the line of communications to Meiktila and also
guard the Brigade administrative elements at Nampandet
made the presence of a fourth battalion imperative. This
was forthcoming, and the Chin Hills Battalion was
promised. But until it arrived there was little to be done
except be content with vigorous patrolling.

On 12th May 1/6 Gurkhas returned to relieve the East
Lancashires, 2nd Worcestershire then being at Nampandet with one company at Kyatsaken, a village six miles
back on the road to Hlaingdet. The latter company

carried out some very effective patrolling and useful
enemy identifications were obtained.[4] At the same time
Brigade Headquarters were supplementing information
from patrols with accounts from civilians from Kalaw
who had managed to evade the Japs. It was quite clear
that both on the Staircase and round Kalaw itself the
enemy were in strength, their main position being centred
on a bluff below the village of Wetpyuye about milestone
49. Formidable bunkers roofed with timber and M.M.G.
and L.M.G. positions had been located.

On 25th May the Chin Hills Battalion arrived at
Pyinyaung, allowing the Gurkhas to rejoin the Brigade
at Nampandet, and plans for an assault on the Staircase
went ahead. The plan evolved depended on a successful
encircling move by 1/6 Gurkhas, who were to move
across country on 28th May and cut the main road back
at milestone 55, nine miles beyond the foot of the
Staircase. On the same day one company of the Battalion
was to occupy the summit of a long ridge which overlooked the road from the north at milestone 53. Positions
were to be occupied early on 29th May, on which date
a frontal attack by the Baluch from the north-west,
supported with the full weight of the artillery available,
was to dislodge the enemy.

The task for the Gurkhas proved a cross-country
commitment which was to tax their little men to the full.
They moved up the Magwe Chaung before tackling the
steep ridge so as to come down at milestone 55 on the
main road. Nevertheless, overcoming all difficulties, they
were astride the road by 1400 hours on 30th May.
Meanwhile "A" Company of 2nd Worcestershire, moving
on a man-pack basis under Major M. R. Ellis, headed
for its objective, the feature known as Beetle, overlooking
the road at Yeyaungma, and by nightfall of 29th May
reached the foot of its northern end. Early the following
morning it pushed on up the hill and reached the south
end of the crest without having seen, or been seen by,

---

[4] On the Japanese side a patrol dressed as Burmans penetrated as far
as Meiktila, where as coolies the Japs were employed on the airstrips.
They found their way back to Kalaw and their information resulted in
only the Japanese 148 Regiment being held to oppose our single
Brigade.

L

1945   the enemy. At the same time another company relieved the Baluch on the hill east of milestone 45, enabling the latter to concentrate for the main assault.

In due course the Baluch attack went in, and by the evening of 30th May they had established themselves in the area of milestone 43 with comparatively few casualties. One squadron of 25 Dragoons had also arrived on the scene from Nampandet and had kept some of the main enemy bunkers under fire. On the morning of 31st May the Baluch occupied the remainder of the Staircase positions without opposition. On 1st June the Baluch and Gurkha battalions linked up, and operation "Staircase" was over. Later considerable evidence was forthcoming to indicate the size and scope of the enemy's defences, and the assumption was that the wide encircling movements of the Gurkhas and the movement of "A" Company, 2nd Worcestershire, produced doubts sufficient to induce him to abandon his positions.

On 1st June the Battalion was still at Nampandet, with "A" Company in the area of milestone 53 and another company at Wetpyuye near milestone 50. After two days' rest, on 4th June the advance continued with the Battalion in the lead and the remainder of the column a mile to the rear. A troop of tanks moved with the Battalion. At milestone 57 another formidable position where the road wound through pine forests following the hill contours suggested certain opposition. But, contrary to expectations, milestone 58 was reached without incident. With Kalaw now only a mile or so away, hopes ran high. Optimism was, however, to receive a jolt, for shortly after the leading company had passed milestone 58 M.M.G. fire was opened on Battalion Headquarters moving behind. "B" Company, forming the vanguard with the troop of tanks under command, immediately went to ground. Heavy fire was coming from the high ground east of the road, and search through glasses failed to locate the enemy machine guns. In these circumstances the Commanding Officer, who had gone forward, appreciated that it would be madness to attempt to attack across the valley on unlocated enemy positions. The remainder of the Battalion were therefore diverted by the

track which took off north of milestone 58 and wound up   1945
across the high ground through pine trees west of the
road. "C" Company now formed the vanguard, "B"
Company assuming the role of left flank guard. In this
manner the outskirts of the town were reached. But
eventually "C" Company also encountered a prepared
position, and the advance was halted. In the meanwhile
"B" Company, reinforced by another troop of Shermans,
were level with the cemetery on the road by milestone 59,
but a long way down the hillside. A blown culvert had
held up the tanks, and it was while filling the gap that
heavy M.M.G. fire again opened up on them from the
same guns which had caused damage earlier in the day.
The Japs had contrived to move their M.M.Gs. down
the east ridge, and it still proved impossible to locate
them. Thus the advance was completely held up.

"B" Company and the tanks appeared to be caught in
the centre of an arc of fire, and the Company Commander,
Major G. Kendrick, could only order his men to take
cover behind the tanks. The opening bursts of fire caused
heavy casualties, and the Company Commander's main
concern was for his wounded. These were sheltered by
the tanks and eventually evacuated by them, the tanks
also effectively covering the withdrawal of the company
in the evening. The casualties were not light. Five other
ranks killed and ten wounded, with two officers wounded,
was the toll within the Battalion, while the sappers and
tanks suffered also. That night "B" Company managed
to rejoin the remainder of the Battalion, which had dug
in making use of the perimeter of a small depression on
the high ground. The tanks, unable to turn round, had
reversed all the way back to the junction of the track
with the main road.[5] A day of sudden set-backs was
followed by a surprisingly quiet night.

It was again necessary to take stock of the enemy
immediately around Kalaw, and so for two days a halt
was called while intensive patrolling probed the country
on the outskirts of the town. To the north a Gurkha

[5] This account, which is based on the account in *Firm* (October,
1946), and on notes submitted by the Commanding Officer at the time,
differs in many respects from the War History of 64 Brigade.

1945   patrol successfully made the ridge which overlooked
Kalaw. The Battalion patrolled forward to three pimples
which marked the extremity of the feature they held
and found them clear. Continuing farther south along
the high ground overlooking the west side of the town,
they drew fire and saw movement. They also successfully
brought in two young civilians to Brigade Headquarters,
who for a suitable reward agreed to walk into Kalaw and
return with information on Japanese troop movements.
The two informers carried out their side of the bargain
and gave information of an enemy party of about thirty
seen at the north-west corner of the town. In the meanwhile the Chin Hills Battalion had relieved the company
at Nampandet, which rejoined the Battalion, still concentrated on the feature by milestone 58.

    With every indication that Kalaw was not now occupied
in strength, plans for its final assault were made. The
Gurkhas were to approach from the north-east, 2nd Worcestershire coming in from the north-west, the two
battalions converging to meet at the town itself. The
plan was put into operation in the early morning of
7th June. The Battalion axis of advance lay along the
main road into Kalaw. All went well, and by 1730 hours
the link-up was completed without opposition. The
honours of the day perhaps went to the sappers, who
toiled unceasingly to deal with the mines and bombs
which were placed at every bridge and culvert. Fortunate
it was that the enemy had been in such a hurry that the
bridges remained intact.

    Kalaw was the first city of any size in which there was
a pause sufficiently long for 64 Brigade to be concerned
with new problems of civil administration. By now
information of the enemy was coming in freely from a
number of civilian sources, and the "I" staff were kept
very busy. Active patrolling continued to supplement the
news from informers, and on 11th and 12th June patrols
from the Battalion sent south to a small village, Myindaik,
inflicted casualties and took a prisoner. Unfortunately,
the prisoner had received severe concussion and all efforts
to revive him failed. It was now known that the Brigade
were to be relieved at Kalaw by 99 Brigade of 17 Division,

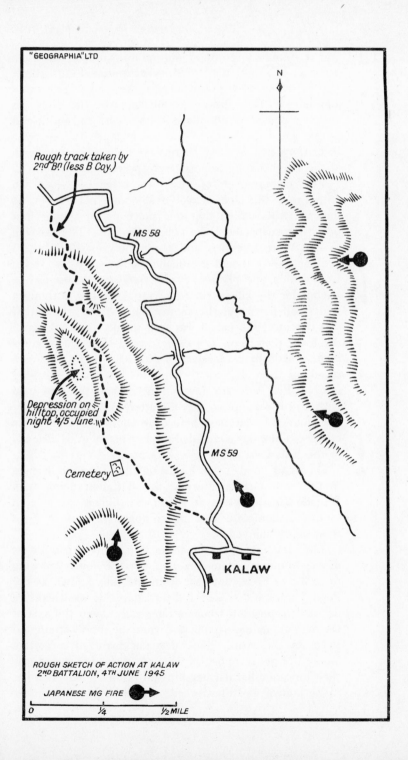

"GEOGRAPHIA" LTD

N

Rough track taken by
2ⁿᵈ Bⁿ (less B Coy.)

MS 58

Depression on
hilltop, occupied
night 4/5 June.

Cemetery

MS 59

KALAW

ROUGH SKETCH OF ACTION AT KALAW
2ⁿᵈ BATTALION, 4ᵀᴴ JUNE 1945

JAPANESE MG FIRE ●➤

0   ¼   ½ MILE

1945   and it became a point of honour to hand on as much
accurate information as could be accumulated in the time.
Patrols were therefore sent out for two and three days at
a time. On 17th June a patrol from the Battalion was
able to report all small villages to the south and south-east
clear. They encountered the Sawbwa of Pangmi, who
had informed them that there were now no enemy north
of the Bela Chaung, though many were still at Hsikip.

The change-over of the two brigades began on
18th June. But since it would obviously occupy several
days it was decided that one more patrol should first
probe the suspected Heko area to the east. The task fell
to 2nd Worcestershire, and accordingly on 19th June a
company set out and established a base west of Heko,
from which one platoon, under Sergeant W. E. Lewis,
set out for the village the following day. It was thought
that small parties of the enemy were in the area, but it
was not until the patrol was well inside the outskirts of
the town that heavy fire came down. The patrol commander skilfully managed to extricate his patrol, one man
receiving three bullets through his pack and escaping
injury. For Sergeant Lewis himself and the two men
with him it was not so easy a matter, and he had to wait
five hours for darkness before he could make good his
escape. Thus was concluded the last patrol of 64 Brigade
in the Kalaw area.

On saying good-bye to Kalaw on 22nd June the Brigade
moved into Central Burma, the Battalion being with
Brigade Headquarters at Pyinmana. There for over a
month a complete rest in comparative comfort was
thoroughly enjoyed.

The remnants of the Japanese 28th Army situated west
of the Mandalay–Rangoon road were obviously massing
in order to break out east from the hills known as the
Pegu Yomas and make a bid for safety. It was therefore
decided to position troops strategically down the axis of
the road in readiness to operate when the enemy attempted
to cross the road. This decision involved a certain
amount of general post, in which 64 Brigade were to lose
their long-familiar partnership and assume a new identity,
to be known as "Flewforce." Accordingly a composite

force under Brigadier Flewett,[6] which included the **1945**
Battalion[7] and six other units with attached troops from
17, 19 and 20 Indian Divisions, concentrated at Nyaungbintha, thirty-eight miles south of Towngoo, on 19th July,
its role being to control operations between Pyn and the
Kun Chaung. To the north of Pyn 98 Brigade held
responsibility, while to the south 63 Brigade, now in
17 Division, watched south of the Kun Chaung. The
orders to Flewforce were to destroy the enemy in the
area to the east of the road after he had crossed and
before he should reach the Sittang river.

The 2nd Worcestershire on this occasion were late on
the scene, and it was not until 24th July that the Battalion
moved into Pyn to relieve the 1/19 Hyderabad Regiment
at the northern end of the Brigade sector. By this time
Flewforce had already rounded up some 700 Japs and
taken prisoners at the cost of trifling casualties. One
company was detached eight miles to the south in
Nyaungbintha, and for the next few days, working eastward along the Pyn Chaung, the Battalion continued to
swell the bag, the villagers offering their enthusiastic
co-operation. Some 2,000 of the enemy had been brought
in. Starved, robbed of clothing and beaten up by the
villagers, they were a sorry travesty of a former proud
army. On 11th August Flewforce ceased to exist, the
figures of enemy casualties then standing at 2,124 killed
and 217 taken prisoner.

The Brigade returned to Central Burma, and the
Battalion reoccupied its former site in Pyinmana. The
Burma Campaign was over, and there was little left to
do but assist the local civil authorities in the reconstruction and rehabilitation of the area.

In the middle of January, 1946, the Brigade left **1946**
Pyinmana and concentrated north in Meiktila. Throughout the country the maintenance of internal security was
now a common army responsibility, and 64 Brigade
carried out this duty in the Meiktila and Yamethin civil
districts. The inevitable disintegration had begun. In

---

[6] Brigadier J. G. Flewett, D.S.O., 1 Punjabis, commanded 64 Brigade
from February, 1947 to July, 1947.
[7] Lieut.-Colonel G. Mander-Jones assumed command from Lieut.-
Colonel Symes in June, 1945.

1946   January the Baluch left for India, while at the same time the 19th Indian Division ceased to exist. The Brigade, however, kept its identity, and in the middle of March a move was made to Maymyo, the Gurkhas being sent to Mandalay.

Maymyo, the old hill station of Upper Burma, has a pleasant climate, and at last in Alexandra Barracks a sense of relaxation was enjoyed and all ranks could start thinking of football, hockey and cricket. Two minor operational commitments had yet to be undertaken. In June the Battalion were ordered to undertake anti-dacoit operations in the plains round Shwebo. Using Kyan-myaung on the Irrawaddy as a base, "B" Company rounded up several wanted bad characters and managed to find time to take on the local villagers at football. "C" Company went to Pakokku and also dealt very successfully with the town football team. "A" and "D" Companies had their respective areas, and companies returned independently when their individual tasks were over. In September the whole Battalion moved hurriedly to Rangoon in connection with strikes and general civil disorder which was then starting to disrupt the civic life of Burma. Fortunately, the Battalion were not called on to perform any unpleasant police duties, but had instead to provide guards both for the Governor and the Japanese War Criminal Crimes Court. At the time the Governor was Major-General Sir H. E. Rance, K.B.E., C.B., who had served with the Regiment in the early twenties, and he was delighted to have men of his old Regiment so near at hand. In November a move back to Maymyo was made, where for the first time for seven years arrangements to celebrate Christmas with traditional festivity went ahead. Inspections by General Stopford and General Briggs[8] drew congratulatory messages on the general turn-out and steadiness on parade, while in

1947   January, 1947, the Governor on a visit to Maymyo added his tribute after a final inspection.

In the world of sport and weapons training the old

[8] General Stopford was now C.-in-C., S.E.A.L.F. Lieut.-General H. R. Briggs, C.B.E., D.S.O., G.O.C.-in-C., Burma ; later to renew acquaintance with the Regiment when 1st Battalion came into his command in Malaya, 1950.

standards were quickly being recaptured. The Battalion team under C.S.M. Hewins won the Burma Army Championship, and most of the honours in the 17th Indian Divisional Rifle Meeting were taken, Major G. G. H. Peace winning the Individual Championship. In their spare time men were busy cutting down the luxuriant "lantana" shrub which had shot up at an amazing rate during their absence in Rangoon.

All the time demobilization and repatriation were taking their toll, and some of the old leaders in sport had, alas, to leave, C.S.M. Ward of "D" Company being particularly missed.

Changes in command had seen the arrival of Lieut.-Colonel J. O. Knight to take over from Lieut.-Colonel Mander-Jones. But health prohibited his full stay, and on 19th December 1946, Lieut.-Colonel F. S. Ramsay, arrived to assume command. Just how capricious can be the play of fate is emphasized when we note that the new Commanding Officer "soon dispersed any qualms about the possibility of suspended animation."

Yet it was exactly that status which a cruel dispensation held in store for the 2nd Battalion Worcestershire Regiment, and on 1st March, 1947,[9] the old 36th paraded at Alexandra Barracks, Maymyo, for their last ceremonial farewell. Fifteen officers and 418 other ranks were on parade in olive green drill, gaiters and jungle hats, belt and bayonet, and the spectators were presented with an example of precision of drill and movement worthy of so great yet melancholy an occasion. The inspection was carried out by Lieut.-General Ritchie.[10] To the tune of "The Lincolnshire Poacher" and "Royal Windsor," the Battalion marched past for the last time, and thus was closed a chapter in the history of nearly 250 years. The records speak of a period of twelve years' extinction. But an Army Council Instruction of 1948 revised the original intention, and the two Battalions are now amalgamated with the designation, 1st Battalion The Worcestershire Regiment (29th/36th Foot). On 16th July, 1947, a cadre

---

[9] 26th March was the official date of suspended animation.
[10] Lieut.-General Sir Neil Ritchie, K.B.E., C.B., D.S.O., M.C., had succeeded General Stopford as C.-in-C., S.E.A.L.F.

1947 commanded by Lieut.-Colonel F. S. Ramsay handed
over their Colours to be laid up in the Officers' Mess at
Norton Barracks.[11] The process of amalgamation suggests
that at any time when a challenging international situation
may require the country to turn again to its armed forces
the 2nd Worcestershire will resume its place in the annals
of regimental history.

---

[11] This ceremony is described in Chapter Fourteen.

CHAPTER NINE

THE SEVENTH BATTALION, 1922–1944

Kidderminster, Dunkirk, Goole, India

SINCE 1919, when on an April morning the 7th Battalion **1920** had been welcomed vociferously back to Kidderminster after four years of service, the Battalion had been centred on its home town, and the normal life of a Territorial Army unit had entered on its uneventful cycle of duty and service which was to bear fruit years later in the jungles of Burma. At Kidderminster the Battalion covered a large area of the north of the county. To the south one company was based on Stourport and Stourbridge, another was isolated away to the south-west in Tenbury, while the remaining two companies included the populous Birmingham suburbs and were based on Dudley, Oldbury and Halesowen. All centres had drillhalls.

At Kidderminster one old building which was shared with the Worcestershire Yeomanry housed the Orderly Room, armoury, offices and drill hall, and also provided permanent quarters for the Regimental Sergeant-Major.

A permanent staff was appointed which consisted of the Adjutant, the R.S.M., C.S.M., three sergeants and a storeman. The average strength of the Battalion for much of the period between the wars stood at about 700, 80 per cent. of whom turned up for the annual camp.

This figure not only reflected a high sense of duty, but also a very happy relationship between the Regiment as a whole and the county whose name it bears.

It should be realized that much of the success of a Territorial unit was without doubt measured according to the attraction which the Social Club attached to a drill-hall is able to exercise on the men of the neighbourhood. A billiard-room, bar, and dart-board in the hands of an enthusiastic and tactful Regular sergeant living on

1930   the spot can play its very real part in creating a live unit.
It was noticeable, too, that those Company Commanders
who were able to encourage personnel to hold their
evening parades in uniform were the first to reap the
benefit of the development of companies with a sense
and spirit of military strength and unity which were
absent when men set about their hour's instruction in
civilian clothes. It proved, for instance, worth while for
a Company Commander to give the first quarter of an
hour of the available time to allowing men to change into
uniform.

While a member of the Battalion could turn up for a
drink and gossip at the Club on most evenings of the
week, the intention, of course, was not to put play before
work. Rather was the Club Room the means to an end.
Apart from the weekly evening attendances, in the
summer four week-ends were set aside for training in
addition to the annual fortnightly camps. Owing to the
difficulty of procuring suitable country for full-scale
exercises, at week-ends it was seldom possible to provide
more than T.E.W.Ts. for officers and N.C.Os. and
musketry for troops. The fortnightly camps were usually
held on Salisbury Plain or in some coastal area, when
space permitted a week's Company training to be followed
by both Battalion and Brigade collective exercises.
Previous to collective training the Adjutant had to put in
some hard work surveying the area, allotting sub-areas
to companies, and preparing the brief outline of exercises
according to the nature of the particular principles to be
taught.

The 7th Battalion took much pride in its musketry
and, apart from week-end shoots, spare Sundays were
also frequently devoted to the range.

Meanwhile the Quartermaster was kept busy getting
in touch with the local supply agencies.

Every year the Annual Officers' Dinner was held in
Birmingham or Kidderminster, while occasionally an
Officers' Dance livened the social life of the Battalion.

1938   The last dance held at the Town Hall in Dudley in 1938
was a very happy function and was marked by the
Battalion Colours standing uncased, with a sentry who

stood duty for half-hourly periods. On this occasion the **1938** sentry was in full dress, sentries being posted and relieved under the command of R.S.M. McCormack.

Another function of significance was the annual "Mayor's Sunday," when a detachment of the Battalion marched to church and the Mayor and Corporation, not to mention boy scouts, girl guides and the Fire Brigade, turned out to emphasize civic interest in their town. On such occasions the Battalion Band would be in great demand.

The members of the Band were mostly professional musicians, and were perhaps naturally apt to think of themselves as bandsmen first and soldiers second. Indeed, at one period there was some indignation when the Adjutant insisted on the Band turning out for instruction as stretcher-bearers on week-end drills. The privilege of being musicians carried with it the obligation of soldiering. That was the Adjutant's view, and it was rightly accepted. In taking note of the Band, it is appropriate to recall that at one period it was under the able direction of Mr. Yarnold, an ex-Bandmaster of the 3rd Battalion, who returned to his former responsibilities as a Territorial. Simultaneously his son was an instructor at Headquarters, destined to go to Normandy in 1939 as R.S.M. The latter, also being a trained musician, would sometimes deputize for his father, so that the Band became a family interest of the two Yarnolds, father and son. R.S.M. S. Yarnold was, alas, later reported as missing, presumed killed, in France in 1940.

Throughout these years Brigade Headquarters were in Silver Street, Worcester, either the Brigade Commander or his Brigade Major always being a Regular officer. On occasions both Brigade Commander and the Brigade Major have been Regular officers.

Early in August, 1939, it became evident that the **1939** annual training would be something more than the routine camp on Salisbury Plain. Previous to moving, companies assembled in their areas. Once in camp at Windmill Hill it was realized that not only were there two Commanding Officers and Adjutants, but that the officer strength was also doubled. It should here be explained that in the

1939 spring of 1939 plans to double the Territorial Army were
initiated, so that by the time the first conscripts were
called up the approximate strength of the Battalion was
55 officers and 1,000 other ranks. Since the swollen
strength included so many newcomers, instruction at
Windmill Hill camp was on this occasion on elementary
lines. Physical training and weapons took the place of
the customary schemes, while the new drill in "threes"
had also to be mastered.

The difficulties of measuring up to the heavy demands
of training new personnel and also launching a new
Battalion will be appreciated when it is remembered that
at the time both Regular Battalions were abroad, and
Regular officers and N.C.Os. were hard to come by.

The process of mobilization was actually completed
after the move to Marlborough, the official orders for the
mobilization of the Territorial Army being dated 1st September. Simultaneously the 9th Battalion took on its
separate identity as the child of its older parent unit, its
association being with the northern portions of the
7th Battalion county area. No record of the 7th Battalion
at this stage would be complete without reference to
Colonel F. M. Tomkinson, D.S.O., who has taken such
an active interest always in the affairs of the Battalion.
Having commanded in World War I, he became its
honorary Colonel, a post he still holds. On at least two
occasions in the 1930's, with the Commanding Officer, he
organized four-day trips to France, where he conducted
most interesting exercises with lectures, covering the
ground over which the Battalion had worked in the war.
The trips were organized on a subscription basis through
Messrs. Thomas Cook and Sons, and were much
appreciated.

It was as the 144th Infantry Brigade[1] of the 48th
(Wessex) Division[2] that the 7th and 8th Battalions the
Worcestershire Regiment, with the 5th Battalion the
Gloucestershire Regiment, concentrated at Marlborough
on 13th September and trained previous to their baptism
of fire in France. At the time the Battalion was com-

---

[1] Brigadier Hamilton.
[2] Major-General A. F. A. N. Thorne.

manded by Lieut.-Colonel J. Parkes, M.C., D.C.M., who   1939
continued to lead through the difficult days in northern
France.[3]

The move to Marlborough went "according to plan."
The men came in on Midland Red buses from their
drill-halls to the rendezvous at the junction of the
Worcester–Stourport–Kidderminster roads by the "Mitre
Oak" inn. The convoy was formed and by 1530 hours
the Battalion was debussing in a field north of the town,
from where it marched into Marlborough, headed by the
Band and Drums. Billets were in lofts, racing stables
and garages, while some lucky ones found themselves in
licensed houses.

The Battalion was down again to 30 officers and 350
other ranks, and the incoming drafts to restore the
strength to establishment were hardly an even entry.
Men from the Royal Berkshire and the Oxford and Bucks
Light Infantry arrived, many of whom had been transferred against their wishes ; while others were discovered
later not to have signed the necessary "General Service"
engagement and had to be reposted to their original units.
Regular reservists would arrive and almost overnight find
themselves with N.C.O. and warrant officer status. In
November, however, a very welcome leavening of 120
healthy strong young men from Norton arrived to swell
the numbers. They were the initial conscript intake of
July and were all over twenty-one years of age. Potential
specialists were being crammed with knowledge at the
various schools of instruction, but even so teachers of
experience were sadly missed. The Battalion signallers
in particular were without an expert instructor until the
last days in France. It is perhaps natural to slip into the
assumption that progress within a keen Battalion proceeded always on an even keel. The difficulties are
stressed only to indicate that in the best-ordered units
there were constant set-backs and handicaps in the
continuous struggle to improve.

Marlborough Downs offered opportunities for more

---

[3] Lieut.-Colonel Parkes assumed command from Lieut.-Colonel
R. H. Edwards, T.D., on 13th September, the latter officer for medical
reasons passing on to the command of the 9th Battalion.

1939 advanced training, and a new Divisional Commander
energetically saw that a modern tactical doctrine was
taught at a bleak spot called Snap Farm where companies
could spend two or three days and nights in the open.
It was a bitterly cold winter and 'flu was the first enemy.

Such was the nature of the constant small difficulties
which the Battalion Headquarter Staff were called on to
overcome, and if it be remembered that small-arms
ammunition was in short supply, that there was little
web equipment, and that for three months the M.T.
consisted of three carriers, five 15-cwt. trucks and an
Albion lorry, it is remarkable that a spirit of optimism
prevailed ; which was perhaps characteristic of the
British Army as a whole up to the last days of the drama
in 1940.

Throughout this period of suspense the Brigade Commander's sympathetic assistance was always at the disposal of his units, encouraging them to improvisation and
the art of making bricks without straw. Quite suddenly
the situation then changed and 48 Division became
"Priority." Equipment of all sorts poured in, and indeed
a message to collect thirty vehicles from Newbury caused
some consternation, for most of the ten drivers were on
week-end leave. Early in December the significance of
the new situation of the Division was left in no doubt
when about 400 officers of the Division came in to
Marlborough Town Hall and heard their fate from the
Chief of the Imperial General Staff himself. The area
"Lille–Arras" was indicated on the map, and 48 Division
could take some pride in the fact that they were to be
the first Territorial formation to reinforce the B.E.F. in
the task of strengthening the "Gort" line. In the light
of after-events it remains one of the mysteries of history
how at that time the doctrine of defence and the infallibility of the Maginot Line were generally accepted.

There followed ten days' combined Christmas and
embarkation leave for the whole Division, and by the
end of the month, with the exception of some casualties
from influenza, the Battalion was assembled and ready
for France.

On 29th December the advance party under Captain

G. B. Hingley left for Southampton. In error they were **1939**
sent to Cherbourg, where they picked up a French
Liaison Officer, a pleasant little schoolmaster but a very
inadequate interpreter. On 15th January the billeting
party were joined by the vehicle party in the staging
area and there they awaited the arrival of the Battalion.

The Battalion sailed from Southampton on 14th January, **1940**
1940, on the *Amsterdam*, and at the time security measures
were sufficient to ensure that officers and men did not ·
know their port of embarkation. The subsequent disembarkation on 16th January at Le Havre was hardly a
happy affair. A high snow-storm was on and they were
met by guides who seemed to have no idea whatsoever
where to lead their companies. They were to lead the
Battalion to St. Nicholas, only ten miles from the point
of detrainment. In the event Battalion H.Q. spent the
night trying to trace its scattered family, and in the
meanwhile Company Commanders had wisely settled into
billets wherever they could be procured. St. Nicholas had
apparently been chosen as a new staging area by H.Q.,
Le Havre ; but nothing was ready and as the Battalion
left a representative of the Royal Engineers arrived to find
out what structures were necessary.

The Battalion transport which, as noted, crossed four
days previously had gone astray. In general, both the
fog of war and of nature governed the introduction to
French soil.

From the Le Havre area 144 Brigade moved north to
the Belgian front. But the 7th Battalion were to leave
the Brigade when (as is noted in the next chapter) the
latter left Moncheaux for the Saar. Thereafter the
Battalion entered 2nd Division.

The move up was made by train, the transport moving
separately and rejoining the Battalion at Le Forest on the
evening 20th January. Le Forest was a typical French
mining village. The Battalion settled into billets in
miners' cottages, and at least there was ample coal to
combat the intense cold. Indeed, at this early stage
casualties incurred were all through sickness, and many
were down with colds and coughs.

It was at Le Forest that orders came to remain in the

M

1940 north and replace the 2nd Royal Warwickshires in the 5th Brigade,[4] 2 Division. The prospect of the change was disturbing, for the Battalion had been settling down very happily in 48 Division. The other two units in the Brigade were the 2nd Dorsets and 1st Cameron Highlanders. While the spirit of co-operation with both battalions needed no encouragement and relations with the Dorsets in particular were of the friendliest nature, it was sometimes difficult to resist the impression that, as a Territorial unit within a Regular Brigade, the Battalion was at a disadvantage. The first few days in February were therefore spent in effecting the exchange, and on 5th February the Battalion marched from Le Forest in the morning and covered some eighteen miles to Rumegies by 3.30 in the afternoon. There companies took up defended localities on the Frontier and went to earth in pill-boxes and block-houses as the staunch defenders of the "Gort" line, in positions which subsequently were never defended. The billets were as good as could be expected, but it was difficult to get a proper bath. Fortunately, Lille was only fifteen miles away, and so once a week the opportunity to clean up in comfort was taken. Musketry and training proceeded on company lines while Battalion Headquarters were busy mustering the various plans of operation set out in connection with the defence of the "Gort" line. One of these, Plan "D," which in the event was to govern subsequent action, involved an advance to the river Dyle, while another amounted only to holding the present position. But they all involved the careful preparation of orders interpreting intentions to the Battalion, and there were some headaches for the Commanding Officer and Adjutant. When not firing their 2-inch mortars or engaged in training, companies worked with R.E. parties on the defences. The apparent sense of static security enabled training to proceed on comparatively normal lines, even Church Parade being regularly observed.

At the end of the month orders came to move to Agny, which was being used by the Brigade as an area for

---

[4] The other two units were 2nd Dorsets and 2nd Cameron Highlanders.

Battalion training combined with rest. Early on the
morning of 28th February the Battalion marched by road
to Orchies, thence by rail to Arras, finally marching into
Agny in the afternoon. The men settled into billets,
mostly barns and empty houses, and after a reconnaissance company areas were allotted, and on 2nd March a
start was made in earnest with Platoon training.

The process continued on through the month until
24th March, by which time Company Commanders had
handled their platoons and Battalion schemes had
rounded off the period. There were naturally many
mistakes, inevitable in a Territorial battalion with few
officers who had more than six months' service. But the
spirit and will to learn were there, facts which sometimes
appeared to pass unrecognized by higher authority in the
day-to-day supervision of training. A brief diversion
from serious training was enjoyed when organized parties
managed to visit the Memorial and preserved trench
system at Vimy Ridge. By 24th March the men were fit
and thought nothing of covering twenty miles in a day
over open fields. There followed Brigade and Divisional
Exercises from 25th to 27th March, and on 1st April the
Battalion returned to Rumegies to put in a few days
practising the occupation of the "Gort" line. More
precisely, the three days 1st to 3rd April were occupied
with the 1st Corps manning an exercise in which the
Battalion again occupied the Rumegies sector based on
three block-houses, with two companies forward, one in
support and one in the Brigade Reserve line at Sarneon.
Brigades retired and recaptured ground, prisoners were
taken and patrols energetically assimilated conditions
which were shortly to prove so far removed from the
final swift reality. This was followed on 3rd April by a
move of the Brigade by M.T. to Pas-en-Artois in the
Doullens area for Brigade training. After the flat country
round Rumegies, the hills, valleys and woods were a
pleasant contrast, and visits to Doullens and Amiens were
welcome relaxation. But the change of scenery was not
enjoyed for long, for on 9th April the Germans invaded
Norway, and early the following morning the Brigade
returned to Rumegies. There followed a brief period of

1940   doubt and rumour with preparations to move at short notice, followed by counter-orders and the opening of leave interspersed with some furious rewiring, burying cable lines and digging anti-tank ditches. It was surely an indication of the measure of our innocence that on 10th May, when Germany invaded the Low Countries, the Brigadier[5] was on leave, while the Commanding Officer had returned from leave only a few days previously.

Plan "D" which was now put into operation allowed for a movement forward, and accordingly at midnight (11/12) the Battalion set out, crossing the Belgian frontier at Howardries. 4 and 6 Brigades were to hold the line of the River Dyle with 5 Brigade in reserve, the Battalion digging in behind the river just north of Genval. Before moving, a Brigade dump of all surplus kit and clothing was formed which, in the event, was never seen again. It included the Battalion drums, and years later these were returned to the local Civil Affairs Detachment by Monsieur Gaston Debuchy of Ennevilin, Nord. This gentleman took care of the drums during the German occupation at considerable personal risk, and the Regiment owe him a great debt of gratitude. The drums were at first sent to the Coldstream Guards, Civil affairs mistaking the badge for that of the Coldstream. One of the drums is now in the Regimental Museum.

In their short-lived optimism the Belgians showered hospitality on our men as they moved through the villages, and it was pleasant to be offered free beer and wine after the extravagant prices demanded in France. By 14th May refugees were streaming back from the forward areas, and the face of the cheerful countryside was within a few hours darkened with human tragedy. So far as the 7th Worcestershire were concerned they had sustained only one casualty[6] and morale was high. Typical of the prevailing spirit was the successful effort of an officer returning from leave to evade orders at the Base and make the journey up by a French taxi.[7]

The position on the River Dyle seemed strong and it

---

[5] Brigadier G. I. Gartlan, D.S.O., M.C.
[6] Private Gilbert, "C" Company, killed by a bomb in La Hulpe.
[7] Captain J. W. Tomkinson.

was with reluctance that orders were received to with- **1940**
draw. On 15th May the Battalion were ordered to occupy
the line L'Argent–Le Grand Etaing, where a Belgian
anti-tank obstacle provided a framework for defence.
The move was completed successfully during the night
15/16 May.

In the meanwhile 5 Brigade had orders to form a
defensive flank on the line Hannonsart–Genval, con-
forming to a general defensive position occupied by
Division. The orders provided for all three battalions
forward, with 7th Worcestershire on the left, the Dorsets
in the centre and Camerons on the right. The Brigade
was involved in these moves when at 1600 hours on
16th May a warning order was received indicating that
the B.E.F. were to withdraw that night to the line of the
River Dendre, 5 Brigade acting as rear-guard to 2 Division, with the 1st Battalion Oxford and Bucks Light
Infantry coming under command, the withdrawal being
covered by 4/7 Dragoon Guards.

Accordingly the Battalion with the Dorsets withdrew
to the line of the River Dyle, while the other two Battalions moved farther back into the Forest de Soignies to
hold the Corps check line. At 0100 hours on 17th May the
withdrawal of 7th Worcestershire and 2nd Dorsets was
carried out over the concrete road bridge at La Hulpe
and back into the Forest de Soignies, the sappers blowing
the bridge as the last platoon was over. By 0400 hours on
17th May the Battalion was in scattered positions in the
thick forest, and at 0900 hours they were on the move
again to Grammourt, the Corps check line having been
abandoned after 4 and 6 Brigades had passed through.

For the 7th Worcestershire the next ten days represented that same vague nightmare and confusion which
was the experience of every battalion of the British Army
in the retreat to Dunkirk. It was a dismal period of
frustration in that so soon as opportunities occurred to
stand and fight the enemy, the flanks were yielding and
orders to break off an engagement and withdraw would
be received. The confusion which appeared only too
evident to Company Commanders and the Battalion
Headquarters staff was but a mirror of what was hap-

1940 pening higher up the chain of command. Thus the Brigade billeting area was changed while units were on the move and there was no chance of letting them know, with the result that, tired of changes and with lack of sleep, units did not finally find their areas until late into the night.

At Grammourt the whole Battalion were grateful for the use of a friendly monastery, and the monks put their kitchens at the disposal of the troops. At 0130 hours on 18th May the retreat continued. The orders were to march to Tournai, 2 Division having now been ordered to withdraw to the line of the River Escaut. The Battalion set out on its feet but was later able to pick up lorries. On arrival at Tournai order and counter-order to occupy alternative positions followed in quick succession. Eventually a position in some factories by the River Escault was occupied, only to be followed on 20th May by the order to make for Guignies. The chaos on the roads was now indescribable. Pitiful hordes of refugees added to the congestion, while the enemy artillery took its toll. The Battalion struck across country to Guignies in artillery formation, but even so were caught by shell fire and lost two officers and thirty-one men killed and wounded.

That night orders were received to push on to Wez-Velvain, where a pleasant surprise awaited the Battalion in that they were to relieve 8th Worcestershire in 144 Brigade. The Brigade War Diary explains the situation by noting that on the night 20th May, 5 Brigade were placed under 48 Division, adding that orders continued to come in from 2 Division ! Such a brief encounter with a sister battalion and with old friends at Brigade Headquarters was a welcome interlude in the relentless conditions of mounting casualties and continuous withdrawal. It was at Wez-Velvain that the Battalion lost their indefatigable Medical Officer, Lieut. R. K. Pilcher, M.C., who was badly wounded in the arm and shoulder.

On 22nd May a move on to Bruyelles was ordered. The move could only be made at night, and when dawn broke the following day the Battalion was in a difficult position with "B" Company isolated in front of Amtoing in the sector held by the Camerons. Somehow the following night the Battalion was extricated, and the next day the move brought the Brigade back to the "Goit" line in the vicinity of Mouchin. Had it been possible to strike the old Rumegies sector it would considerably have simplified the immediate tactical problem. As it was, valuable time was taken up in the necessary reconnaissance, while the unpredictable movements of elements of the retreating French Army further confused the issue.

The retreat continued the following night, first by march route and later by M.T. The route lay through Sedin into the La Bassee district, where billets were taken up in scattered farmhouses in the rear of Givenchy. The transport was doing heroic work, for it was no easy matter to line up vehicles in the dark in their correct order on the road and get them away in the right place and at the right time.

From billets a position forward of Givenchy was occupied along the bank of the La Bassee canal from the bridge over the canal in front of Givenchy on the right to some lock gates two and a half miles away on the left. "B" Company was now so weak that the Commanding Officer decided to keep its two remaining platoons under his direct control, with "D," "A" and "C" Companies up. On the right "D" Company under Captain J. Tomkinson was in touch with the Dorsets. But on the left and in the centre "C" and "A" Company positions remained obscure, though "C" Company were in touch with the Cameronons. It was in attempting to trace "A" Company that the Commanding Officer's truck ran into machine-gun fire and his party had to jump for it and make for the ditch by the road. The Commanding Officer escaped injury, but the three officers with him received wounds and injuries. It was clear that the Germans had penetrated "C" and "A" Company positions, and an attempted counter-attack by the two platoons of "B" Company could make no progress. "A" Company had in fact been overwhelmed. Thus dusk fell on 25th May with the Battalion in a very precarious and exposed position. Tank support which was promised never materialized. Instead the enemy tanks appeared and

1940 opened up on company positions with H.E. and incendiary shell. By now heavy casualties had been sustained and every available man, including the Orderly Room staff, was in position. Six of the ten Bren carriers had been knocked out. Early on the morning of 26th May a message from Captain Tomkinson came in saying that "C" Company was completely surrounded, but that he was hanging on as long as possible, and in this situation a sorely wounded battalion fought on through the following morning. When in the afternoon a message came from the Brigadier to break off the engagement, together with the Dorsets and Camerons, only a skeleton battalion remained to receive orders. The forward companies could only be left to their fate and the remnants of the reserve company and Headquarters were all that were mustered for the final move to Dunkirk. On the night of 28th May, Lavantie was reached. By now the transport had destroyed their trucks and so a small party, consisting of the Commanding Officer, two officers[8] and some 150 other ranks, in answer to a last call from Brigade, made for the north.

Unsuccessful efforts were made to contact Headquarters, 2 Division, and instead advice from 1 Division was forthcoming which amounted to "keep going." The message from Brigade, scribbled hastily across three pages of a small note-book, made no mention of Dunkirk, the rendezvous named being St. Jan sur Bitzen. On reaching the rendezvous, 1 Division H.Q. were able to direct the party on to Dunkirk.

On reaching the suburbs of Dunkirk on the evening of 30th May, the Area Commandant was anxious to get the small party away as soon as possible owing to the food shortage ; and the final stage was an anti-climax in which the remnants of 7th Worcestershire on 31st May walked along the sea wall and waited for the first boat to come in. Then with simple formality they stepped aboard and were soon away from the coasts of France.

Later another party under Major T. G. Vale, and one under Captain J. W. Tomkinson with 2nd Dorsets,

---

[8] Lieut. R. H. K. Evers and Lieut. G. P. P. Chesshire.

arrived and embarked. Out of a total of 800, approximately 250 men were killed and wounded and another 150 remained as prisoners, some 400 men finding their way out of Dunkirk.

On 6th June a small nucleus arrived at Dewsbury, in Yorkshire, and Battalion H.Q. occupied the Yorkshire Penny Bank building, with the remainder in billets near by. On 14th June a large draft of fifteen officers and 210 other ranks arrived, to be followed by one officer and 165 other ranks on 15th June. The 7th Worcestershire was once again a living unit with that core of men who were to fight through to victory in Burma. On 22nd June the whole Battalion moved by bus to Burton Constable, the home of Colonel Chichester-Constable, who was a cousin of Major Nugent Chichester, who was Adjutant of the Battalion from 1936 to 1940. Companies camped under the trees in the park and the kitchen in the house became the battalion cook-house. The officers were lucky to be able to make use of one whole wing of the house for their Mess and quarters.

On 29th June Lieut.-Colonel Parkes relinquished command of the Battalion, with which he had shared the fortunes of a vital episode in history, and he handed over command to Lieut.-Colonel T. L. Molloy of the 2nd Dorsets.

The role of the Battalion was now that of the greater proportion of the British Army—namely, the defence of the country from invasion. The records of *Firm* at the time are so constricted by the demands of the censor, that for once no true picture of the period is to be had from studying the Battalion notes.

On 23rd June the duties of Reserve Battalion in the Brigade were taken over from a battalion of the Border Regiment. Companies took over road-blocks and wiring parties were kept busy in the coastal area. The War Diary quoted an Operation Order covering invasion measures known by the code word "Cromwell." It tells of coastguards ready to fire red flares emitting stars and the ringing of church bells to indicate parachutists.

The Battalion remained in Yorkshire for the remaining months of 1940, moving in January, 1941, to Hull. From

1941   February to June, with the Brigade, it was stationed some thirty miles inland at Goole, where the role of 2 Division was that of mobile reserve, the object being to counter-attack any force that might fight its way on shore or land by parachute. On 20th August a move was made to Ripon, to be followed by the transfer of the whole Division down to Adlestrop, near Kingham in the Cotswolds. When at Adlestrop khaki drill was issued and topees fitted, suspicions that a trip overseas was impending were confirmed.

1942   On 11th April, 1942, the Battalion embarked at Liverpool on the *Reina del Pacifico*, a ship which in peace time used to carry a luxury tourist traffic on the round of the South American ports. The 2nd Battalion Dorsets and a battery were their companions on board. Once at sea, it was realized that the many components of 2 Division were bound for an eastern destination in about the largest convoy which had yet left these shores. To put it mildly, on deck there was hardly a dull moment. With the example of other formations which had put to sea and suffered from failure to prepare for subsequent events, 2 Division were determined to keep fit. Thus for the first time, boots were worn by all until midday. While much time was devoted to intensive P.T., many lectures ensured that mental exercise was not to suffer at the expense of the physical. Not even the overwhelming hospitality of Cape Town succeeded in undermining the will to fitness, a will which resulted in friendly rivalry between the Battalion and the Dorsets being carried to almost exaggerated measures of competition, the Dorsets going to the length of publishing an order that "sea sickness *will* cease" ! The third unit of the Brigade, the Camerons, were in another ship.

On 2nd June the great convoy arrived at Bombay, and by 5th June the Brigade were up at Kirkee. Thus there opened a chapter of Battalion history which could be summed up as one uninterrupted process of tuning-up for the exactions of the Burma jungles and mountains. Very soon after disembarking on 16th July at Secunderabad, the routine at sea was to be tested out in a march in which fifty miles were covered in twenty-four hours !

Not all completed the twenty-five miles out along the Ahmednagar road and the return journey. Nevertheless it was an achievement of endurance by any standard. **1942**

The Battalion spent the Christmas of 1942 at Borsad, near Ahmedabad, with a rear party at Ahmednagar, and on 18th January it was back again at Bombay. Juhu Beach in better times is as attractive a stretch of sand for a bathing holiday as can be found in the world. But on this occasion 2 Division had little time for such relaxation, all units being busy with training for combined operations. A "tropical assault" Division was the title it assumed, and the rumour was that the Andaman Islands were to be the first objective. On 20th April the Battalion put out to sea for an exercise to test out the whole machinery of getting ashore in face of opposition. It then seemed certain that they were for an adventure off distant coasts. But it was not to be, and on 3rd May they were up at Mahableshwar Khud, climbing and patrolling through the thick jungle, which was in effect a very useful imitation of the kind of country which was later negotiated in Burma. **1943**

In the latter months of 1943 there were constant moves, and at least two camps, Nira and Gulunche, outside Poona, were as dismal, soul-destroying experiences as a keen unit could wish for.

Once again, in November, a sea exercise was undertaken from Bombay, this time for operation "Sword Fish," with a practice landing at Ratnagiri just south of Bombay.

There followed more jungle training at Khanapur and Benoli, and Christmas, 1943, was spent in camp on the maidan at Belgaum.

As the year 1944 progressed it became clear that a long period of intensive training, with constant moves and an uncertain future, was beginning to tell on the efficiency of 2 Division (which was in fact in danger of becoming stale), so much so that the A.D.M.S. advised that the brake be applied. The result was a decision to scatter the three Brigades, and while two trained, the third was to rest and enjoy some leave from Ahmednagar. 4 and 6 Brigades were thus to continue training, while 5 Brigade settled down at Ahmednagar for a little relaxation. It had **1944**

1944   however, only enjoyed five days' rest when orders to move
were received ; and this time at last the move was of
deeper significance than those months of rumours which
had dogged the Division for the past year and a half.

It was in high spirits that on 6th March the Battalion
entrained across India, leaving its transport to find its
own way by map and rejoin in Burma. The Japanese
were to make their last bid for Indian soil, and among
others the 2nd Division was ready to meet the challenge.

CHAPTER TEN

THE SEVENTH BATTALION, 1944-1950

Ahmednagar, Dimapur, Kohima, the Irrawaddy,
Ava Bridge, Mount Popa, Secunderabad, Muzaffarpur,
Calcutta, Worcester

EARLY in 1944 the situation in Burma was critical. The 1944
Japanese intention was nothing less than a full-scale
invasion of India with a subsidiary objective to gain
possession of the all-weather Manipur road and threaten
our air bases in the Brahmaputra valley, upon the continued existence of which our air supply to China over
"the hump" depended. Three Japanese Infantry Divisions and two brigades of the Indian National Army
composed the army of invasion; and the speed and
assurance with which they set about their task betokened
a fanatical zeal which could only spring from a totalitarian
system, unscrupulous in its propaganda and incautious
in its underestimation of likely opposition.

In the first week of April troops of the Japanese 31st
Division had cut the Manipur road between Kohima and
Dimapur, while farther south they were again across the
road a few miles north of Imphal. As a result of the
enemy's astonishing advance the 4th Corps were therefore
completely isolated in Imphal, and it was to move to their
assistance and open the Manipur road that the 33rd Corps
under General Stopford was hurried into Assam. Speed
was essential and 2 Division were rushed up by rail, road,
and air. Inevitably there was a certain amount of administrative confusion with brigades and units arriving the
other end spasmodically, and a lot of improvisation and
guess work enforced on harassed Unit Commanders and
their staffs.

On 1st April the 7th Battalion crossed the Brahmaputra river at Gauhati and entered the operational area
of Assam, being the first troops of the Division on this

1944 occasion to taste the conditions of the Burma war, though
previously 6 Brigade had fought a campaign in the
Arakan. Almost immediately they moved on to railhead
at Dimapur. On 2nd April a perimeter was formed to
cover the approaches to Dimapur from the north. The
site was a typical wet patch of jungle with teak trees and
their dripping creepers as an effective introduction to
tropical warfare.

From 5th April onwards the Battalion was busy patrolling the Kohima road, working in with the armoured
cars. But it could hardly have been expected that the
road would remain open much longer. On 10th April
"A" and "D" Companies moved up to milestone 32 with
the object of reinforcing two companies of the Assam
Regiment who were astride the road. In happier circumstances it would have been pleasant to have taken stock
of the magnificent scenery, the road winding and climbing
its way up the west slopes of the dense green hillside.
The village of Zubza was reached by "D" Company in
M.T. Thence progress was on foot, the immediate
objective being a blown bridge, the main responsibility
falling to "D" Company. In the darkness they failed to
make their objective by dawn and were caught in an
ambush, whereupon they concentrated at Zubza and were
joined by the rest of the Battalion.

The 12th April found the Battalion with Brigade H.Q.
and two companies of the Dorsets within the perimeter
at Zubza. Thereafter the Zubza box was to remain the
Brigade base and administrative centre for the subsequent
Kohima battle. So far as the Battalion was concerned,
Zubza will be remembered for a successful beat through
the thick undergrowth after some Japs who had worked
round to the rear. The mortars finally took their toll and
no "partridge drive" could have been more skilfully
managed.

Some fifteen miles to the south-east lay Kohima, out
of which ran a track due north to Bokajan. The Japanese
used the track for supply to the north, and it was now
decided to cut across east on to the track to a feature,
Merema, some 4,900 feet high. Thus it was hoped to
dominate the Kohima position. In the meanwhile 4 and

6 Brigades were to move down the main road, 5 Brigade 1944
delivering its left hook to the main movement and thereby
assuming by far the most difficult task in the general plan.

The move from Zubza on 22nd April involved covering
only some three miles, but the route led up and down a
formidable hillside through thick jungle. There was no
track so that mules could not be taken and the Brigade
moved on a man-pack basis, with no blankets, cookers or
creature comforts in any form. The method of advance,
which was to deploy the whole Brigade in single file,
would not have won approval at a Staff College exercise.
But, in fact, it was unorthodox enough to be highly
successful and Merema was taken without opposition on
24th April. It was clear from the manner in which
Japanese supply columns continued to dribble innocently
up and down the Bokajan track that they had been taken
completely by surprise.

A tribute is here due to the Naga stretcher-bearers.
Throughout the campaign the evacuation of the wounded
up and down the thickly jungle-clad hills presented
superhuman difficulties. But in all weather the Naga
hillmen rose to the occasion.

On 27th April the Brigade at Merema were ready for
the next phase in the advance to Kohima, four miles to
the south, and the method adopted was to leap-frog
battalions forward through each other. In Kohima itself
a small garrison was fighting a gallant battle of resistance.
The 1st Assam Regiment were protecting some hospital
units and the 161st Indian Infantry Brigade had already
been flown in to their assistance from the Arakan. But
only the 4th Royal West Kents had succeeded in fighting
through to Kohima, and the rest of the Brigade had been
withdrawn to a few miles from Dimapur. This small
force had gallantly withstood a siege against overwhelming
numbers of savage, fanatical Japanese.

The advance from Merema once again involved movement in as hazardous circumstances as could be conceived.
Certain track junctions had first to be secured and the
Battalion was given this arduous responsibility. Three
pickets, each of one company, were furnished. They
moved by night and successfully established the screen

through which the rest of the Brigade could advance. Secrecy and surprise were essential and, in order to assist movement and make less noise, gym shoes were requested. Accordingly 3,000 pairs of shoes were dropped for the Brigade from the air. Slowly by the light of a moon which appeared spasmodically through the drifting clouds, the companies secured their objectives. The difficulties will be appreciated in noting that the farthest company took four and a half hours to cover a mile and a half.

The objective was now a high feature, Point 5120, which constituted the main Kohima position. A Brigade attack went in, and the Camerons at first succeeded in gaining the main position. But they were subsequently forced to abandon it. The Brigade now found itself in a situation which seemed fantastic. About a mile to the north of Kohima lay Naga village on top of a small hill some 200 feet higher than the surrounding Kohima ridge. Round this village the whole Brigade formed a perimeter, while only 200 yards away the Japanese were firmly dug-in on a feature known as Church Knoll. There was little cover and the Battalion had to go to ground like rabbits. Strong bunkers, each for three or four men, were constructed. All maintenance for some days previously had been by air. Some of the drops fell outside the perimeter and it was then a case of either collecting in the mist, or at night, or shooting at supplies on the ground to render them unserviceable.

Preparations to capture Church Knoll went ahead and on 16th May a track was made with bulldozers and later tanks were winched up for close support purposes in the coming attack. On 18th May a concentrated air strike by the Hurribombers thoroughly frightened our men round Naga village since with the target only 200 yards away it seemed as if bombs would surely occasionally drop short ! At 0830 hours on 19th May the artillery fire plan opened up on Church Knoll and "A" and "D" Companies moved forward to the attack. Intense as had been the preparation, it proved insufficient to carry the day. The Japanese, making skilful use of the five-foot terraces, were able to site their bunkers so that as each terrace was scaled the attack came under withering fire from bunkers in the

next terrace, while bunkers were able to afford each other 1944
close mutual support. Thus forty lives were lost in a
gallant but fruitless battle, among them Lieutenant Wood-
ward, who was killed in the act of storming a bunker
from which he had driven the Japs with a flamethrower.
Another bunker from behind fired on him and he fell at
its edge while making straight for it with a grenade.

On 23rd May the Brigade was relieved and moved
back three miles for a short rest, the subsequent invest-
ment of Kohima being left to the other two brigades of
the Division. At this time the Battalion were sorry to
lose their Commanding Officer, Lieut.-Colonel Stocker,[1]
who was moved on to command the 1st Royal Welch
Fusiliers, the Second-in-Command, Major Brierley,[2]
taking over from him.

The Glorious First of June was not forgotten and the
evening meal was supplemented with extra rations. But
the enemy showed scant appreciation for regimental
tradition and "A" and "B" Companies had to break off
and were hurried away to come under the command of
6 Brigade, where they were put on to escorting mule
columns for an attack on a prominent feature, Aradura
spur, which continued down from Mount Pulebadze
(7,522 ft.) and sprawled across the main road some three
miles south of Kohima. On 2nd June "C" and "D"
Companies moved up to join the remainder on the spur,
a movement which was hampered by hurricane rain-
storms. The monsoon had now set in and superhuman
efforts had to be exerted to keep forward companies
supplied. Mules in places would sink up to their bellies
in mud and many were lost over the steep hillside.
Indeed, no small measure of success had been won due
to the fact that the Japanese had undoubtedly appreciated
that we could not conduct a monsoon campaign.

On 3rd June the Battalion were not sorry to revert to
5 Brigade, now on a feature, Jail Hill, which after Aradura
seemed comparatively free of waterlogged trenches,
jungle creepers and rain drip.

It was no surprise to realize that Aradura Spur was

---

[1] Lieut.-Colonel J. Stocker, D.S.O. (South Wales Borderers).
[2] Major J. B. Brierley, M.C.

N

1944 proving too exacting a proposition and that further
advance was to be attempted through the less formidable
country east of the main road. Accordingly on 7th June
the Battalion joined the Dorsets in the village, Pfuchama,
some two miles east of the road. The familiar night
advance was involved with the usual opposition of nature
to offset the lack of opposition from the enemy. Movement was particularly hampered across the terraced fields
since the terraces were just too high to take in the normal
stride.

From Pfuchama the course was set back on to the main
road, which was struck at milestone 53 with little opposition, and on 9th June a day of rest was taken at Kigwema,
just short of milestone 60 in a hospital building. It was a
welcome sight to see the cooks coming along the road
with a hot breakfast. A beer ration was issued and with
indications that the Japs were on the run there was a new
confidence abroad. On 10th June for two days the
Battalion formed a perimeter at milestone 59 for the
protection of Brigade H.Q. But on 13th June they were
again on the move, and the subsequent episode at Viswema certainly deserves record as a small action of high
merit, particularly in its successful co-operation as between
the infantry and its artillery support.

The attack on Viswema was carried out at first light on
15th June and was a complete success. Previously the
5.5 Medium Artillery had put down a twenty-minute
concentration, to be followed up by a similar softening
up by the Divisional Artillery, during which "A" and
"B" Companies moved up as near to the objective as
possible. Leading positions were indicated by 77 smoke
grenades every fifty yards. This enabled the Bofors Light
A/A guns which lay out at right-angles to the attack to
fire just in front of the leading companies. It was a
technique which was to be repeated later with frequent
success. As a result of the attack, Viswema itself was
burnt out, but much material and some useful documents
were captured, and on 16th June the Battalion took a
well-earned rest.

If, however, the enemy were to be hustled out of Imphal
it was essential that he should receive no respite. No

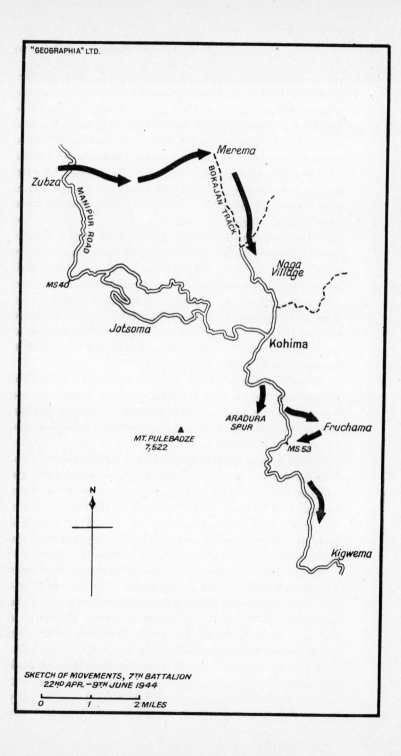

"GEOGRAPHIA" LTD.

Zubza

MANIPUR ROAD

Merema

BOKAJAN TRACK

Naga Village

MS 40

Jotsoma

Kohima

ARADURA SPUR

MT. PULEBADZE
7,522

Fruchama

MS 53

N

Kigwema

SKETCH OF MOVEMENTS, 7TH BATTALION
22ND APR. – 9TH JUNE 1944

0   1   2 MILES

1944　sooner was Viswema captured than, on 17th June, orders
were received for an attack on Mao Song Sang, the
highest point (6,500 ft.) on the Manipur road. The
Battalion moved by M.T. to Khuzama, about two miles
short of the objective, and thence across wet paddy fields,
through jungle to the edge of the ridge on which the
village was situated. At night patrols pushed forward
through the jungle and failed to reach the village, since,
in the words of one who was present, "You could not see
your hands in front of your face." On the morning of
18th June, after a silent night approach, an attack was put
in which went home with clockwork precision, and by
0800 hours the Battalion was back again on the road,
ready for a hot breakfast. Having embussed and moved
forward to milestone 71, the Battalion took over the lead
from the Dorsets and advanced on foot. A blown bridge
proved the only immediate obstacle, and it was cleared
on the night 18th/19th June in a neat minor operation in
conjunction with the Sappers.

At the same time a night patrol discovered that Maram
village was held. A high ridge with the village on the
left running up to a feature known as Telegraph Spur on
the right constituted a formidable position. A block across
the road itself proved to be covered by an enemy 75 mm.
gun, but it was quickly dealt with by the 25-pounders.
The subsequent attack on Telegraph Spur was a complete
success, enabling the Commanding Officer to throw in his
reserve, "A" Company, in an attack on the village. Thus
yet another quick success was the reward of a tireless
pursuit, the captured documents indicating that the Japs
had had orders to hold Maram for at least ten days !

There followed three days' welcome rest. The Corps
Commander visited the Battalion to offer his congratulations on the series of achievements, and meanwhile the
remainder of the Division passed through. By the time
the next move forward was made to milestone 107 on
22nd June, Imphal had been relieved.

After the relief of Imphal the Battalion moved back
six miles, where for nearly a week a perimeter was formed
astride the road to protect Brigade H.Q. from many
parties of Japanese who, cut off from their units, were

roaming the countryside. It fell to Lieutenant Spalding 1944
with two platoons to be lucky enough to round up and
account for seventeen Japs, including three officers, without loss to his own detachment. Even the cooks with "B"
Echelon accounted for a prisoner, much to the quartermaster's surprise. On 29th June Lieut.-Colonel C. A.
Street took over command and the Battalion moved into
Imphal, the occasion being marked by an open-air film
show the same evening. Three weeks passed in Imphal
with refitting and training and with visits from the
Commander-in-Chief, S.E.A.C., and the Army and Corps
Commanders.[3] But on 20th July once again the Battalion
were on the move, and finally Moreh, just above Tama on
the Burma side of the frontier, was reached on 3rd August.
During this fortnight, though there had been little enemy
opposition, weather conditions hampered movement
almost as effectively as enemy action. The role of the
Brigade had been to support 23rd Indian Division in
clearing the Imphal–Palel road. This Division had so
effectively dealt with the enemy at Palel that it now only
remained for the Brigade to follow up as quickly as
possible. Very heavy rain had brought on landslides, and
in the result troops had to march the forty-odd miles
from Palel to Tama, the Battalion being the first troops
to cross the Burma border since the Japanese invasion.
Tama presented a scene of horror. Typhus, cholera, and
malaria had taken their toll of the Japanese and their
dead bodies lay around in heaps, the Buddhist temple
sheltering many of their skeletons. Eventually bulldozers
were used to bury the bodies and the village was burnt.
Not the least of the captures of importance was a complete
nominal roll of the Gandhi Brigade of the Indian
National Army.

For the next three months the Battalion was to retrace
its steps, and a move out of the Kabaw valley of disease
was made back to Maram on the familiar ground of the
battle in June, half-way between Kohima and Imphal.
There, at last, was opportunity for relaxation. Training

---

[3] Admiral Lord Louis Mountbatten, K.G., P.C., G.C.S.I., G.C.I.E.,
G.C.V.O., K.C.B., D.S.O.; General Sir William Slim, G.B.E., K.C.B.,
D.S.O., M.C., Fourteenth Army; Lieut.-General M. G. N. Stopford,
C.B., M.C., D.S.O., 33rd Corps Commander.

1944 and refitting continued, and the new drafts in particular needed to be brought up to the high standard the older hands had achieved. Nevertheless there was time over for "housey-housey" in the evenings, and the Divisional Concert Party and an occasional E.N.S.A. show were much appreciated under the shelter of the fine Divisional theatre which the Sappers had put up from Bailey bridging covered with tarpaulins.

There was time, too, to remember comrades who had fallen in the fighting, and today the traveller down the Imphal road will perhaps be not unmindful of those to whom he owes his security when he notes the Memorial Tablet to the men of the 7th Battalion The Worcestershire Regiment in the Maram Rest House.[4]

When on 1st December a move forward was again made, this time travel was in comparative comfort, and in three easy stages in M.T. the Battalion reached the Divisional concentration area at Yazagyo down in the Kabaw valley. Twenty miles farther down the road the 18th (East African) Division were fighting to establish a bridgehead at Kalewa where the road met the Chindwin river. When it was realized that the Battalion might well be in action on Christmas Day, arrangements were made to celebrate on 18th December. With extra beer and rations it was not difficult to assimilate a festive spirit, though the neighbouring jungle seemed a somewhat different world to that of holly and mistletoe.

On Christmas Eve the Battalion left Yazagyo, and by 0630 hours it was over the Chindwin river, crossing by the longest Bailey bridge in the world, and had arrived at Chaungzon in the bridgehead area. All around lay the derelict tanks of our Army in retreat in 1942 which had been unable to make the river crossing. But there was little time for reflections on the play of fate, for ahead 6 Brigade were making rapid progress, and after four days of moves by M.T. the Battalion were on the outskirts of Ye-u in the heart of Burma. Opposition now

---

[4] This tablet was dedicated by 3rd Brigade Padres and unveiled by the G.O.C., 2nd Division, Major-General C. C. G. Nicholson, C.B., C.B.E., D.S.O., M.C. It is a fine work carved from native teak by the Pioneer Platoon.

stiffened, but 5 Brigade only encountered the enemy in **1944**
force when the Shwebo plain was entered. At Ye-u the
Dorsets bore the brunt of the fighting, capturing the
village after a bitter fight. The Battalion then pushed
through and continued on down the Shwebo canal,
encountering only minor opposition.

On 6th January a halt was made at Myothit, the reason **1945**
being that the Division was outrunning its supply, while
maintenance entirely from the air was proving extremely
difficult. But on 7th January the advance continued and
was only disturbed by an intense but surprisingly ineffective enemy air attack which drove all ranks into a hurried
dispersion in the paddy fields, but which, apart from
puncturing some vehicles, wounded only one man and
killed a mule.

On 8th January Myingatha, to the east on the Mandalay–Myitkyina railway, was captured when a link-up with
36 Division, which had come down the railway corridor
from the north, was effected. Turning south only patrols
and stragglers were encountered on the move down to
Shwebo and the Battalion had the satisfaction of leading
the advance, with the help of the tanks, and entering the
town in the face of ineffective opposition. Afterwards it
became apparent that in the easy capture of Shwebo, luck
had been with our men. The only way into the town lay
across a single causeway over a moat and through a hole
in the wall. The leading platoon took a bold chance,
rushed the bridge and were through the wall before the
astonished Jap on guard had time to operate the charge
which should have blown the causeway. The first troops
of tanks were also lucky in that their tracks were wide
enough to go either side of the charge. The entry into
Shwebo was at first regarded as something of an event,
for here at last was a real town with parks laid out and
tarmac roads. But second impressions were disappointing.
The local population were scared and depressed and much
of the town was burnt out. Later, however, when a moral
revival had set in they graciously presented the Battalion
with a hand-painted bowl as a token of gratitude on their
release.

5 Brigade were now concentrated for a short rest while

1945 4 Brigade took up the chase.   For the Battalion this meant
a stay of a few days in Moksogyon, a small village on the
Mandalay–Myitkyina railway, which was reached on
12th January.   On the way there was a brief but memorable break of a couple of hours when the 2nd Battalion,
from 19 Division, was encountered and a hurried reunion
was celebrated on the banks of the Moksogyon canal.
They had just completed 300 miles on their feet and there
were many experiences exchanged between old friends.
All too soon the time to go their respective ways arrived
and the Battalion was "on the road to Mandalay."

Once again progress was ahead of maintenance so that
two weeks were put in at Kadaw, some eleven miles down
the road from Shwebo, while supplies were concentrated
for the coming big push over the Irrawaddy.   There was
time for some light relaxation.   Toc H organized gramo-
phone concerts, and an E.N.S.A. party, the first token in
Burma of Mr. Basil Dean's endeavours, not only amused
personnel of the Brigade but also thoroughly startled the
local inhabitants !

On 27th January the Battalion left Kadaw and marched
twenty miles through the night to Sadaung, repeating the
process the following night to Kinwya.   "D" Company
actually pushed out patrols to Maungdaung, which lay
some 5,000 yards to the north of the great Irrawaddy
river.   Such resistance as was being encountered came
over from the east, where 4 Brigade were heavily involved.   Thus for a day or so the Dorsets had gone over
to their assistance, but they returned to Maungdaung on
4th February, by which time 5 Brigade were deployed
along the river on a front of about 8,000 yards.   The
Battalion had in the meanwhile moved down the east
bank of the Mu river to its junction with the Irrawaddy
and was thus on the right of the Brigade deployment.

At this stage some assessment of the general situation
will help to an appreciation of the great task which lay
ahead ; that of crossing the Irrawaddy river in face of an
enemy for whom the fate of the river line was obviously
a turning-point in his fortunes.   If the Japs could stem
our advance along a river front of 120 miles from about
Thabeikkyin, due east of Shwebo, round to the Mu river

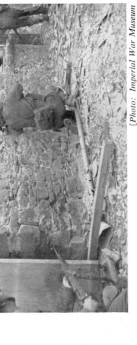

From Cameron Ridge: Pinnacle, Pimple and the Keren road

[Photo: *Imperial War Museum*]

Benneville, Normandy: 1st Battalion searching for snipers

[Photo: *Imperial War Museum*]

A Regimental Signpost between Imphal and Kohima, Burma

[Photo: *Imperial War Museum*]

Men of the 7th Battalion in Burma listening to "the other war," April, 1945

junction he might conceivably take hope in holding Cen- **1945**
tral Burma and staging a counter-offensive. Yet to hold
our thrust the Jap could apparently deploy only four
divisions, totalling 10,000 men.

The Shwebo plain, which was now 30 Corps theatre of
operations, is a stretch of flat, heavily cultivated country
intersected with water-courses, bounded on the east and
south by the Irrawaddy as it turns sharply to the west a
few miles south of Mandalay. On the west the Mu river
marks the edge of the plain. Only in the south-east
corner of the plain, where a line of hills runs twenty miles
north from Sagaing on the west bank of the river, was
there a position which the defence could exploit. For the
rest, 30 Corps, with its greater mobility, rejoiced in the
open spaces after the frustrations of the jungle.

The plan evolved for turning the enemy off the river
needed a high degree of deception. While 19 Indian
Division were to effect a crossing in the north-east of the
Corps area near Thabeikkyin, on the west 20 Indian
Division were to operate about the confluence of the Mu
and Irrawaddy river, with a view subsequently of iso-
lating Mandalay from the south and west.

Within 2 Division area it was hoped to deceive the
enemy into a belief that the thrust would come in the
south-east corner of the river through the Sagaing hills.
5 Brigade, deployed eastward from the Mu river, had
therefore to appear to be very thin on the ground, even
to the point of disguising sentries as natives pounding
maize !

By the beginning of February the Battalion had felt its
way forward to the line of the river, "B" Company being
on the banks in two hamlets, Tadaing and Dawete, "D"
Company half a mile to the north-west at Shwele, and
Battalion H.Q. in a pleasant grove of trees among some
pagodas a few hundred yards back from " B" Company.
On the right 20 Indian Division were just across the Mu
river. It almost seemed that enemy opposition north of
the Irrawaddy had melted away. But such hopes, if they
existed, were to be rudely dispelled when on the night
7/8 February the two platoons of "B" Company in
Dawete were heavily attacked. The telephone line to

1945 Battalion H.Q. had been cut, and it was with difficulty that the Commanding Officer with "A" and "C" Companies could move to their assistance. With first light an attack was put in on Dawete, "A" Company taking up a position west of the village and "C" Company moving round the east flank, hoping to pinch the enemy out. The latter ran into heavy machine-gun fire so that "A" Company took the initiative and attempted to rush in, firing their weapons on the move. By 1120 hours "A" Company, after two attacks, were held, and had suffered heavy casualties : not only that, but the Commanding Officer and three other officers had lost their lives. Late in the morning the village was set on fire by the Japs. Accordingly "B" and "A" Companies withdrew to a position between Dawete and Tadaing, which covered the approaches to the river from the north. Lieut.-Colonel T. Irvine of the Cameronians arrived to assume command, and the Battalion was relieved by the Dorsets and withdrew to an area north of Legyi.

For the next fortnight the Battalion was busy reorganizing and preparing to take its place again in the first flight in the crossing of the Irrawaddy. The 1st Royal Welch Fusiliers had come over from 6 Brigade to augment the strength, and the Brigadier had decided to cross with three Battalions up, 7th Worcestershire being on the right. Accordingly, after practising the plan intensively, on 24th February once more a march was made back to Dawete, and at 2030 hours the first flight, "A" and "B" Companies, carried their craft forward through the heavy sand. But their luck was out. Any hopes that the crossing would be accomplished without detection were to be disappointed. After paddling for a few minutes silently in the moonlight, a sudden burst of machine-gun fire from the opposite bank splashed around the leading boats. It had been previously decided in the event of opposition to lash boats together in groups of three, the middle boat which had a motor then taking on the motive power for the other two. But when the order was given only one motor sprang to life. Boats became waterlogged and began to sink ; and swimming in the Irrawaddy in full equipment in the night proved unpleasantly cold and

confusing. There was nothing for it but to call off the   **1945**
crossing and return to Tadaing.

These are but the bones of a crowded hour in which
the tragedy of those in despair struggling in the swift
torrents of the Irrawaddy weighed under by their equipment, the confusion of orders and counter-orders shouted
across the moonlit water, and the dashed hopes of men
eager only to close with the enemy contributed to a scene
of dramatic intensity and grief. The colourful account of
the *Daily Herald's* War Correspondent who set out with
the first flight is far more appropriate to the occasion.
But, as always, when the fictional and factual aspects of
military operations compete in historical record, the
dramatist yields to the historian.

On the left the Camerons had been luckier and a move
was accordingly made on 26th February across the
Cameron beach, some 2,000 yards up-stream from
Dawete. Both the Camerons and the Dorsets were across
the river and had established a bridgehead at a point
about two miles down-stream from the important town
of Ngazun, which lay almost due south from Cameron
beach and was the largest town on the southern bank and
an important road centre. It was to share with the
Dorsets in the capture of Ngazun that the Battalion
crossed the river, this time in comparative comfort, and
took the position on the right of the Dorsets, facing east,
preparatory to a two-battalion attack staged in unre-
hearsed but surprisingly auspicious circumstances. To
the north of Ngazun spreading across the main stream
was a marshy island. There Brigade Tactical Headquarters, with a company of the 2nd Manchesters, was
admirably placed to control the artillery support by the
Divisional Artillery still on the north bank and at right-
angles to the infantry advance. In addition, the Brigadier
promised an air strike "bigger and better" than any air
support yet offered. It is a tribute to the standard of
Brigade co-operation attained that details were elaborated
by the Brigadier with his two battalions on the radio with
1/25,000 maps and from an air photograph.

The approach lay across flat, open cultivation interspersed with a few trees and the essence of its success lay

1945 in the ability of the infantry attack to get right up to Ngazun under cover of the air strike and the guns. An Aldershot demonstration could hardly have been executed with greater precision in artillery and air co-operation. From 1300 hours to 1350 hours the enemy received such a pasting as must have shattered all will to organized resistance. Even so a suicidal Japanese party in position in a pagoda at the south of the village met the leading companies with machine-gun fire, and the mortars and some machine guns with "D" Company were dropped to deal with the opposition. The final assault went in with bayonets fixed, and was covered by the close support of the 75's from a troop of tanks and the Manchester medium machine guns from the left flank. The whole operation had been a triumph of co-ordination for the Brigadier and the two Battalion commanders, who had mutually worked out their objectives and the details of the infantry plan. Some credit, too, is due to a local native of Ngazun, who, having mastered the correct way up to hold an air photograph, gave valuable confirmation of enemy positions to the east of the town.

The 28th February was spent in mopping-up at the south end of the town, and a period of so-called "rest" followed while supplies were being built up and the bridgehead enlarged. 6 Brigade then passed through and took the lead, but by 4th March 2 Division was well set for an advance due east along the river for Ava and Mandalay on a two-brigade front, with 6 Brigade on the right and 5 Brigade on the left.

At the beginning of March the enemy must have realized that his hopes of holding Upper Burma were shattered. 4 Corps under their indefatigable leader, General Messervy, had suddenly reappeared and were lapping round the left rear of the Japanese with infantry and armour and making for Meiktila. On the right of 2 Division, 20 Division were across the river west of Myinma and were enlarging their bridgehead. North of Mandalay the 19th (Indian) Division were making rapid progress and the race for Mandalay was on. But the Jap is a tenacious fighter when on the defensive, and there were many suicidal small packets of the enemy fighting

last-ditch battles long after their main formations had   **1945**
lost cohesion. General Stopford could, however, regard
33 Corps as over the Irrawaddy, and so far as the 5th
Brigade was concerned the advance started in earnest on
7th March with the capture of Letpantabin on the river
bank, three miles east of Ngazun, by the Camerons.
About a mile and a half to the south-east of Letpantabin
was a feature, Dirty Pagoda Ridge, which covered the
main road running parallel to the river. On 8th March
the Battalion ran into heavy opposition from this locality
and also from a secondary feature, Worcester Ridge, which
lay a few hundred yards to the west across the rear position by Pagoda Ridge. The two positions were obviously
held in strength and very effectively protected by mines.
The Camerons on the left were also held up, and eventually the first ridge was captured by midday without heavy
casualties. That night the Dorsets passed through the
Battalion and secured Pagoda Ridge in the dark, while on
10th March the Camerons again leap-frogged through
the Dorsets and on 11th March occupied Kyauktalon on
the river bank, which constituted the right flank of the
Japanese position running south along the road from
Kyauktalon to Myotha. On 12th March the Battalion
moved up to a position just behind the Camerons and
on 13th March, with a squadron of tanks in support,
occupied Letpanzai without opposition. The Kyauktalon
position had been regarded as a proposition possibly as
tough as Kohima. Yet here was the Jap being hustled
out of one position after another by bold night advances
and a refusal to recognize fatigue when in other circumstances men could have slept the clock round.

The advance now was on a narrow one-battalion front
across open country broken only by small oases of trees
sheltering the ubiquitous pagodas. The Battalion was,
therefore, moving on a widely deployed two-company
front supported by tanks. It was while nearing a group
of pagodas on 14th March that a young officer, Lieutenant
Phillips, leading a patrol on the outskirts of a village,
Letpanzin, lost his life, the enemy withholding their fire
until the patrol was on them.

On 16th March the Battalion, with "D" Company in

1945   the lead, raced on to Ava fort, which lay at the tip of the
loop in the river as it turned west some ten miles south of
Mandalay. It fell to the Camerons to capture the fort on
the afternoon of 17th March, and the Battalion, hard
behind them, passed through and were planning to cross
the next obstacle, the Myitinge river, before the startled
inhabitants had time to realize that the British Army was
really back again.

The Myitinge river half a mile south of its junction
with the Irrawaddy is 300 yards wide. First an officer,
Lieutenant Plumley, and his batman crossed in a small
native boat which was the only craft available and which
took two men. They landed without opposition, and wisely
the Brigadier decided to send the whole Battalion across
and push on to the east end of Ava bridge on the Irrawaddy. "A" Company reached and secured the bridge
before last light with only a skirmish with an enemy
pillbox to hinder them.

On 18th March the advance continued along the main
road towards Mandalay, the first metalled road seen for
many days. On reaching the suburbs of Mandalay the
Battalion halted, and on 19th March the Dorsets passed
through. Operations had assumed the aspect of a race for
Mandalay between 5 Brigade and 19 Division from the
north. The latter were now fighting for Fort Dufferin in
the middle of the city. Our supply line across the Myitinge was once again being strained and stretched to
capacity, and it was as well to apply the brake gently.
Amid the flush of a stimulating advance it was good to
note the spontaneous delight of the inhabitants at their
delivery. At Bono, a large village on the outskirts of the
city, Burmese, Anglo-Burmese, Anglo-Indians, and
Indians turned out to welcome our men, and fruit, eggs,
vegetables and even watches were gladly offered as
presents.

At 1000 hours on 19th March the Battalion was on the
move again, the Brigadier having decided to switch the
Worcestershire round to the south of the old ruined
Hmandan Fort. By now the Japanese forces in Mandalay
were in real distress. For them it became a matter of
urgency to bolt for the south before they were wiped out.

On the left the Dorsets held the north-east corner of the
fort, while to the south the Battalion had put down a
road-block across the main Rangoon road. Thus when
a Japanese convoy attempted to run the gauntlet on the
morning of 20th March, after the Dorsets had left their
mark on it, it came in for a hot reception from the anti-
tank guns and small-arms fire of "B" and "D" Companies. The mortars put down a smoke-screen to slow up
the convoy, and when the dust had cleared twelve enemy
vehicles were out of action.

. In Mandalay itself on 20th March they were cele-
brating the entry of 19th Division with a ceremonial
parade and the raising of the Union Flag by the Army
Commander on the site of Government House, but the
Dorsets alone were able to represent 5 Division. But
Mandalay after months of Japanese occupation was a
shadow of its former greatness and nothing was really
missed by the Battalion, which now awaited the next
phase from the village of Tadundaing on the outskirts of
the city.

The word went round that more than ever was it
necessary to push on so as to make Rangoon before the
monsoon broke. Already 4 Corps were on the outskirts
of Meiktila, sixty miles to the south, so that it looked as
if the next lap would be an unopposed scramble for the
maintenance services to keep pace with the advance, and
meanwhile the remnants of three Japanese armies were
sandwiched in between 33 Corps in the north and 4
Corps in the south. Some re-sorting of Divisions was
necessary, in which the 2nd Division had to find its way
from the Mandalay area to Myingyan, an important road-
and river-head on the Irrawaddy some eighty miles to the
south-west. Nevertheless for a very few days the 5th
Brigade group was able to concentrate at Ava and enjoy
a brief rest.

On 27th March the long, hot journey to Myingyan was
undertaken by M.T. The road was extremely dusty and
parties of roving Japs slowed the pace down; though
only once were they actually encountered, and even then
an Indian battalion was effectively dealing with them.
On 28th March the concentration of 5 Brigade around

1945 Myingyan was complete, and the Japs in the area looked like being caught in a pincer movement between 5 Brigade and 4 Brigade bearing down on them from the east. In effect this is what happened, and by 31st March the task of the 2nd Division so far as Myingyan was concerned was over.

Meanwhile at higher levels, something in the nature of an administration crisis had to be faced. In a few weeks the monsoon would be putting the airfields out of action, while even with Myingyan available as a river port it was not going to be possible to accumulate sufficient supplies for the Burma Army as now constituted.

In these circumstances a decision to reduce the forces in Burma had to be taken, and it was inevitable that 2 Division—an all-white formation and thus the most difficult to maintain—should be chosen for dispatch to India. The days of 7th Worcestershire in Burma were therefore numbered. Already 6 Brigade had started to fly back to Calcutta, and it was clear that 4 and 5 Brigades now faced the last lap.

The first leg was fifteen miles south to Welaung in open six-wheelers across country by tracks. At Welaung on 1st April the most comforting signs of disintegration in the forces on the other side were first noted in the surrender of small parties of the Indian National Army. For the next few days a preliminary trickle was to develop into a constant stream. They were hardly the fanatics of the early days of the campaign, and many were obviously loyal soldiers of the crown who had been pressed into service against their will.

At Welaung the Brigade were on to the Rangoon road, and the milestones now provocatively numbered out the distance from the coveted goal.

The small village Legyi, which was covered by a rocky position astride the main road, proved the next obstacle. It lay ten miles to the south of Welaung, and the Camerons, who were in the lead, had failed to dislodge the enemy though supported by both field and medium artillery. The Brigadier then decided to work the Battalion round the right flank, a movement which was

executed very successfully in co-operation with the 1945
Grants of 3rd Dragoon Guards. The Dorsets then
passed through on 4th April to complete the "right hook"
and secure the main road at milestone 414. But the
resistance in Legyi itself was stubborn, and it was not
until 9th April that the village fell after the combined
efforts of the Camerons and the Worcestershire. From
9th April to 12th April three welcome days of rest
brought the opportunity for much needed dhobying by
a small stream. But on 12th April a move forward was
made, and the following day the Battalion in the lead
made milestone 409.

The Brigade now confronted a position which appeared
as tough a proposition as any it had faced within the last
year. Four miles south of Legyi the rough sand and rocks
give way to rising ground, culminating in the great massif
of Mount Popa which rose to 5,000 feet above sea-level.
The road ran up through a gorge on to the plateau, and
the ravines and spurs afforded the enemy a magnificent
defensive position. On 13th April the Dorsets reconnoitred forward to feel the measure of the enemy's
strength, and it was quickly realized that the Jap was on
the ridge with the intention to stay there.

There followed five hectic days when the Battalion was
busy in heavy fighting on the edge of the Popa plateau.
In a staged attack on the early morning of 14th April,
"B" and "D" Companies moved forward on either side
of the road. "D" Company, in fact, successfully made
the crest after four hours of crawling and dragging themselves up on to their objective. But the effect was to
leave large parties of the enemy infiltrating forward while
their main position remained intact. It proved impossible
to supply "D" Company with ammunition, water or food,
and the Brigadier ordered their withdrawal. By 1600
hours the whole Battalion was back astride the road at
milestone 409.

Preparations now went ahead for a planned attack by
the Dorsets and Camerons on the Popa Massif on 22nd
April. But on the morning of 20th April the headman of
Popa, in his best clothes, appeared with the news that the
Japs had cleared out and our men had only to dodge the

o

1945 mines to walk up and receive a welcome. This episode
was, however, of interest mainly for the Dorsets and
Camerons, for previously on 18th April the Battalion had
moved back to Legyi[5] and it had thus seen its last encounter with the Jap in Burma.

The 5th Brigade had been the first brigade of 2 Division to arrive at Dimapur, the first to inflict a defeat on
the Japanese, and it was now the last to leave the theatre
of operations. Except for short halts never of more than
a few days' duration, the Battalion had been without
a break in the battle area fighting through the monsoon
and the heat of a Burma summer. The most assiduous
attention to hygiene and matters of health could hardly
combat such conditions with complete success ; and thus
a change of environment perhaps did not come too
soon.

On 26th April a move back to Myingyan airfield was
made and soon the whole Battalion had emplaned for
Chittagong, way back in Bengal. The 27th April found
the Battalion steaming down the Brahmaputra on a
pleasant day in a ferry steamer, having embarked at
Chandpu. Eventually Bandal, some twenty miles from
Calcutta, was reached in the pouring rain. There, for a
time, it seemed that 2 Division might be due for Rangoon
and a sea-borne operation. But Rangoon fell and May
passed in a sense of anti-climax, reinforced by the normal
reactions to the sudden available flesh-pots of Calcutta
and Darjeeling. It was almost difficult to relax ! Daily
passes and seven days' leave in the great city were
available, and it was pleasant to experience a change from
conditions in camp where the monsoon rain threatened to
flood the area. Two parades in May should be recorded :
the first, 14th May, in celebration of VE Day in Europe ;
the second, an investiture when the Commanding Officer,
Lieut.-Colonel T. A. Irvine, received his D.S.O. and six
others received decorations for gallantry. On 1st June,
the G.O.C.-in-C., Eastern Command, General O'Connor,[6] inspected the Battalion on the occasion of the
annual regimental celebration, and in a short address

---

[5] Not to be confused with Legyi, near the Irrawaddy.
[6] General Sir R. O'Connor, K.C.B., D.S.O., M.C.

reminded his audience that he owed his life to the action of a platoon of the 1st Worcestershire in Palestine. Secondly, he drew attention to the fact that the Worcestershire Regiment on a former 1st June in 1794 had set the fashion for "Combined Operations."

On 4th June the Battalion set out on one of those long rather monotonous train journeys familiar in India, and detrained four days later at Kamaredi Camp in the Deccan. The journey was uneventful. After cleaning up the camp, training cadres were started up and trainees started to train for the specialist activities, signals, mortars and pioneers. Three months were passed in camp and a move was then made to Trimulgherry, outside Hyderabad city.

In July the Battalion had to part with some good men who were due for release, and the Corps of Drums played R.S.M. Brain and a large party out of camp. In the following month it was sad to say good-bye to Lieut.-Colonel Irvine, Major F. G. Burrell, M.C., assuming command until the arrival of Lieut.-Colonel J. B. Brierley, M.C. At this stage an uneventful period of monotony set in, partly to be accounted for by a sense of anti-climax after the war years and the break-up of many friendships cemented in action. The War Diary for the time is a meagre record, "normal routine" being the most frequent entry. Cross-country runs were introduced, and in September a visit from Mr. Jack Lawson, the Secretary of State for War constituted an event of comparative stimulation. In October the Battalion moved into the Haig Lines in Secunderabad. At the same time it appeared that a decision to end their existence had been taken and some 500 men left for home. But almost immediately orders were issued to re-form. Conditions, however, were not easy. Men from Worcestershire were not available and every rank from the highest to the lowest had to be found from the young entry newly landed in India. Of 550 who arrived from reinforcement camps, 50 had to be selected as N.C.Os. in the first few days.

Meanwhile the men for home sailed from Bombay on 31st October on the *Winchester Castle* and docked at Southampton on 15th November. After some very wel-

1945   come leave they were greeted by the Mayor and Corporation and people of Kidderminster at a great reception in
the Town Hall. There were addresses from the Mayor,
Alderman A. E. Meredith, Brigadier Clarke and Colonel
Tomkinson. Fallen comrades were not forgotten as the
gathering stood for a few moments in silence, to be
followed by the "Last Post" and "Reveille." It was a
great and appropriate occasion to mark the end of two
memorable years.

While the men from Burma were being welcomed
home, the few who remained in India were for a time the
neglected and bewildered victims of administrative indeci-
sion. Thus at least it must have seemed to the handful of
officers and men who remained at Secunderabad, not
knowing exactly what status they enjoyed as a unit. The
fifty or so men who were left were those under three years'
service. In the circumstances it was hardly to be expected
that they would accept their unknown destiny with
enthusiasm. A melancholy entry in the Diary records a
football match with the remnants of 2nd Dorsets. Serious
routine training was obviously not practical. Fifteen
minutes' P.T. opened the day. There were E.N.S.A.
shows, and efforts were made to interest the men in local
affairs, successful visits to the Hyderabad tombs and the
State Mint being organized.

The exact stage at which the nucleus party realized
that the 7th Battalion was by no means extinct is difficult
to assess. Drafts started to arrive. Command of the
Battalion changed hands in rapid succession, and in
November two officers[7] held command pending the
arrival of Lieut.-Colonel S. H. C. Stotherd on 29th
November in permanent replacement of Lieut.-Colonel
Brierley. The "silly season" continued and "normal
routine" still figured in the Diary as representing an
absence of incident.

1946   Early in the new year the situation in Bengal was
unsettled. India was hardly a happy country, and its
misfortunes were reflected in increasing demands on
British troops in the role of internal security. Normally

---

[7] Major J. R. P. Montgomery, M.C., Major J. P. Stilas. Lieut.-
Colonel S. H. C. Stotherd came from the Cheshire Regiment.

regarded as unpleasant, the assumption of strenuous
police duties was to prove a blessing in disguise so far as
7th Worcestershire were concerned.

The Battalion was accordingly warned to move up to
Muzaffarpur in North Bihar, and on 15th January once
again a train journey covering four days was endured, the
Battalion detraining on 19th January and taking a camp
from 26/1 Punjab Regiment. The available strength still
only represented a skeleton unit, but in February 136
reinforcements arrived to swell the numbers, and were
duly lectured on the intricacies of "internal security" in
North Bihar by the sub-area Commander. The few
veterans from Burma might have been forgiven had they
found their new role comparatively tame after the stimulation of jungle warfare ! Yet the situation was not to be
accepted lightly, as the Bihar Police were themselves not
in a happy condition, and plans had to include the
concentration of the European population within the
camp if necessary.

The month of March passed with the departure of
Age and Service Group number 26 and the arrival of a
draft of sixty men. The Duke of Aosta's Band of Italian
prisoners of war from Eritrea visited the camp and
delighted all with a high standard of performance, while
as an antidote to light music an official from the Ministry
of Labour lectured on "Release and Resettlement."

In April "D" Company left by road for Samastipur, an
important railway centre, some thirty miles distant in
the direction of Calcutta. A Battalion Concert Party,
"Worcester Sauce," presented its first show. But they
had later to yield to an E.N.S.A. party which remained as
welcome visitors for four days. In May the Battalion
moved on to South Bihar into camp at Ratu Piska in the
Ranchi area. Apart from innumerable visits from sub-
area commanders, auditors and others, life was uneventful. Thus July came. Shillong was opened as a leave
centre and the Commander-in-Chief, Sir Claude Auchinleck, paid a visit of inspection. Although Muzaffarpur
had been only a pre-war one-company station, it represented civilization itself as compared with conditions at
Ranchi. The camp was at the twelfth milestone on the

1946 road south of Ranchi, and for accommodation, bamboo
huts of the "basha" type sufficed.

On 23rd July the Battalion moved to Kanchrapara into
camp thirty miles from Calcutta. After weeks of comparative inactivity, the trouble in Calcutta was to provide
a role and purpose which was needed for young troops
from England. On 29th July communal riots broke out
and assumed serious proportions, the centre of rioting
being the Ochterlony Monument, where a crowd of ten to
fifteen thousand refused to disperse. Reconnaissance
parties left for the city, encountering road-blocks on the
Grand Trunk Road. Companies stood by ready to move,
and on 30th and 31st July "B" and "A" Companies were
summoned in by lorry. A welcome accretion to the
strength was a platoon of young Danes who were included
in a draft at Kanchrapara. How or why they arrived is a
mystery, but in every way they proved an asset.

Throughout August and September the situation
remained unpleasant. Finally on 1st October at 1400
hours the Battalion left Kanchrapara and moved into
Calcutta,[8] arriving in their allotted area at 1630 hours.
A detachment of tanks from 25 Dragoons reported for
duty and companies quickly got down to intensive
patrolling, chiefly concerned with the enforcement of the
curfew order. With the emergence of a real job of work
the young National Service men rose to the occasion.
Responsibility proved a tonic and leadership was quickly
forthcoming where previously there had been apathy.
The post-Burma period which had represented an anti-
climax took on a fresh orientation. Towards the end
of the month the rioters became more active, and on
28th October "A" Company's bag of curfew-breakers
was twenty-eight. "D" Company, however, who were
operating from the Y.M.C.A. building in Keshab Sen
Street, came in for the greater share of hostile demonstration. The rioters had taken to throwing acid about
indiscriminately. "D" Company were able successfully
to deal with a house which harboured acid-throwers,
where they located and destroyed an effective signal

---

[8] In Calcutta the Battalion was brigaded with two Regular battalions,
2nd Green Howards and 2nd York and Lancaster Regiment.

system. November came and companies changed and **1946** extended their areas, but were unable to relax their efforts. Fortunately, liaison with the police was excellent and arrested rioters were quickly passed on.

By the middle of December the situation had improved sufficiently to allow the whole Battalion to return to Kanchrapara. The strength for the last three months had stood at about 500 all ranks, and an effort was made to mark the recent events by staging an inspection by Sir Frederick Burrows, the Governor of Bengal, who was himself a West Countryman from Herefordshire. But sickness prevented him from coming and the District Commander deputized.

About the middle of February a warning order arrived **1947** for suspended animation to be completed by 12th March, leaving just under a month to dispose of the Battalion. Many men who were not eligible for repatriation were accordingly posted to other battalions in India ; while the small nucleus of about two dozen Regulars found their way to the 2nd Battalion in Burma after they had first been attached to 179th Field Regiment, R.A., in Kanchrapara.

In the meanwhile the decision had been taken that 7th Battalion would be the regimental representation in the Territorial Army, and on 1st March the Battalion at home officially rose from the ashes from a suspended status which had never really been assumed. It was in these circumstances that a meticulous Indian auditor attempted to insist on the return of Battalion funds from England in the belief that the Battalion no longer existed. The Commanding Officer[9] had, however, seen to it that the cheque was beyond the grasp of the Indian finance authorities, and about £1,000 of funds were duly lodged with the Depot at home.

Thus once again 7th Worcestershire had experienced the curious uncertainties of defence policy, the new Battalion with its home at Worcester being formed from entirely fresh material. After Burma few Worcestershire officers were available to maintain old associations. A

---

[9] Lieut.-Colonel T. A. W. Bolland from the Royal Irish Fusiliers succeeded Lieut.-Colonel Stotherd after Christmas, 1946.

1947 Canadian officer, Captain J. E. O. Davies, who had served with the 1st Battalion in Europe was a welcome arrival in February, 1946, and one officer, Captain J. F. Styles, served through from early days until March, 1946. With the exception of a few romantic liaisons of a local nature in India, only two wives braved the primitive conditions of the last few months, and in general the Battalion was deprived of knowing the India which the Regular battalions had experienced in the spacious days of pre-war routine.

Since only one Territorial battalion has been raised, the 8th Battalion bides its time until the next emergency !

In the meanwhile the new 7th Battalion occupy the offices in 16 Silver Street. Lieut.-Colonel H. J. C. Lattey, T.D., commands. Recruiting started on 1st April and by October eighty recruits had joined, which included men who had served in the Royal Navy, the Royal Marines, the Royal Air Force and the Home Guard.

1948 Throughout 1948 and 1949 the strength of the Battalion continued to increase, but hardly in a manner commensurate with the amount of work and publicity which was being put in by all concerned. It was to draw attention to the Territorial Army and its vital role in the defence of the Commonwealth that His Majesty the King held a public Review in Hyde Park on 31st October, 1948. One hundred per cent. of the Battalion volunteered for the great occasion, and eventually a ballot was held to decide the lucky party of fourteen which assembled for the occasion. The party was led by Major E. R. W. Tooby, M.C., and experienced a strenuous but memorable parade, the element of a ridiculous after the sublime being furnished by the train arrangements for the return journey. It was apparently thought that Birmingham in the small hours of a Sunday morning was an alternative way back to Worcester.

1949 By 1949 the familiar cycle of week-end camps and annual training had been fully re-established. Drill halls and clubs were active again and in good order. True to tradition, the Battalion was highly successful at the County Rifle Association meetings held in 1948 and 1949. In 1949, entering for the Western Command Rifle

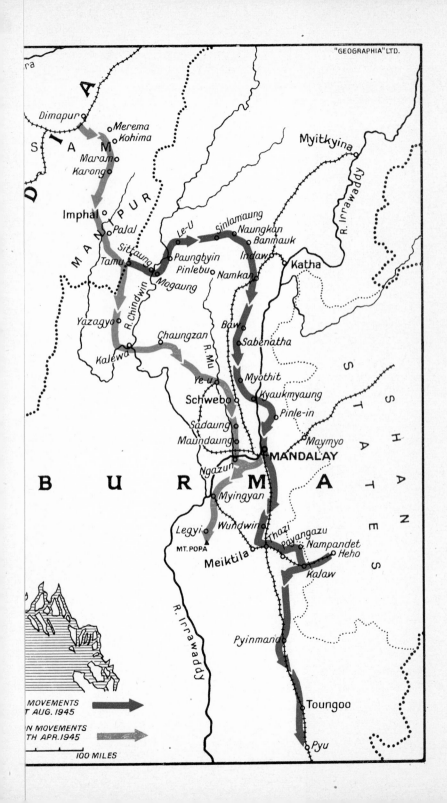

"GEOGRAPHIA" LTD.

Dimapur
Merema
Kohima
Maram
Karong
Imphal
Palal
Sittaung
Tamu
Le-U
Sinlamaung
Naungkan
Banmauk
Paungbyin
Indaw
Pinlebu
Namkan
Katha
Mogaung
Myitkyina
R. Irrawaddy
Yazagyo
R. Chindwin
Chaungzan
Baw
Sabenatha
Kalewa
Ye-u
Myothit
Schwebo
Kyaukmyaung
R. Mu
Sadaung
Pinle-in
Maundaung
Maymyo
Ngazun
MANDALAY
B U R M A
Myingyan
Legyi
Wundwin
Thazi
Payangazu
Nampandet
MT. POPA
Heho
Meiktila
Kalaw
S H A N   S T A T E S
R. Irrawaddy
Pyinmana

MOVEMENTS
T AUG. 1945

N MOVEMENTS
TH APR. 1945

Toungoo

100 MILES

Pyu

Meeting at Altcar for the first time, the Battalion had   1949
outstanding successes, winning both the Warrant Officers'
and Sergeants' match and the T.A. unit team match.

It now remains to welcome the National Service entry
expected in 1950. If the Battalion can pass on to the new
generation the spirit which animated all ranks at Kohima,
they can be certain that the Territorial representation of
the Worcestershire Regiment will be in safe hands in
the years to come.

CHAPTER ELEVEN

THE EIGHTH BATTALION, 1922-1946

*Worcester, The Saar, Moncheaux, Bois de Soignes,
Bambecque, Dunkirk, Kington, Devonshire,
Lincolnshire, Glanusk Park*

1922   IN the period which we know as "the years between"
the corporative life of the battalions of the Territorial
Army could not and did not vary greatly as between one
unit and another. Thus many of the features and episodes
in the life of the 7th Battalion at the time are repeated
in the case of its colleague, the 8th Battalion, based on
Worcester. The 8th Battalion, however, suffered from
having to cover a wider area of the country, and the
training and development of a scattered battalion presented certain problems which did not arise in the case of
the battalion at Kidderminster.

    The area covered included Pershore, Evesham, Red-
ditch, Bromsgrove, Droitwich, and Malvern Link,
1928 although in 1928 for a short time Pershore had to be
abandoned as a half-company station owing to the fact
that training in August was always difficult for the fruit
pickers.

    Just as musketry might have been considered as a
strong feature of life in the 7th Battalion, so the 8th
Battalion could claim a leadership in sport. The Battalion football team once reached the final of the T.A.
1929 Championship, once the semi-final, and for three years in
succession it won the 48th Divisional Cup. In February,
1929, there is a record of a game played at Plymouth,
when the 2nd Battalion acted as hosts, in which the
5th Devons were defeated to the tune of 16-2 ! Much
credit for this record must go to Sergeant H. Kite at
Worcester, who was indefatigable in his efforts to improve
both the standard of football and boxing.

    During these years the Battalion Band, under Band-

master J. Martin, was able to build up a great reputation, **1928**
and its services both in Worcester and outside were in
constant demand. A particular occasion in the summer
of 1928 in Gheluvelt Park was marked by fireworks and
attracted some thousands of Worcester citizens to the
park.

In spite of recruiting drives and demonstrations at
Worcester, Evesham, Malvern, and Redditch, numbers
remained under strength. In the past a certain amount of
promiscuous recruiting had resulted in men joining who
were not up to the battalion standard. Subsequently it
was rightly felt that mere numbers were not necessarily
indicative of a high standard, and the Battalion aimed at
quality rather than quantity. Nevertheless numbers had
to be maintained, and the ingenuity of the staff at Worcester was fully taxed in keeping enlistment abreast of
discharge. In the summer of 1929 the strength of the
Battalion stood at just over 450.

It was a sad day for the 8th Battalion when on 30th **1930**
September, 1930, the 2nd Battalion sailed away for its
term of duty abroad. For two years from Plymouth its
services in assisting in many problems of training and
instruction had been invaluable. At the time the recently
formed Machine Gun Company was the subject of much
speculation, and expert assistance in training was very
welcome.

The year 1930 saw the provision of one motor vehicle
for the Machine Gun Platoon, the first introduction to
training for the mechanized age.

On 1st November, 1938, however, the Battalion ceased **1938**
to be "mixed" and became a rifle battalion armed with
Bren guns, anti-tank rifles and 3-inch and 2-inch mortars,
a transformation which involved no little amount of
administrative reshuffling.

Windmill Hill had become almost a traditional centre
for the annual camp, and by 1937 the Battalion had
become perhaps over-familiar with the topography of
Lamb Down Copse and the wooded slopes of Clarendon
Hill.

During this period the 7th and 8th Battalions formed
a solid Worcestershire representation in the 144th (T.A.)

1938   Brigade. In 1939 the 4th and 6th Battalions of the
Gloucestershire Regiment who had completed the Brigade
left for reconstitution, the one as a searchlight regiment,
the other as a mixed tank battalion. Their places were,
however, taken by the 5th Battalion the Gloucestershire
Regiment. Thus the association of the annual battles of
the "Bristolites" and "Worcesterites" over the downs of
Salisbury Plain was not broken.

1939   It has already been noted that in September, 1939, the
144th Brigade concentrated at Marlborough after the
annual camp. At Windmill Hill in August, 1939, camp
had been attended by the Battalion at a strength of a
thousand. For some weeks the young men of the countryside had been coming forward in a new enthusiasm under
the vague threat of events to come. Recruits who had
joined since April together with a cadre from the Battalion
now formed the new 10th Battalion, which continued with
elementary training. Hardly had the Battalion returned
from camp when the international crisis came to a head.
The 1st September marked the day of mobilization. For
a while training continued on "the home ground." But
a move was soon made to the concentration area at
Marlborough, where the Battalion settled down for three
months and was tuned up for the day of embarkation. In
between periods of concentrated training there was time
to collect a pack of beagles. Through a Mrs. Cole, the
Malmesbury Farmers' Beagles were generously lent, and
good sport and exercise were enjoyed after an abundance
of hare.

1940   Early in the new year His Majesty the King inspected
the Brigade in Savernake Forest ; while as an exercise in
silent movement under control, the Brigade spent a day
rounding up the deer in the forest, finally taking leave of
the enemy after they had all been successfully coaxed into
the deer park. The operation, if demanding no bravery,
certainly required careful signal co-ordination and infi-
nite patience, in that if hustled the deer were apt to
double back on their tracks in a manner hardly familiar
to a more dangerous biped.

When the great day came, the difficulty of coping with
nature proved more exasperating than any suggestion of

enemy interference, and the irritations of the first two **1940**
days on French soil in a heavy snow-storm have already
been stressed.

The Battalion landed at Le Havre on 16th January,
1940, and moved up to a concentration area at Tourville
before moving on to Moncheaux, near the Belgian
frontier, which was reached three days later. It will be
recalled that at this stage the B.E.F. on the left of the
Maginot Line, with a neutral Belgium to its front, was for
months out of touch with the enemy. Such activity as
took place was to be found farther to the south on the
Saar front and within the French area. For obvious
reasons of a political nature, it had become a matter of
policy to hold some British troops in the French sector ;
and it was in accordance with this policy that, soon after
sett ing into Moncheaux, the 144th Brigade moved south
to Lorry-le-Metz in the Saar, which was reached on 22nd
March. Thereafter during April the Battalion was constantly on the move. The Saar experience might have
been regarded as a continuation of training which had
initiated at Marlborough ! In spite of the fact that
German patrols were from time to time encountered,
there were no casualties. The task allotted was to patrol
about ten miles in front of the Maginot Line. Under the
French, defence had been organized with a *Ligne de
contacte*, supported by a *Ligne de soutien* some 1,500 yards
behind. The set-up was hardly in keeping with our own
education in principles of defence in depth; and had a
heavy attack fallen on the area, the enemy could certainly
have been quickly through what amounted to a linear
system. It was during this period that Sergeant Donald
with a patrol captured a Nazi flag which now hangs in the
Regimental Museum. The Battalion had woken one
morning to find a large Nazi standard flying high up over
the church in a deserted village. That night a patrol
procured it, substituting a piece of old red cloth.

Battalion H.Q. were first at Waldeistroff in the
Ligne de soutien, with companies near by in Bizing and
Halstroff. But Waldeistroff, which was the H.Q. of both
battalions in the *Ligne de contacte* and the *Ligne de soutien*,
was occupied in rotation by the other two battalions of

1940   the brigade, 2nd Royal Warwickshires and 5th Gloucester-
shires, thereby allowing a rest in a third area back in
Kedange, which was some fifteen miles behind the
Maginot Line. Here the Battalion was directly under
French orders, and once again some differences of
opinion and method were noticeable in attempting to
interpret the local French Commander's views on what
constituted an *alerte* position. The general tendency of
the French to accept passing rumours and mild shelling
as occasions for movement, order and counter-order did
not encourage that confidence which should have been
the background to a close liaison.

The countryside was densely wooded in patches. Such
as had formerly held crops lay untended, as the civilian
population had long since disappeared. The frost of a
bitterly cold winter had added to the general barrenness
of the landscape. To the left and right of the Brigade
sector the ground was held by the French Foreign Legion
and some Algerian troops and patrolling was co-ordinated.
But it was a queer kind of warfare and of a pattern calculated to mislead young troops as to the true nature of war.
As an example of the deceptive calm that enveloped the
area, Waldeistroff, which accommodated a mass of
French miscellaneous units, was regarded as secure and
was not shelled until the last day, when the Battalion
was relieved by the 2nd Battalion The Black Watch.

On 24th April, the Battalion arrived back at Moncheaux with Brigade H.Q. near by at Le Forest. It was
to spend another month digging anti-tank defensive
positions in the area and carrying out reconnaissances up
to the Belgian frontier. The dreadful weather continued
into the spring, so that digging became a slow, messy
process, and in the event proved subsequently of no avail.

But the war of mud and static defence was abruptly
concluded when Germany invaded the Low Countries,
and by 14th May the Battalion was way up at Dan Hoek
on the outskirts of Brussels, and for the next fortnight
was to experience its first and last taste of grim reality.
During that short period it acquitted itself in a manner
which indicated that, had the fortunes of war demanded
its services on a second occasion, it would have come

away with all the honours and more, of which it was to be 1940
deprived by the luck of the draw.

Leaving behind many good friends among the civil
population of Moncheaux, the Battalion packed up and
by daylight on 14th May was across the Belgian frontier.
In looking back on the months in France and Belgium
there were few colourful moments on which the mind
could focus. But no record would be complete without
mention of the episode which, for all its humour, nearly
caused an "International situation." The Commanding
Officer had managed to evade all restrictions and had
successfully brought over four ferrets, presumably to
deal with the French rats. It was at Moncheaux that a
private soldier detailed to look after the ferrets thought
he would test them out in the rabbit copses round the
Moncheaux mines. Alas, a French game-keeper was
waiting for them over an exit hole and duly confiscated
the offending animals. It then needed all the diplomacy
of Lieut.-Colonel Johnstone and the H.Q. Staff to
negotiate the subsequent hand-over, the French Liaison
Officer being the medium through which, at a price, they
were eventually returned. The ferrets were last seen
scampering away in freedom in a Belgian field.

The 48th Division was moving by M.T. The frontier
barriers were up and as the columns moved through the
Belgian villages they received a wild welcome from the
inhabitants. Everywhere at the street corners groups of
women and children had gathered to speed them on
their way with shouts and cheers.

Up at Dan Hoek the Division came into reserve to the
1st Corps, which was already in action away to the east,
and instructions were issued to carry out reconnaissances
for three alternative situations. The Second-in-Command[1] found that the great "Lion" Memorial marking
the battle of Waterloo made as good a viewpoint as any
and a long reconnaissance was made. But no sooner was
this over and plans formulated than orders were received
to reinforce a French formation. The French, however,
could not be found, and the only French troops encountered were some columns of Colonial units moving

---

[1] Major S. W. Jones.

1940 rapidly to the rear in undignified confusion. Finally, after the Brigadier had contacted Divisional H.Q., confirmation was received that that particular plan was no longer operative.

The plan chosen involved a move on to the Bois de Soignes, forward of the field of Waterloo, and accordingly on 16th May a move was made. The Brigade spent a rather fruitless day entangled in the thick forest. Good roads intersected the forest, but otherwise there was no field of fire. There were some large private houses round which desultory patrolling took place. But the day passed with nothing more eventful than the spectacle of some race-horses from a racing stable galloping madly around in wild confusion.

For the next few days it was a matter of marching, halting to fight spasmodic rear-guard actions, then on again, with little news coming in to give a picture of how the Division in general and the 8th Worcestershire in particular were fitting into the entangled movements of the B.E.F., the French, the Belgians and the enemy. For the soldier in the ranks it meant marching all night to a full moon, arrival in the early morning, waiting for the task allotted and contact with the enemy. Tentative orders to go would be received late in the evening and by midnight the Battalion would be again on the move. Encounters with the enemy were nearly always of an isolated nature so far as the Battalion was concerned. The bridges were all being blown and there was constant anxiety lest some portion of the Battalion should be caught on the wrong side of a blown bridge.

On 18th May there should have been a brief rest at Wez-Velvain, where the Battalion came into reserve and harboured for the night in the grounds of the chateau. But that night some enemy mortars ranged on to Battalion H.Q. and there were many casualties, among them a very gallant medical officer, Captain Jones.

The Division was now on the line of the River Escaut, and all ranks were heartened by a message from the Divisional Commander to the effect that the 48th Division was now to stand and fight, and there would be no further withdrawal. Accordingly the Battalion moved up to Bruyelles on the Escaut, relieving the 5th Gloucesters in the forward area in a defensive position of two battalions up and one withdrawn.

Throughout 22nd May the enemy was held. The country was enclosed with low scrub down to the banks of the river, and it was not difficult for the enemy to work forward under cover. Nevertheless only small parties succeeded in crossing and these were mopped up by our patrols. In spite of heavy casualties, the morale of the 144th Brigade stood high, and it was a bitter disappointment when that evening orders came to withdraw over the French frontier. The explanation—though it was not known at the time—proved to be the surrender of the Belgians on the left.

It was not easy to extricate the Brigade in the darkness, but the Brigadier[2] handled it superbly without fuss. Standing at a road junction, he watched his weary, disappointed troops march slowly on, many turning to their comrades for support.

Planard was reached on 23rd May and French troops were in position on the frontier. But their general attitude to the situation and the numbers of them who were roaming around lost and unarmed was not an encouraging background for speculation on the future. Nor was it possible to remain for long unmoved by the pitiable spectacle of refugees, old people, women and children, who, with their paraphernalia, crowded the roads everywhere and hampered movement.

On 24th May the Battalion staggered into Avelin. They had covered some 200 miles in the last ten days, fighting all the way, and they were reaching the limits of human endurance. The supply system had broken down and there was precious little to eat. At the best low rations could only at moments be supplemented by buying and scrounging in the villages.

In the fog of war it was unwise to pay heed to the many rumours. At Battalion H.Q. there was a story of an officer who had driven by, standing up in the turret of a British armoured car, shouting out to the effect that the German tanks were through and resistance was hopeless. But he

---

[2] Brigadier J. M. Hamilton, D.S.O.

P

1940 carried a duelling scar on his cheek, and on second
thoughts it seemed that he must have had a day out
sowing alarm and despondency in our columns before he
got back to his right side of the line.

At Avelin the Battalion tumbled into motor transport,
and few were awake to note Armentières, the Menin
Gate and Ypres as they drove north-west to Beveren.

It is difficult to know to what extent the fighting
battalions of the 48th Division could follow the general
situation. But the move to the north was an effort to hold
the Germans who were pushing up the coast from the
south. Though it was known that the French had col-
lapsed, there was yet no talk of evacuation and Dunkirk
was still just a name of another French port.

A tribute is here due to the Divisional Cavalry Regiment, the 12th Royal Lancers, who had worked back with
the Brigade to Avelin. It was comforting indeed at the
end of the long night to march through their road-blocks
and find their cars tucked into the hedges ready to help
the Battalion in.

Whether or not the decision of Dunkirk had been taken
at this stage is hardly relevant to this story. The fact
remains that there was news of a German tank formation
moving up from the south-west, and from Beveren the
144th Brigade were sent off to meet and hold the threat in
order to give the Division and other formations the
freedom needed to reach the coast.

On 26th May the Brigade was therefore concentrated
in and around Wormhoudt. Both Battalion and Brigade
H.Qs. were in the chateau. Two companies were in the
chateau grounds, the other two being some distance away
to the north in touch with the defenders of Bergues. The
Warwicks were in position in Wormhoudt village, while
the Gloucesters on the left held the main road from
Cassel.

On 27th May there were hopes of a quiet day, but the
Brigadier explained that there was a difficult time ahead.
The job in hand was to save precious hours for others to
get to the coast. If the pressure became too great, then a
withdrawal of a few miles would be undertaken, another
stand would be made, and the process repeated over again.

Later this was interpreted in an order which came in to hold the Wormhoudt position until midnight of the 28th.

And so on the morning of 28th May the Battalion was still in and around the chateau of Wormhoudt. Everyone was in high spirits and the very serious situation elsewhere was fortunately hardly realized.

That night the weather, which had hitherto been so kind, broke in a tremendous thunderstorm, and in the event the drenching rain and darkness may well have imposed a welcome fog of movement over the enemy tanks. In the circumstances the withdrawal was put forward from midnight to 2100 hours.

About a mile from Battalion H.Q. to the north-east, "A" and "D" Companies had organized an all-round defence of the village Wylder. These were left out to protect the right flank of the Brigade while Battalion H.Q. and "C" Company withdrew along the road to Herzele. With them came the survivors of one troop of the 52nd Anti-Tank Regiment (The Worcestershire Yeomanry). This troop alone had accounted for some twenty-six German tanks and had man-handled its guns after its transport had been destroyed. On the way to Herzele, "B" Company, which had held the southern extremities of Wormhoudt, were met swinging along at a good pace, wonderfully fresh and in high spirits.

Only a short halt was called at Herzele, and thence a march was made north-east to Bambecque. It was here throughout 29th May the Battalion was to fight a rearguard action worthy of the finest traditions of the Regiment. Orders were received to hold Bambecque until 2100 hours. "B" Company took up a position north of the River Yser covering the road from Herzele, with "C" Company just west of the village itself. Battalion H.Q. was in the village.

By 1130 hours Captain Farrar had successfully withdrawn "D" Company half a mile to the east on to the road from Bambecque to West Cappel. At Battalion H.Q. the doctor had found time to deliver a French woman successfully of a son and "both were doing well." German tanks were now coming on in large numbers from Wormhoudt in the south-west and Bergues in the north-west.

1940   Tanks would come up first to draw fire and then to break
through for the lorried infantry behind. The L.M.Gs. of
"A" and "D" Companies were having good shooting, and
Private Turton of "D" Company successfully shot up a
M.O. party off-loading from a large tank. By 1700 hours
an enemy tank attack had closed in on "D" Company
H.Q. and set it on fire. Captain Farrar was last seen
firing an anti-tank rifle at enemy tanks at close range. By
1800 hours both companies were so badly cut up as to
make further resistance impossible, and the survivors,
three officers and about sixty other ranks, dribbled into
Battalion H.Q. in threes and fours to reorganize.

Meanwhile stragglers from other units were coming in
and it was difficult to organize them effectively in support
of the defence. By 1730 hours the circle was beginning to
close around Bambecque and "B" and "C" Companies
were heavily involved. Captain E. W. Berry organized a
working party and built a very stout road-block of farm-
carts and tractors on the Bambecque road below Battalion
H.Q. The same officer had previously had a great shoot
round the Wormhoudt market square from a carrier, sending German infantry scuttling like rabbits into the houses.

At about 1800 hours a Liaison Officer from Brigade
H.Q. arrived with orders for a withdrawal at 2100 hours,
and a route to Bray Dunes, on the coast north-east of
Dunkirk, was given. The Adjutant then had to get
out marked quarter-inch maps to as many subordinate
commanders as could be found, no easy task in view of
the fact that the enemy now had every possible route
under observation. Various runners volunteered to take
out the orders, but none of them got through to their
destinations. At last darkness fell and at 2105 hours a
start was made thinning out the defenders, who began to
wind their way in single file along the road to Rexpoede.
The last detachment finally left at about 2200 hours under
the command of Captain Berry. But "B" and "C"
Companies had suffered grievous loss. "B" Company
indeed, which had been widely deployed, fought on until
its ammunition was exhausted and then, with the net
drawn tightly around it, had no alternative but to surrender. The survivors as they trudged the long miles to

Bray Dunes all through the night at least could know that, **1940**
despite heavy sacrifices, their endurance had ensured the
safety of thousands.

The above is all too brief an account of an action in
which many moments of individual heroism must remain
unsung. A British infantry battalion had fought and held
an armoured enemy attacking in overwhelming strength.
In doing so, its Commanding Officer, Second-in-Command and Adjutant had set an example of leadership and
disregard for personal safety which had quickly become
infectious. In such conditions it is invidious to single out
individuals for merit where so many contributed to the
common heroism of some ten long days of fighting.

The march to Bray Dunes has been summed up as a
nightmare. All transport had been destroyed at Bambecque. For many this involved the abandonment of a
mass of trinkets, of personal kit collected laboriously over
the winter. The Second-in-Command and Adjutant also
had the happier task of burning all secret and confidential
documents over a kitchen fire.

On either side of the road the dykes were flooded and
for miles an interlocked shambles of transport jammed all
movement. Here and there an exploded vehicle burning
itself out added colour to the confusion. Sometimes the
only way round was to take to the water in the dykes. At
other moments troops had to climb on to and over the
vehicles. At Rexpoede it was hoped to find British troops
in position, but the place was a mass of burning hamlets
with bewildered villagers adding to the chaos. A few
minutes' contact were made with the Brigadier and then
on to Bray Dunes. An enormous dump of army vehicles
blazing away in some fields was grim evidence of the
German domination.

The flooding of the countryside may have handicapped
the enemy, but it meant precious little to drink for the
troops ; and it was good to find the Brigade water-truck
within a mile or two of the beach near by one of the few
pure water supplies.

On the beach a massive, immaculate military policeman
was sorting out arrivals by divisions. As far as the eye
could see, thousands of troops—British and French—

1940   crowded the beach, while at the time only one solitary
destroyer and two small merchant ships stood a mile out
to sea. Surely, some may have thought, here was no
salvation but a death-trap ! Officers and men lay huddled
together in the dunes, sleeping the sleep of exhaustion.
Others were chatting to each other or staring silently out
to sea. Here and there an officer or N.C.O. was busy
sorting out his particular flock. Hundreds were slowly
wandering to and fro searching for their comrades. Confusion there certainly was, but no panic. Discipline was
unshaken and gradually the situation was resolving into
such order as was possible.

At last a count could be taken, and about a hundred
men of the Battalion could be mustered. The tale of
losses is simply told when it is remembered that 533
replacements were sent to join in England. On the beach
throughout the day, seven men of "C" Company turned
up ; none, alas, from "B" Company.[3] Later a total of
149 men boarded the *Glengower*.

That day on the beach the Battalion performed its last
service for the welfare of its comrades in the B.E.F. It
had been evident that there were no orders covering the
arrangements for the rowing boats to come and go between
the shore and the ships. The Commanding Officer and a
Major of the Royal Engineers took the situation in hand.
Volunteers were called for to swim out and bring in many
of the boats which were floating idly in the sea, and
rowing gangs from men who professed to row were
organized. The men of the Battalion formed three sides
of a square on the beach facing away from the sea, and
into this box parties for the boats were passed as they were
made up. It was a fine job of work. Earlier the Colonel
had decided that parties of waifs and strays without a unit
should take precedence ; and so it was that 8th Worcestershire came away having seen many another to safety first.
Yet it was not immediate safety. For some who fell
asleep on the *Glengower* awoke two hours later with

---

[3] Captain E. J. Haywood, whose account in *Firm*, May, 1941, was of
much value in reconstructing this story, wrote later : " 'B' Company
were cut off and when we withdrew that night we could still hear
fighting. We concluded that 'B' Company was still holding out, but
there was nothing we could do."

visions of the English coast in sight, only to find that they were still at Dunkirk ! The ship had steamed five miles down the coast to pick up 200 wounded before heading for Harwich.

The *Glengower* proved to be a paddle-steamer, familiarly known on the Bristol Channel ferry service. Her decks were packed with troops. Rifles were stacked to save space, and her captain had a busy time shouting instructions to obtain an even distribution of weight on his decks. "Move right down the car, please !" In such a way he balanced his paddles evenly in the water.

So far as enemy interference was concerned it was a lucky day. Only at Dunkirk a German plane straddled the *Glengower* with a stick of bombs and one caught it with a glancing blow. Of the 1,400 men on board, only four or five were hit.

And so to Harwich ; and for once "the Glorious First of June" passed uncelebrated !

Those few who lay awake on the journey to Harwich might perhaps have wondered at the kind of reception which awaited them from the people of England. Hardly could they return triumphant as conquering heroes. Yet would there be credit for the stubborn heroism of the past few weeks ? Would there be some recognition of the magnitude of the task the B.E.F. were called on to perform at a time when it was being deserted by those on whom it had depended to form a common front against the German armour in its sweep across the Low Countries ? They need not have been anxious. In the case of the 8th Worcestershire, a battalion of the Welsh Guards were to be their hosts for a few hours, and they made the small party feel that whatever the circumstances, it was good to be home. First, there was the joy of getting clean, and afterwards a "high tea" of ham, salad, bread and butter, cheese and cake seemed a veritable banquet after the scanty rations of the past three weeks. As the men formed up to catch the train to Derby, a crowd collected along the railings by the station and gave them a cheer. It was the tonic they needed ; and once again the old spirit was alive.

In such ways the return of an army in its grievous loss

1940   was to shake the people of England from their apathy and brace them to meet the danger ahead.

It was not until 4th June that at Kington the Battalion was able to halt and take stock of its resources. Unlike many units, it had brought away its rifles and some had managed to carry their L.M.Gs. At Kington for a month it re-formed. Two large drafts were received, one from the Depot at Worcester, the other from the Royal Welch Fusiliers at Wrexham. With the arrival of about 400 new recruits, new clothing and light equipment, the Battalion was once again an active unit ready to train for the next phase. From Kington on 3rd July a move was made to Somerset, where billets were found in two villages, Castle Cary and Bruton, with Brigade H.Q. at Frome. The role of the 48th Division was now that of "anti-invasion," and in this capacity they proceeded into Cornwall. Transport was by single-decker Western National buses, and the Battalion went into camp at Lanhydrock, near Bodmin.

On 5th August the Battalion moved to Penryn and Falmouth, where, under the orders of Admiral Kitson, it was responsible for the defence of Falmouth. Once again it was a matter of digging and wiring round Falmouth and Penryn, with heavy guard duties by night. The usual alarms and rumours interrupted work with frequent orders to "stand-to." On 12th October they returned to Truro. Exmoor and Amesbury provided the areas for anti-invasion exercises and weapon training. All the time further additions in arms and equipment were

1941   arriving, and by May, 1941, the 48th Division, though still in an anti-invasion role, was complete in equipment, was mobile with all its transport services and up to full establishment.

On 21st May a move was made to Tiverton, Brigade H.Q. being close by in Cullompton. The Battalion left the Brigade for a short period from 20th June until 19th July for Brixton, near Plymouth. This allowed for the 11th Battalion The Devonshire Regiment to take its place in the Brigade for training purposes and afforded all ranks a welcome rest.

Yet another move followed to St. Austell, in Cornwall,

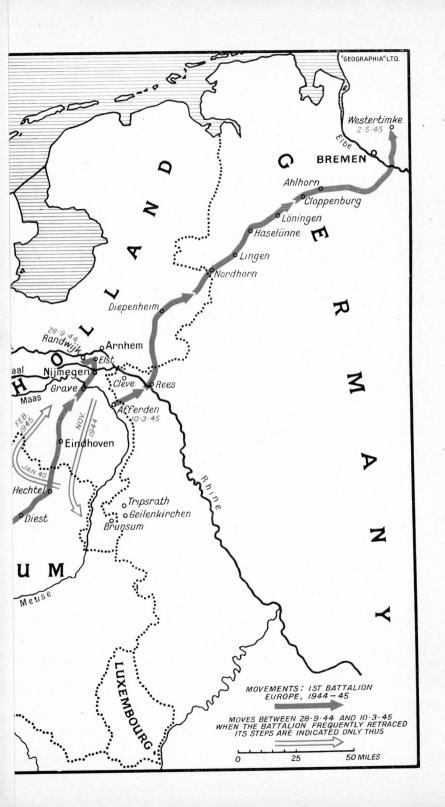

"GEOGRAPHIA" LTD.

Westertimke
2·5·45

BREMEN

Elbe

G

Ahlhorn
Cloppenburg
Löningen
Haselünne
Lingen
Nordhorn

Diepenheim

E

H   O   L   L   A   N   D

R

28·9·44
Randwijk
Arnhem
Elst
Nijmegen
aal
Grave
Maas
Cleve   Rees

M

Afferden
10·3·45

FEB.
1945

NOV
1944

Eindhoven

JAN 45

Rhine

A

Hechtel
Diest

Tripsrath
Geilenkirchen
Brunsum

N

U   M

Meuse

Y

LUXEMBOURG

MOVEMENTS: 1ST BATTALION
EUROPE, 1944–45

MOVES BETWEEN 28·9·44 AND 10·3·45
WHEN THE BATTALION FREQUENTLY RETRACED
ITS STEPS ARE INDICATED ONLY THUS

0   25   50 MILES

on 21st August, the Brigade going to Bridestow, near   **1941**
Okehampton. It was at St. Austell that for a brief period
the whole Battalion became screen artists for the purpose
of making the film "Next of Kin." The new role, however,
was interrupted on 26th September when the whole of the
48th Division took part in exercise "Bumper" and finished
up at Woburn, in Bedfordshire. The exercise was on a
large scale with tanks in battle on both sides and was a
clear indication of the degree to which our armed forces
had been able to recover and equip since the tragic days
of Dunkirk.

By 5th October the Battalion was back at St. Austell to
complete its film work. But on 15th October it rejoined
the Brigade at Okehampton, and early in November the
whole Division moved north to Lincolnshire, Battalion
H.Q. being at Hungerton Hall, Grantham, with companies scattered around. On 29th November, 1941, the
Battalion moved to North Somercotes. Thereafter north
Lincolnshire was to remain the training area for many
months. Constant moves for the sake of movement
seemed at times to be the policy of higher authority, and
in 1942 Louth, Woodhall Spa and Market Rasen were   **1942**
visited, with frequent exercises at Rufford and elsewhere.

First at North Somercotes and then at Louth in
January, 1942, where H.Q. was set up in a new drill hall,
the role was coastal defence. The War Diary reflects the
monotony of the period after the campaign in France, and
entries tell of snow, frost, voluntary church parades and
coastal exercises. It is almost with a sense of relief that
reference is made to the successful baling out of the crew
of a Manchester bomber which crashed in the Battalion
area. It was a constant struggle to maintain and stimulate
interest. For the work in hand, the preparation of the
48th Division in a role to meet the threatened invasion,
was still of vital significance. District exercises were,
however, frequently packed with interest. The allowance
for fifth columnists provided with false identity papers
lent a certain excitement to the proceedings. But it is a
little incongruous to find in the same orders covering such
matters that "special care will be taken not to alarm flocks
of sheep by firing blank owing to the lambing season !"

1942   Wisely, much ingenuity was shown in variation with lectures, training films and demonstrations of all sorts, leavened with plenty of inter-unit sport.

At the beginning of October, 1942, the Battalion was back at North Somercotes, where it remained until the **1943**   end of January, 1943. Thereafter throughout 1943 it was based on Market Rasen, where it settled down to an uneventful training cycle. It was to remain at Market **1944**   Rasen until 24th July, 1944, when a move was made to Whalley, in Lancashire, the troops being accommodated in a disused mill with H.Q. near by at Milton Hall.

Much to the disappointment of all, on arrival at Whalley the link with the 48th Division was broken. Together with 5th Royal Warwicks, the Battalion now entered the 80th Division, which changed its identity again and became the 38th Division. The old 48th Division received many new units after Dunkirk, and in 1944 it moved north to Scotland and was to play no further part in the life of 8th Worcestershire.

Finally, on 21st September the Battalion moved to Glanusk Park Camp at Crickowell, in Breconshire.

During the past two years a series of Commanding Officers had come and gone in quick succession, and Lieut.-Colonels Moss, Hallowes, Vale, Harrison and Knight covered the period from 1943 to 1945.

1945   At Glanusk Park all ranks found Lord Glanusk a kind and thoughtful host. The house was used as an Officers' Mess, Lord Glanusk himself living in a small house the other side of the river. One mile of fishing on the River Usk was placed at the disposal of the Battalion. Until the end training was carried on with an intensity which should have merited the reward of a second era of service overseas. The Brecon Beacon provided a realistic background and enabled safety precautions in regard to the use of live ammunition to be cut to a minimum. But as a training battalion, the Battalion had, alas, to be content with providing general reinforcements, first for the European theatre and, after VE Day, for the Far East, with all the emphasis on jungle warfare.

Every fortnight or so drafts were dispatched to different

destinations, one large draft going to the 9th Battalion.   1945
Men would arrive having completed preliminary training,
and it was the task of the Battalion to complete the job.
At one stage an element of variety was introduced by the
arrival of a few Belgians.

"The Glorious First of June" was celebrated in Glanusk
Park in 1945 with combined ceremonial and entertainment
on a great scale. After a parade at which the Colonel of
the Regiment took the salute, the Battalion dispersed to
the park, where those farmers over whose land the
Battalion had trained were entertained with pony races,
a sheep dog exhibition and various side-shows with prizes.

Thus 1945 passed away in an atmosphere of disappointment that so much training and enthusiasm was not to lead
to the full use of the Battalion again as a unit. Inspecting
Officers testified to the fine training which was being
lavished on the drafts which came and went. But it was
poor consolation for those few with memories of Bambecque and Wormhoudt. A nucleus of some forty men
were all that remained from the 1940 days, while Major
A. Graham was the only officer who had served through
to the last days at Glanusk.

On 1st February, 1946, orders were received to take   1946
the first steps towards "suspended animation," and 28th
February the process was complete. Dust had returned
to dust; but memories linger on to quicken the spirit
which is indestructible.

CHAPTER TWELVE

THE NINTH AND TENTH BATTALIONS, 1940-1944

It has already been noted how at a summer's Territorial Army Camp in August, 1939, the 9th Battalion had taken on its separate identity with the assistance of its parent, the 7th Battalion. Its area was accordingly based on Dudley, Langley and Halesowen.

1940 In January, 1940, the Battalion was back on familiar ground at Kidderminster. But on 15th January a move was made to Adderbury, near Banbury, where it was to spend the next few months in the unspectacular but extremely important role of preparing and waiting for Hitler's invasion. In addition, internal security duties were carried out at the R.A.F. stations at Bicester, Little Rissington and Brize Norton. In June the Battalion moved to Winchcombe, near Cheltenham. It had hardly settled down to training in the Cotswold hills than news came through of an impending long journey. Embarkation leave followed and an atmosphere of expectancy prevailed. But no sooner had the Battalion collected again than it was learnt that the first orders were cancelled and they were due to move to Northern Ireland.

Portrush in normal times is a pleasant holiday resort, and for a few days it seemed that life was going to be unexpectedly normal and comfortable. But moves followed one another swiftly, and on 24th June the Battalion was at Coleraine and a month later at Strabane.

Free from the demands of draft finding or any internal disintegration, the Battalion made rapid progress. Internal security duties meant constructing defences. At the same time there was always the prospect of having to move into Eire if things did not go well in the Battle of the Atlantic.

For the next two and a half years the Battalion's home was in Northern Ireland. A move was made to Belmont
1941 Park, Londonderry, on 23rd June, 1941, and to Cooks-

town on 5th November in the same year.　In the new year　**1941**
further moves to Tynan and Ballycastle continued the
process of general post, the Battalion remaining all this
time a unit of 182 (Birmingham) Infantry Brigade in the
61st Division.

It was an ambiguous kind of period, for while the
situation demanded that the Army in Northern Ireland
should be on its toes, those opportunities for sport and
leisure which are associated with peace-time soldiering
were also at hand.　Thus at Tynan the Battalion were able
to uphold the Regimental reputation by winning the
Brigade Association Football League Cup, and at the same
time captured the Brigade War Weapons Competition in
February, 1942.　Conditions are reflected in the nature of
the daily orders published which ranged over a variety of
miscellaneous headings.　Learning up American badges
of rank, debates to discuss current affairs, church parades
and penalties for indiscreet conversation are matters which
received attention.　Every day orders closed with a slogan
demanding attention.　"Famous last words : watch me
make her do fifty," is the type of advice which frequently
occurs as an afterthought.

In September Lieut.-Colonel R. R. Cripps handed over
command to Lieut.-Colonel W. E. Tolley, M.C., from the
Royal Lincolns, who by now had a very complete unit to
direct, the strength mustering just on 40 officers and 780
men.　But the ambiguity of the period is emphasized in the
fact that whereas the peace-time cycle of training was
quite unpractical, the imminence of active service was
always in doubt.　Thus training became a matter of mixing
up exercises, demonstrations, digging defences and
throwing in platoon and company training periods in haphazard sequence.　There was no doubt that a toughening
process was effectively under way.　In February the
Battalion marched back twenty-seven miles from ten
days of work on defence construction without noticing
the distance.　The drums met them on approaching
camp, and the Divisional Commander sent his personal
congratulations on a fine performance.

Particular attention was paid to night training, which
included patrol work, night firing and tank hunting.　The

1942   country lent itself to exercises with situations involving rivers as obstacles, and on more than one occasion the Battalion stoutly defended the line of the river Blackwater. The record of an exercise in May sadly mentions that after fighting a fierce battle with a battalion of the Northamptonshire Regiment, they were attacked by the 10th Worcestershire !

On 28th May the Battalion moved to Ballycastle, in County Antrim, where the tempo of training noticeably increased and exercises were more elaborate and exacting. Throughout this period one company was ready always to furnish a mobile column and an anti-parachutist platoon.

In June the Matilda tank showed its paces in a demonstration and the Battalion simulated Germans in a fight against a battalion of the Warwickshire. But in July training reached a level of sterner reality when in exercise "Atlantic," Antrim Force, consisting of 61 Division and an American Division, fought out a situation with 59 Division and the American Armoured Division. A Brigade field firing exercise which was to have included a full programme of artillery support was spoilt by the weather, and July closed with an exercise "Guerilla" which introduced an element of novelty. The three battalions of 182 Brigade were allotted different secret areas in the hilly country between Ballycastle and Cushendall. There then followed a free-for-all contest in which the Battalion was about to profit from an attack on the other two units which had already closed in battle. It seemed unfair that an umpire then thought it legitimate to disclose the situation to the other side as a spy on the grounds that the situation might otherwise get out of hand.

In August yet another large-scale exercise, "Defiance," was staged between "Purple Force" and "Green Force," the former composed of 61 Division with an American Medium Tank Regiment, the latter comprising the American 1st Armoured Division. The exercise was interesting as revealing some impressive handling and control of their armoured units by the Americans. In the same month the Battalion received a single 2-pounder anti-tank gun, and immediately short courses were started

in the hope of further guns being received in the near   **1942**
future.

In September the River Bann once again presented an
opportunity for an exercise to test out the crossing of a
river at night in face of opposition. In the meanwhile
relations with the local inhabitants had developed on a
very friendly basis, and the feeling was expressed in such
small ways as a bowls match with the Ballycastle Bowling
Club and a two-guinea donation to the Club by the
Battalion. Exercise "Haversack" in October was designed
to test out physical endurance, and the Battalion covered
thirty miles in poor weather at a "walk and run" pace
without mishap. More rivers were crossed in exercise
"Thrust" in November, and the Battalion staged a very
successful demonstration of "night infiltration" for the
benefit of the officers of 61 Division.

A dance in the Town Hall at Coleraine encouraged the
belief that Christmas would be celebrated with traditional
festivity. And so it proved. Turkey and Christmas
pudding were consumed and the town went gay with
dancing, whist drives and a healthy consumption of beer.
In days of balanced hard work and necessary recreation
the hand of bureaucracy was never absent, and a Battalion Order records that "the flaps of envelopes in
multiple green envelopes must not be tucked in"!

In January, 1943, Lieut.-Colonel J. H. O. Wilsey took   **1943**
over command from Lieut.-Colonel Tolley, and under
him the period of hope and suspense in North Ireland
was closed, for on 3rd February 61 Division was ordered
back to England and the Battalion found itself at Clacton-
on-Sea. But the halt at Clacton appeared to be only for
the purpose of exercise "Spartan," and on 27th March a
move on to Hertford was made where for nearly eight
months the Battalion concentrated on assault and combined operations training.[1] Confidence in employment
on service abroad was reflected in a lecture by the Divisional Commander, Major-General C. B. Wainwright, on
11th June, when he told his audience that 61 Division
had been earmarked for future military operations. There

---

[1] On 3rd April, 1943, orders to mobilize **were received**, mobilization
to be completed by 10th May, 1943.

1943   followed a role as a "follow-up" Battalion; and then
quite suddenly without warning the Battalion was placed
on a lower establishment.

On 23rd October the Battalion moved to St. Margaret's
Bay and the 61st Division was given an anti-invasion
role. A few days previously Lieut.-Colonel Wilsey in
announcing his own departure had broken the news of
the impending change.[2] In the words of the Adjutant,
Captain W. G. Wright, "It was strange to hear we were
to defend beaches after having trained for so long in
attacking them!"

Simultaneously insult was added to injury when the
task of "heavy draft finding" was allotted. Nevertheless
training, intermingled with cross-Channel shelling and
some flying bombs, continued, and the Battalion gave a
good account of itself whether in preparation for war or
in billets. At this stage a very high standard of training
had been reached and on exercises the Battalion had
distinguished itself. It was a happy family which Lieut.-
Colonel Wilsey had to leave, a condition for which the
departing Commanding Officer with his qualities of
leadership was responsible.

1944   In June, 1944, the task of drafting lay heavy, for in
that month the majority of N.C.Os. and men were sent
away, being replaced by category men from the 77th
Division. The Battalion moved on to Folkestone and
thence to Shorncliffe. Shorncliffe will be remembered as
a station of attraction for the flying bombs and the
measures taken to meet them. It was in fact the height
of the flying bomb season and, with an effective anti-
aircraft barrage within half a mile, orderly room and
parades were often conducted over a continuous roar of
gun fire. Nevertheless not a single casualty from flying
bombs was ever sustained. Simultaneously two new roles
were added, those of training ex-L.A.A. personnel for
conversion to infantry and retraining returned wounded.

In October, 1944, a welcome interlude for some lucky
ones was afforded by a visit to Sandringham for guard

---

[2] Lieut.-Colonel K. G. Exham assumed command on 16th October.
Lieut.-Colonel J. H. O. Wilsey, C.B.E., D.S.O., later became Chief of
Staff, Rhine Army, and commanded 5 Brigade, 2 Division, B.A.O.R.

duties. A composite company was made up and the men **1944**
spent spare time providing parties of beaters for the
royal shoots, which were followed by the traditional bottle
of beer and an excellent lunch. The officers had the
honour of dining with His Majesty, who visited the
Officers' Mess in York Cottage on Sunday morning after
Church.

In May, 1945, a move was made to Hothfield Camp, **1945**
near Ashford. "The Glorious First of June" was duly
celebrated, and the Band of the 1st Battalion The Duke of
Cornwall's Light Infantry was fortunately available for
an inspection parade by a distinguished officer of the
Regiment (Brigadier-General Grogan). Information was
now received that the Division was to reorganize as a
Light Division. This involved being transportable by air
and being trained to fight in any theatre of operations.
It was evident that there was some prospect of meeting
the Japanese in the Far East and hopes once again ran
high. But with the collapse of Japan in August, 1945,
this last project was abandoned and in November the
61st Division was disbanded. For a short time the Battalion came under command of the East Kent District for
internal security duties until finally it accepted "suspended
animation" on 31st December, 1945.

In the six and a half years of its life the Battalion had
been commanded by twelve Commanding Officers. Some
of these had had their full share of active service with
other battalions of the Regiment or with other regiments.
They were able to bring a constant fresh experience to
the heavy demands of training: and thus, if the 9th
Battalion were to be deprived of their opportunity of
service abroad, they at least could claim to have been a
practical school for passing through men from many
sources on to many destinations. Nevertheless in their
sense of frustration after so long a period of preparation,
watching and waiting, there will be ready sympathy
for those good officers and men who staffed so fine a
school.

The 10th Battalion saw the light of day in much the **1939**
same manner as its colleague, the 9th Battalion, when in
August, 1939, the annual camp of the 8th Battalion at

Q

1939   Windmill Hill mustered some 1,000 men, and two Commanding Officers and Adjutants turned up for training. Indeed, since both battalions were destined to serve in the same Division, the circumstances governing life in Northern Ireland differed little as between the two. From the few surplus personnel the 10th Battalion was formed at Worcester under Lieut.-Colonel A. R. Kettle, and when the 8th Battalion mobilized at Marlborough at the beginning of September, the new Battalion took over much of the area and were located at Malvern Link, Upton-on-Severn and Pershore. For some time the small numbers available only permitted the formation of Headquarters and two companies, "C" Company being regarded as the training unit and "D" Company holding men who were considered as trained but who naturally still required further experience and training. "D" Company accordingly had the privilege of responsibility for so-called "Operational" roles. Thus, from Malvern they were almost immediately moved to Quedgeley, near Gloucester, for the defence of No. 7 R.A.F. Maintenance Unit, where they guarded valuable technical equipment and aeroplane engines. In the meanwhile "C" Company had set up at Pershore, having first filled a gap guarding Badminton tunnel in Gloucestershire. Later "D" Company returned from Quedgeley to guard Pershore aerodrome. These opening moves saw the old year out, and as the new year was entered the numbers rose and Londoners came to join the men from the Midlands.

     In September, 1939, Lieut.-Colonel D. Chesney, 1940   O.B.E., had assumed command, and early in June, 1940, he took the Battalion down to Kingsclere, outside Newbury. Here for a few days it seemed that the 61st Division might be for France. The last troops were away from Dunkirk, but there was still some slender hopes entertained of a counter-landing much farther down the French coast. They proved abortive and the Battalion, now a unit of the 183rd Infantry Brigade in 61 Division, under the redoubtable Major-General Carton de Wiart, entrained for Stranraer in Scotland and embarked for Larne in Northern Ireland. Here, the staff arrangements had gone awry, for some futile movement and counter-move-

ment ensued. On 17th June from Larne the Battalion   1940
entrained for Portrush, which was reached in the early
hours of the morning of 18th June. Within three hours it
was discovered they should have gone to Belfast, so they
entrained again late in the afternoon for Belfast, where
they enjoyed the unique experience of moving by tram
with bands playing. This must surely be the only
occasion on which a battalion of the British Army has
been transported by tram.

Outside Belfast the greater portion of the Battalion was
in Sicily Park, with elements in the adjoining Balmoral
show ground.

At Sicily Park all ranks got down to the business of
preparation to meet the threat of a German landing in
Southern Ireland. It was an anxious time for a raw
battalion. At that stage the new entry under canvas in a
wet summer knew nothing of camp life or organization.
The move to Ireland had been carried out with an issue
of five rounds per man and one anti-tank rifle, while
officers were even without their revolvers.

On 1st December a move was made to Cookstown.
Here, carriers and anti-tank rifles began to arrive and
training was accelerated. At the same time Lieut.-Colonel
A. T. Burlton assumed command and Lieut.-Colonel
Chesney left. Nearly a year passed at Cookstown in the
unstimulating precincts of the local hospital and the
work-house. But by June, 1941, officers and men were   1941
hard. Although men with active service were difficult to
come by, the Battalion managed to collect and retain a
small invaluable core of Regular officers and N.C.Os.

From Cookstown a move was made to billets in Castlerock in November, 1941. It was a bleak, uninviting station
and the anti-parachute role of local protection proved
unspectacular. On 22nd January, 1942, the Battalion left   1942
Castlerock with few regrets and moved on to Ashbrook
on the border of Eire. Lieut.-Colonel Wills took over
from Lieut.-Colonel Burlton, and under his leadership
the Battalion was to attain a standard which merited a
more spectacular role than that of continual preparation
for situations which never arose.

At Ashbrook hutted accommodation was shared with

1942 the 7th Battalion The Gloucestershire Regiment, on Sir Basil Brooke's estate, and some of the officers were lucky to enjoy his hospitality at dinner during week-ends. It was at Ashbrook that a useful draft of fifty trained officers and men had to be passed on to India. Nevertheless the lessons of experience were being absorbed and essential personnel were retained. It should be appreciated that throughout this period the Division was still training for an active war role. Indeed, the various exercises reflected the process of tuning up in a manner which kept hopes of active service always just round the corner. Thus exercise "Atlantic," which has already been referred to, ushered in the Christmas of 1942. It proved a severe physical test covering eight days with an approach march culminating in taking up a defensive position against armour : and with the new year the whole Division felt it was ready for war.

Ashbrook will ever be remembered for a very close liaison which had been developing for some time with the 172nd Field Regiment, R.A. This unit had been working with the Brigade throughout training in Northern Ireland. It was formerly the Berkshire Yeomanry, and their officers and men seemed to have much in common with our men from the Midland counties. At Ashbrook for a time one of their batteries lived with the Battalion.

In June, 1942, the Battalion moved on to Londonderry into hutted accommodation. But not much was ever seen of the town for the process of hardening went ahead, and four or five days a week out on the Irish hills proved tough training by any standards. For a time the Commanding Officer was out of action from a useless explosion of a Bangalore torpedo at a Divisional R.E. demonstration, his Second-in-Command, Major Harrison, deputizing for him.

Londonderry was full of troops. Not only were there soldiers and sailors of our own Services, but men of the United States Army and Navy also thronged the streets. There were some lively scuffles at times between our men and the Americans. The formation staffs of both sides met to decide what should be done. But they concluded that there was nothing really serious in exuberance which

sometimes overstepped the mark and the situation was   1942
accepted in a spirit of "boys will be boys."

In January, 1943, the Battalion returned to England   1943
still as a unit of 61 Division. Hope and belief in great
adventures to come persisted. At first the Battalion was
split up at Southminster and Burnham-on-Crouch, in
Essex, where training at high pressure continued. Later
they moved to Chalfont St. Giles, in Buckinghamshire,
where Lieut.-Colonel Wills rejoined. A new Brigadier[3]
of great energy drove his team to maximum capacity, and
his approval of the 10th Worcestershire, which was no
secret, was a tribute to the standard attained.

It was from Chalfont St. Giles that it chanced on a
training march that the Battalion bivouacked at Halstead.
Some officers found themselves in a private house, and
the late Captain FitzMaurice Stacke's name appeared in
the visitor's book. It then transpired that much of his
monumental history of the Regiment had been written on
the spot, a unique coincidence if weighed against the
chances of that particular house being chosen for a visit.

In April, 1943, the Division was busy preparing for a
full-scale assault role. A later change to a status of
"follow up" involved no modification in training, and by
July a period amounting to a repetition of mobilization
seemed to confirm the rumours of an imminent move
overseas. Postings away ceased and leave was restricted.
The latest luxuries of equipment and arms were to be had
for the asking and new 6-pounders and anti-tank rifles
poured in.

But suddenly in September all these preparations col-
lapsed. Mobilization measures ceased and the Battalion
was called on for drafts, and with a move to New Romney
high hopes melted away. The seal was set on the most
unkind of anti-climaxes when it was realized that the new
role was that of playing "enemy" to the 43rd Wessex
Division ! Nor did it have the consolation of a friendly
encounter with the 1st Battalion, which for a short time
was ranged on the other side.

It is to the lighter side of life that one must turn for
relief in these gloomy days, and we therefore note a

---

[3] Brigadier Sir Alexander Stanier, D.S.O., M.C.

1943 special visit of the "Norton Follies" as a feature of an
otherwise black period. This talented concert party had
started life from Norton Barracks as a regimental party
and had toured the British Army, retaining always something of its regimental identity. It had included such
well-known artists as Frederick Ferrari, "the voice" in
Charlie Chester's radio show.

In the late autumn some welcome interest in a more
concrete rôle of useful purpose crept into the daily round
when for a short time the Battalion was earmarked for a
counter-attack task in connection with the project known
as "Pluto." Later this proved to be a bold plan to pipe
oil from England across the sea to France and assumed a
well-merited notoriety. All that the men knew of their
duties was that they were guarding what seemed to be
some innocuous bungalows round Hythe and Dymchurch
from sea or air-borne attack. Only the Commanding
Officer was aware of the secret and knew that his collection
of seaside villas housed concrete pumping installations
and tanks of precious oil. The good mark for behaviour,
however, was not so much for complete tactical preparations to meet various situations as for the successful
manner in which the secret was kept. On such occasions,
when the British soldier knows that so much is at stake,
he will keep a stiff upper lip through all the temptations
to gossip.

But "Pluto" was soon to be followed by a yet more
important operation of secrecy; and the fact that inevitably all ranks had to realize the nature of the great
deception in which they participated added colour to the
work which was taken in hand in December, 1943.

Just before Christmas the Commanding Officer was
summoned to H.Q., 21st Armoured Group, in High
Holborn and was briefed for the Battalion's role in the
great deception known as operation "'Quicksilver." The
task was to be shared out with the 4th Northamptonshire,
the latter based on Yarmouth and Lowestoft, while the
10th Worcestershire were to work from Dover, Folkestone
and the estuary of the River Orwell at Harwich.

The more detailed plan (operation "Overlord") involved a period of intense training from January to April,

1944, at Harwich, near Ipswich, on a small tributary of
the River Orwell, and once again all ranks played the
game and the strictest secrecy was observed, the area
being closely ringed and all contact from outside prohibited. Briefly the plan was to construct a large dummy
fleet of landing craft to deceive the Germans into an
assumption that a landing was imminent across the
Channel from the Kent and Essex coasts. During the
training period building was undertaken either at dusk or
in the early morning, eventually being carried on into the
night.

Eventually the Battalion was deployed with H.Q. and
the Support Company at Dover in the Duke of York's
School, "B" Company at Folkestone, "A" on the right
bank of the River Orwell and "C" and "D" on the left
bank. Sub-units took turns to train near Ipswich. The
ships were made of tubular scaffolding on wheels appropriately covered with painted canvas and sail cloth, and
floated on sets of oil drums. The final standard achieved
represented the construction of one ship over eight hours
—from 5 p.m. to 3 a.m.—by a party of forty men. No
deceptive details were forgotten, even down to the construction of dummy anti-aircraft guns.

In May the training phase ended and the actual operation was initiated (the great day being fixed for the
24th May). The stores arrived by night from an unknown
source and Company Commanders camouflaged them
with aeroplane netting. At Dover the main street at the
sea end, where construction was to take place, was
barricaded off and the surrounding houses evacuated.
Sappers constructed concrete launching ramps and the
Navy prepared tie-up buoys. Later motor boats and
pinnaces scurrying from one ship to another contributed
to the illusion of a fleet making ready for the open sea.
All went well except that up on the River Orwell, where
four ships should have been in the water on the first
night, only one was successfully launched due to the fact
that no previous training with the sappers had been
possible. At Folkestone use of the tide facilitated the
task of launching.

Ultimately construction was speeded up to a rate of

1944   ten craft taking the water each night. The Battalion had
122 craft to its credit and, together with the Northampton-
shires, a fleet of some 250 precarious phantom vessels
were afloat by 6th June.

We know now that the deceit was complete. It was no
easy task to make the project sufficiently obvious to attract
attention without overplaying the part, which would have
aroused suspicion. Air activity and radio deception added
to the illusion, and in the event much of the German 14th
Army around Calais was kept guessing. As if to confirm
their doubts, the Germans bombarded the fleet and some
forty shells fell in Folkestone and Dover, and at one
period their radio announced in triumph that they had
successfully held off the British invasion ! By then the
first elements of the great invasion Force were fighting
their way over the Normandy beaches and the two
battalions concerned with operation "Quicksilver" could
take pride in a good job of work carried through to its
complete success at the expense of three men wounded
in Dover.

In July one of those vague decisions was taken to
disband the Battalion which remained untranslated into
action, and in October they packed up and left the Duke
of York's Royal Military School, Dover, for Sheffield
Park, five miles from Lingfield in Sussex. Sheffield
Park was the home of a family, Soames, and in their
spacious park grounds the hutted camp accommodation
provided was very adequate. As the Battalion settled into
Sheffield Park it became evident that they were destined
for a role as a training unit. All fit personnel had been
posted away and in their place war-wounded men who
had undergone a period of rehabilitation started to arrive
for re-training.

The process by which 10th Worcestershire passed to
their final end was never clearly defined. In November,
1944, after the majority of the men comparatively fit had
been posted away, a party of about 200 strong made their
way to the Cavalry Barracks at Redford up at Edinburgh,
where they encountered a welcome friend in Lieut.-
Colonel L. G. H. Bryant of the Regiment, who was then
commanding another Primary Training Centre in the area.

Previously most of the stores had been returned to various
Ordnance depots, but the process of disposal continued
from Edinburgh in driblets. At Edinburgh the role of a
Primary Training Centre was definitely assumed and for
a time the title of changed status was known as 61st
P.T.C. (10th Bn. Worcestershire Regt.). Men from civil
life poured in at the rate of 1,000 per month and passed
on after six weeks of basic training. Gradually the
association of the Primary Training Centre with its parent
Battalion faded. In effect the 10th Worcestershire had
ceased its task at Sheffield Park, and one more war-time
offspring of the Worcestershire Regiment had passed
unostentatiously into the annals of regimental history.

CHAPTER THIRTEEN

THE ELEVENTH AND TWELFTH BATTALIONS, 1940-1942

Colchester, Haselbech, Harrow, Burton, Llanelly,
Iceland, Gravesend

1940 THE story of the two New Army Battalions of the Regiment is not only of concern to those who served with them during their brief career, but is also linked closely with the interests of the 1st Battalion. For it was from personnel of 11th Battalion that the 1st Battalion was able once again to re-form and participate with fresh vitality in the concluding phases of the war in Europe, while as gunners, 12th Battalion were to meet and co-operate with 1st Battalion in that historic campaign.

The 11th and 12th Battalions were raised in June, 1940, the former at Worcester, the latter at Burton-on-Trent. Only a cadre of 150 men of the Regular Army was available at Norton Barracks on which to build 11th Battalion and these included only four Regular officers. For three weeks Major de Courcy-Ireland[1] acted as Commanding Officer, with Captain A. Chichester[2] as his Adjutant. A Regular soldier who was early on the scene and who was to become an institution with the Battalion was Lieutenant and Quartermaster Yeates, formerly a well-known C.S.M. of 1st Battalion in the days of Plymouth and Aldershot. After three weeks this hard core of the Battalion moved into camp on 12th July on the race-course at Hereford, where two drafts of freshly enlisted civilians, each of 400 strong, joined to form eventually the body of the Battalion. It was fortunate that they were of the right age-group and they proved magnificent material on which to build the new unit. The greater number came from the Midlands and the neighbourhood of Birmingham, so they

---

[1] Major G. B. de Courcy-Ireland, M.B.E., M.V.O., M.C.
[2] Major A. E. Chichester, War Office (M.S.I.), 1950.

could also claim some territorial association with the
Regiment with which they were to link their future.
Even so, it will be appreciated that the work of the nucleus
of Regulars in equipping and training so many with no
military experience whatsoever was exacting. After Dunkirk there was a general lack of all weapons and for a
short time the new entry found themselves literally
learning their arms drill with broom-sticks !

From July onwards 11th Battalion was constantly on
the move, and by the time it had settled into Haselbech
Hall, in Northamptonshire, it knew something of camps
at Hereford, Bedford and Yarmouth. At Hereford Lieut.-
Colonel Court,[3] a senior Regular officer of the Regiment,
had assumed command and was to remain with them
until May, 1941. The parent formation was 13th Infantry
Group, under Colonel J. V. R. Jackson, late of the Buffs.
On 17th October a move was made to Yarmouth, halting
at Bedford for a few days *en route*. Here the Battalion
came into 213 Infantry Brigade under the command of
Brigadier Baker[4] and set to work on the task of placing
some four miles of the coast from Caistor down to Yarmouth in a state of defence. By night the men disappeared
into pill-boxes and by day they worked like ants on
road-blocks, wiring, anti-tank obstacles, camouflage and
all the hurried means of preparation which were to meet
a problematical invasion. Had the enemy ever managed
to make the crossing he would have found that particular
portion of the coast held by a brave and determined unit,
but sadly lacking in weapons and with little training or
experience.

In November the Battalion moved to Haselbech Hall,
near Northampton. Battalion H.Q. and the H.Q. Company were in the Hall itself, but rifle companies were,
perforce, scattered around in billets three to four miles
away from Headquarters. At last the opportunity had
arrived to put in some intensive training, which was
indeed essential when it is realized that specialists such
as the mortar personnel and signallers had yet had no
training, as such, whatsoever. At Haselbech the Battalion

---

[3] Lieut.-Colonel C. V. W. Court, M.C. (2nd Battalion).
[4] Brigadier E. E. F. Baker, C.B.E., D.S.O., M.C., T.D.

1941   formed part of the 9th Support Group, a formation
equivalent to a brigade, which was to be included within
9th Armoured Division, then in the process of formation.
At that time there was still doubt as to the correct in-
gredients of an armoured formation and tactical doctrine
for its use was still in evolution. To put it mildly, the
Battalion lived in a state of flux which nevertheless did
not prevent the foundations of a fine unit, fit for war,
being firmly laid. Fortunately, the Worcestershire Regiment were old friends of the Corps Commander,[5] who as
Brigade Major to a Brigade which included the 1st
Battalion before the war had charge of a Junior Officers'
Course, when he had made a point of getting to know the
young officers. Before the Battalion had passed on from
Haselbech it had collected a very large proportion of
officers from the home county, while no less than eight
officers were Regular officers of the Regiment.[6]

Reading the records, the layman cannot fail to be
impressed by the fine spirit of comradeship and the
determination to maintain regimental traditions which
animated the new entry. As time went by there seemed
to grow a very natural impatience at the inability to put
so much enthusiasm in training to the test. As an example
of the spirit abroad one notes the Signal and Carrier
Platoons indulging in healthy rivalry on route marches,
with the last mile of a twenty-mile march being covered
at five miles per hour.

Training was seldom interrupted by any features of
interest outside the local level of normal life. But those
who served at the time will recall a memorable occasion
when H.R.H. The Duke of Gloucester, with several
celebrities in attendance, arrived to inspect at Battalion
Headquarters. He was accompanied by the Army Commander, General Sir Ronald Adam, and others of lesser
rank—sufficient, however, to represent a galaxy of seniority
such as had not yet been welcomed in the short life

---

[5] Corps Commander, Lieut.-General Sir B. G. Horrocks, K.B.E.,
D.S.O., M.C. Divisional Commander, Major-General M. B. Burrows,
C.B., D.S.O., M.C. Group Commander, Brigadier F. C. F. Cleeve,
C.B.E., D.S.O., M.C.
[6] At Haselbech the C.O. was Lieut.-Colonel J. T. Milner, O.B.E.,
who took over on 27th May, 1941.

of the Battalion. With great difficulty a bugle had been **1941**
procured and a bugler trained, just in time, to blow the
Royal Salute ! Such were the exigencies of the service in
times of much improvisation and intensive preparation.

Haselbech was to remain the Battalion home for over a **1942**
year, and then on 14th June, 1942, the process of general
post was repeated. By December the Battalion had done
the round of Ashridge, Ipswich, Colchester and Purley,
before finishing up at Harrow.

At Ashridge the Battalion settled into tents in the
seclusion of Ashridge forest and for a time seemed no
one's child. R.A.S.C. drivers drove away the vehicles
which brought them from Northampton and the reality
and purpose of the 9th Armoured Division seemed a long
way away. The local Area dealt with administration, and
the only operational role allotted was an obscure commitment to guard an alternative but unoccupied site for the
Headquarters of Bomber Command in case of a hypo-
thetical parachute attack.

There was some interest attached to liaison with the
R.A.F., for this offered scope to use the high-powered
wireless sets which they had retained with them after
leaving the Armoured Division. Otherwise the main
preoccupation became drill and weapon training ; that
fine servant of the Regiment, R.S.M. Hurd, putting
in a lot of hard work to keep the young entry up to the
mark.

On 4th July the Battalion said farewell to their popular
Commanding Officer, Lieut.-Colonel J. T. Milner, who
was posted away to the Staff, and in his place they welcomed Lieut.-Colonel W. R. Cox of the King's Shropshire Light Infantry. This officer soon became a very
staunch supporter of the Worcestershire Regiment and it
was indeed by his tireless efforts that many drafts were
prevented from splintering away to other units.

Ipswich was the next home and here the Battalion was
attached to 223rd Independent Infantry Brigade under
Brigadier Sir Alexander Stanier. Companies were housed
in town billets and training was therefore somewhat
restricted. Nevertheless, undismayed by the somewhat
uneventful daily round, the Quartermaster set about

1942   procuring drums, bugles and fifes, which had suddenly
been noticed as featuring in the latest Equipment Tables.

There followed a few weeks at Colchester in Roman
Way Camp. The twenty miles were covered by march,
at the end of which it was pleasant to find quarters in a
concentrated area with a central parade ground. There
were, of course, all the training facilities of a normal
garrison town and much time was put in on the ranges.
But Colchester is to be remembered for one of those
unimportant decisions which yet attract attention. For it
was here that the 11th Battalion adopted the very obvious
shoulder badge of its motto "Firm" against a green cloth
background. At the time, the name of the regiment as
now universally worn was confined to units of the Brigade
of Guards. There was some outside speculation as to
the meaning of the new badge, but our men were quite
equal to the occasion when the inquisitive tried to be
facetious.

From Colchester the process of general post brought
the Battalion to Purley and thereby into the 24th (Guards)
Independent Brigade Group. The Battalion conformed
to Brigade practice and surrendered their green shoulder
badges for the conventional pattern. Thus the small green
strip emblazoned by the regimental motto after its brief
use passed to the collectors' purview and has found a
home in the Museum at Norton. At the same time the
Battalion took the Brigade badge, which carried the
family crest of its founder, Lieut.-General Sir Frederick
Browning. The standard of drill and alertness expected
was naturally extremely high. But there was a welcome
absence of red tape and the informal friendliness of the
senior officers of the Brigade was noticeable.

The last lap was now in sight as the Battalion moved
to Harrow on 5th December, thereby again changing its
formation and coming within 33rd (Guards) Brigade
Group under Brigadier J. Jefferson. Headquarters was in
the town, with companies scattered around in the surrounding country. The one unexacting operational role
was the defence of Northolt aerodrome, for which purpose
one company was at the West London Shooting School
on high ground overlooking the airfield.

It was then that a fine new Battalion had to surrender   1942
its identity, luckily in the great cause of the reconstitution of the senior battalion of the Regiment.

THE 12TH BATTALION

The 12th Battalion throughout its period was com-   1940
manded by Lieut.-Colonel A. P. Watkins. It was raised
as the 50th (Holding) Battalion, the permanent staff
coming from the 1st Militia Training Group at Dover and
from the Worcestershire Company of the 8th Holding
Battalion at Crewe. Three companies were raised from
men called up from civil life, a fourth company being
formed from "old soldiers" and men of Worcestershire
returning from Dunkirk. Immediately after Dunkirk the
Battalion housed and re-clothed some 250 officers and men
of the B.E.F. and were, in consequence, inundated with
gifts from the kind folk of Burton.

At the time, all emphasis was on "invasion." Rumours
of enemy parachutists sent companies scouring the
countryside, while a more deliberate task was to prepare
the River Trent as a "stop-line." As a diversion much
assistance in training was given to the Home Guard, while
throughout August and September "D" Company enjoyed the doubtful distinction of guarding a camp of
French sailors at Trentham Park, outside Stoke, who had
been removed from their ships. They were a tough lot,
with an unpleasant habit of shining lights at night when
German planes were overhead. It was not until 9th
October that the Battalion was designated 12th Battalion
The Worcestershire Regiment, and became a Rifle
Battalion.

From Burton a move was made to Dudley on 15th   1941
October, yet another transfer to Llanelly taking place on
25th February, 1941. The three months at Dudley passed
quickly, for the hospitality of the town to a battalion of
their county regiment was phenomenal. At this time the
raids on the Midlands were increasing and the men were
constantly busy in Birmingham clearing the debris. A
melancholy duty which also came their way was assistance

1941 to the people of Coventry on the morning after the disastrous raid on that city.

At Llanelly the Battalion's chief concern was the defence of the beaches, the old machine gunners coming into their own with an issue to beach companies of the Vickers machine gun. The Battalion was scattered over a wide area, with "C" Company on Pembrey beach near a large R.A.F. fighter station, "D" Company at Ashburnham beaches, and the other two companies in the town, the whole area stretching a length of about fifteen miles. A humorist at the time has aptly described the daily round as "digging sand-castles"! On 4th June the Battalion sailed from Greenock for Iceland.

While German air and sea power could penetrate the Atlantic, Iceland remained a strategic centre of obvious significance. The role of the 12th Battalion, while being neither spectacular nor stimulating, was of the first importance. On 8th June the Battalion disembarked at Reykjavik, the capital of the island, and by 13th June it was encamped in Reykjaskoli, with H.Q. and two companies billeted in the school and in tents, the remaining two companies being scattered, "D" Company at Blonduös and "B" Company at Borganes, a hundred miles separating the two. The school was most fortunately found to be heated very effectively by water from hot springs from the mountainside near by. At the time 49th West Riding Division (Territorials) held Iceland, and the protection of the north-west sector, an area one hundred miles in length, fell to the Battalion, which had a battery under command.

Boredom was perhaps the first enemy! Occasional leave parties enjoyed a visit to Reykjavik for a dance, where they were put up by a battalion of the Manchesters and could meet the girls of the town. Fishing parties were organized and in the afternoons would set out in hired boats to catch cod for breakfast next morning. There was golden plover shooting and salmon fishing for the more experienced anglers. An unfortunate sergeant who shot a salmon suffered for his slip with having to pay compensation of 200 kroner to the owner of the fishing.

The Iceland landscape is not exciting. There are no   1941
trees and very few bushes or flowers : and although the
49th Division took the polar bear on their badge, no
polar bears were ever seen on the island ![7] Occasional
E.N.S.A. parties and the 16 mm. films of the Army
cinema organization were welcome high-lights in long
periods of monotony.

Away from Headquarters, "D" Company at Blonduös
perhaps enjoyed a slightly more varied programme than
their companions, "B" Company at Borganes. Blonduös
was the staging camp between Reykjavik and Akureyri,
the latter being the only port in the north of the island.
At Company Headquarters a visitors' book recorded the
passage of travellers and registered about a hundred sig-
natures in three months. At least one concert was staged
in the guest house, and the Sergeants' Mess held a couple
of dances. But the young ladies of the town were shy of
emerging until after dark since they were apprehensive of
local gossip.

At the time heavy air raids were developing over the
Midland Counties at home and, with a lack of wireless
sets to pick up the news, the men from the Midlands were
naturally restless.

Blonduös was the scene of an episode, small enough in
the general perspective of the war, yet sufficiently sensa-
tional to give an isolated company of 12th Worcestershire
something to discuss for a short period in their uneventful
era. A small Norwegian vessel one day suddenly appeared
which had sailed from Spitzbergen on only a child's atlas
and pocket compass. The captain brought a story for the
G.O.C., Iceland, about the German intentions in regard
to the Spitzbergen coal. He was passed on from Akureyri
to Reykjavik by plane, and, whether through his initiative
and courage or whether through other intelligence available, a month later Canadian troops landed at Spitzbergen
and destroyed the coal dumps.

Paradoxically, with slender chances of enemy inter-

---

[7] The stretch of sea on which Blonduös is situated is called the
"Hunafloi," "Huna" being the Icelandic for "Bear." A bear was known
once to have floated ashore at Blonduös. But the adoption of the sign
was perhaps as faithful to fact as the dispatch of a R.T.O. to Blonduös
to work on 100 yards of railway line at the docks.

R

1941   ference, the training facilities were excellent and musketry
enthusiasts would have found the fulfilment of their
ambitions in the opportunities the country offered for
field firing. To encourage initiative reconnaissance parties
went off for days at a time and were left to their own
devices. The area covered was, of course, far too large
for the Battalion ever to concentrate for unit training.
The Icelanders were not at first very forthcoming hosts.
It was said that the Americans had previously aroused
their suspicions of the wealthy world outside. But at
least it was with many regrets that Battalion Headquarters
said good-bye to the schoolmaster at Reykjaskoli, who
had successfully filled an invaluable role as interpreter.

From Reykjaskoli a move was made to Borganes and
later to Brautarholt. In both places accommodation was
in Nissen huts. It was at Borganes that a fine N.C.O. of
the Battalion, Colour-Sergeant Church, the Orderly Room
Sergeant, lost his life in a useless vehicle accident. Thus
a good Worcestershire man today lies buried in the
Borganes churchyard in distant Iceland.

From Brautarholt, after handing over to the 6th Bn.
U.S. Marine Corps, a move was made on 19th September
into the Faroese[8] tented camp just outside Reykjavik.
Finally on 25th September the Battalion disembarked at
Greenock and set out for Milton Barracks, Gravesend.
They quickly settled down to the normal routine of
training, with companies going out for three weeks to
guard airfields in Kent. It was then that General Paget,
the G.O.C., Home Forces, broke the news that, along
with some seventy other battalions, the 12th Battalion
Worcestershire Regiment were to be converted to gun-
1942   ners; and accordingly on 28th February, 1942, the
Battalion changed its identity and became the 179th
Field Regiment, R.A., and as such were destined to meet
the 1st Battalion in close co-operation two years later in
France[9]. But a change in name connoted no change in
spirit and the old tradition passed on.

Today the Commanding Officer of the 12th Battalion,

---

[8] Personnel from the Faroe Islands had been brought in to build
the aerodrome.
[9] 45 Infantry Training Centre, being formed at Chichester, took
2 officers and 60 other ranks.

as secretary of the Victory Club in London, is responsible   1942
for an association of some 19,000 members, among whom,
one likes to think, may be some of his former comrades of
the bleak coasts of Iceland.

Milton Barracks, Gravesend, has sad memories for
soldiers of the Worcestershire Regiment, for it was there
that the old 3rd Battalion had also had to face disband-
ment in 1923.

CHAPTER FOURTEEN

NORTON BARRACKS

1921 THE old order changes ; and in the interests of history those changes must be faithfully recorded. We therefore turn from the action of life in the battalions of the Regiment in peace or war to the less spectacular and sometimes extremely complicated measures in administration which marked a transition in organization from 1939 until the present day. This chapter is also devised to cover those many episodes and matters of interest which in one way or another have had their focus at Norton though their alternative association may well be with the units of a family which has been scattered in different corners of the world. Amid much change Norton Barracks represents all that is permanent in the life of the Regiment, and for that reason alone it demands its separate record.

Over the years the Barracks have seen little structural alteration, and within the period of this History they have remained the solid homely mass of red brick which housed the soldiers of the Queen. Outside the Barracks, during World War II, hutted accommodation was constructed to take in the additional personnel required by the new Infantry Training Centre, and this area is now held by a unit of the Royal Artillery, the 49th Anti-Tank Regiment.

In 1939 the function of the Depot was still to train recruits and administer the regimental home. Early in 1940 a principle was established by which training divided into "Primary" training, covering the first six weeks of service, and "Corps" training, which concentrated on the more advanced training for infantry as such. To meet requirements the Infantry Training Centre (I.T.C.) was set up at Norton with two Primary Training Companies and two Corps Training Companies, the old Depot dwindling to a small Depot party and reduced to a strength 1940 of four officers and a few other ranks.

In July, 1946, orders were received for the Corps Training Companies and Headquarters to move to Oswestry to establish a new Infantry Training Centre. But a Primary Training Wing of two companies was left behind at Norton to be administered by No. 20 Holding Battalion, which had just arrived.

On arrival at Oswestry four companies were formed to represent the four regiments of the I.T.C., and these were respectively No. 1 (Cheshire), No. 2 (Worcestershire), No. 3 (South Staffordshire) and No. 4 (North Staffordshire). The new I.T.C. was now known as the West-Midland I.T.C., and was shortly afterwards redesignated "The Mercian Brigade Training Centre." At Norton in the meanwhile No. 20 Holding Battalion had been disbanded, and on 28th November, 1946, No. 29 Primary Training Centre (P.T.C.) was formed under the command of Lieut.-Colonel L. G. H. Bryant with two Primary Training Companies.

Throughout these changes the Regimental Depot party had continued to function. Not the least of its duties was to guard jealously the interests of the Regiment in the face of many minor problems raised by officers in authority who had only a passing interest in Norton Barracks as the permanent regimental home. In addition, it was, of course, responsible for the permanent records and administration of all matters pertaining to the Regiment.

Administrative changes followed thick and fast. In January, 1948, the Mercian Brigade I.T.C. moved from Oswestry to Lichfield. Thus at this stage personnel trained in the P.T.C. at Norton due for the Worcestershire Regiment completed their training at Lichfield. A further change was effected when the four-company organization which had functioned at Oswestry gave way to the existing arrangements by which one Regular battalion of the Mercian Brigade Group became the recognized centre for training all personnel selected for regiments of the Mercian Brigade from the various P.T.Cs. Battalions of the group now take it in turn to function as "the Mercian Brigade Training Battalion,"

1948 to which is attached a Group Training Centre with a small administrative Staff. The background to these changes was clearly and convincingly set out in a letter of June, 1948, from the Colonel of the Regiment, Brigadier B. C. S. Clarke, to all officers.

"An even greater change is the introduction of the group system by which regiments are brigaded together in county Groups. It was found to some extent in the 1914-18 war, but very much more so in the recent war, that more often than not it became impossible to post reinforcements to their own regiments. As an alternative to a Corps of Infantry it is thought that by confining such postings within brigades much of the regimental spirit may live again within the brigade group. We have been grouped with the Cheshire, North and South Stafford-shire Regiments under the name of the Mercian Brigade. Unwelcome as these changes undoubtedly are, it must be admitted that it is difficult to find a practical alternative, and officers and men may now be called to serve in any regiment of the group."

In April, 1948, it was decided that all personnel, both Regular and National Service, should undergo "basic" training, as primary training was now designated, with their own arm of the service. P.T.Cs. were therefore disbanded. Thus a recruit for the Regiment now joins at Lichfield.

The conditions of modern war demand that personnel be available for posting over a far wider field than previously obtained. A modern recruiting system has to be both fluid and flexible ; and in fulfilling these require-ments the old personal attachment and interest of a recruit for the regiment of his choice must to some extent be sacrificed in general administrative interests. The Regiment has taken these changes with calm resignation ; and it is some slight compensation that in April, 1948, the Depot Staff was increased to four officers and twenty-two other ranks with a clear-cut function as the custodian of all regimental property and with general responsibility for the regimental home. The new functions of a Depot were defined as to act as the Headquarters of the Regiment, to provide administrative facilities for Territorial

Army and Cadet training, and to hold various categories 1948
of personnel. Simultaneously with the Depot increase in
establishment, the appointment of an Administrative
Officer was recognized, a serving Captain or retired
officer being eligible. Thus it was that Norton Barracks
was able to welcome back Colonel S. W. Jones, who has
assumed control of many matters of regimental administration outside the sphere of normal Depot responsibility.
The duties of an Administrative Officer are varied and
manifold, and must vary greatly according to conditions
in different regiments.

It was with the object of ensuring that subsequent to
the infantry reorganization in June, 1948, the full weight
of preserving the regimental home should not fall on the
small Regimental Depot that the Colonel of the Regiment
issued an appeal to all officers, past and present. In
particular, attention was drawn to the difficulty of main-
taining the Officers' Mess, a difficulty accentuated when
officers of the Depot lived out. The appeal covered
proposals for an annual subscription from all officers. As
a result the Regiment still has its own Mess at Norton
Barracks, which is a gathering place from time to time
for numbers of officers, past and present. In the same
way the Sergeants' Mess is also now a Regimental Mess,
fulfilling the same function for past and present members
of the various Sergeants' Messes of the Regiment.

The recent establishment of the Regimental Room at
Norton was a happy way of realizing the need to provide
a room for present and past other ranks of the Regiment
to meet and use as a home. It is now furnished and
decorated with pictures and trophies and readily combines
the pleasant atmosphere of a club and a home.

The above is but a recital of the bare bones of drab
administrative matters. Behind the facts are many small
episodes of human interest which must be left to the
ready imagination of all with experience of the "correct
channels" of military administration.

Before passing to other matters of regimental concern,
a record should be made of an association of interest
which logically can have no particular claim to any
definite point in Regimental History either in time or

location. After World War I two Australian units, the 29th and 36th Australian Infantry Battalions, were appropriately allied to the Regiment, the former stationed in East Melbourne, the latter in Haberfield. There was unfortunately never an opportunity to translate the association into more than an alliance on paper, and on the reorganization of the Australian land forces after World War II these battalions were not re-raised.

In describing the high-lights of work or play an attempt has been made to touch on those achievements which merit a record as they occur in the lives of the battalions of the Regiment. But there is one aspect of play which is particularly associated with Norton Barracks and which therefore seems to demand a separate reference ; for cricket is a game which has flourished from an encouragement and interest directed from the Depot in a manner which does not apply in the case of the other methods of chasing a ball or in athletics. It is natural that it should be so, for not only are the hopes of a great home of county cricket centred round a well-known setting down by the River Severn within the city of Worcester, but also the shady seclusion of the green field within the Barracks has come to be regarded as the appropriate home of a regiment which reflects the devotion of its county to the great game.

After World War I the annual cricket week was held during mid-July. Cricket waned during World War II, to be revived in 1946, and since 1947 the week has been held during the last week in June.

Arrangements for the week of four days' cricket have always been the prerogative of the Officer Commanding the Depot and his staff. If team-building proved the major problem before the war, more than ever is it a headache in modern times when, without a Regular battalion at home, and with the Territorial battalion occupied in building up its strength, the services of officers and other ranks who have left the Regiment have been sought and exploited : and very readily they have responded to the call.

The machinery for assembling the regimental team has to be put into operation as early as March, and after much correspondence and many frantic telephone calls the team is ready to take the field at the end of June. An air of relief then pervades the Depot orderly room. Over the years a number of friendly foes have afforded annual fixtures. "The Worcestershire Gentlemen," "Hereford Gentlemen," "Shropshire Gentlemen" and "Warwickshire Imps," all well-known clubs in the Midlands, have been welcome visitors with whom many exciting finishes have been fought out. In 1925 at Worcester and 1926 at Aldershot matches were played against "our cousins," the Royal Lincolnshire Regiment. Unfortunately, there then ensued a long gap ; but in 1947 the contest was revived and has now been an annual fixture, being played alternate years at Lincoln and Worcester. The honours are so far equal, "our cousins" being victorious in 1948 and 1950, and the Regiment winning through in 1947 and 1949. Of the many performers with both bat and ball who might claim distinction, the name of Lieut.-Colonel A. C. Johnston[1] as a batsman during the period 1922-1939 will not be forgotten. His sterling efforts on many occasions in defeat or victory were an example always for the young entry. In recent years it is not too much to say that the enthusiastic direction of Lieut.-Colonel L. G. H. Bryant has been mainly responsible for the effective revival of regimental cricket. And so amid many difficulties and with absences through service abroad the game goes on. May it always be so !

Veterans of World War I must view with some bewilderment the many modifications and changes in dress which have been adopted by the infantry of the British Army in recent years. In 1922 officers were still wearing khaki breeches, puttees, and laced leggings. In 1925 dismounted officers took to plus-fours. In 1937 mounted officers gave up leggings and took to the "gunner-boot" with three straps. But with the passing of the horse and the need for a practical dress to stand up to all conditions, the Army as a whole went into battledress shortly before the outbreak of war in 1939. At the same time another sign of the times was the passing of mess dress, a new blue uniform being introduced which is to take the place

---

[1] Colonel A. C. Johnston, D.S.O.

of mess dress, blue patrol or full dress. The changes in head-dress have been more erratic. Between the wars a green and blue forage cap was introduced, Field Officers being distinguished by gold piping. When battledress appeared this gave way to its khaki counterpart, known officially as the "F.S. cap." This in turn was found unsuitable and a khaki beret in imitation of the Royal Tank Corps was adopted, which was later changed to the present dark blue beret. It was on the orders of the G.O.C., 43rd (Wessex) Division, that before embarking for Normandy his units took to a coloured backing to the badge on the beret, and thus it was that the 1st Battalion assumed the green backing for the first time at home in April, 1944, with the approval of the Regiment. A green backing to the badge on the topee had, of course, been worn in India for many years.

So far as the Regiment were concerned, interest was not so much in the general changes as with the more personal small problems of badges, facings, buttons and ties. Between the wars facings on the full-dress tunic changed from white to green, and it is on record that at a Levee at St. James's Palace on "The Glorious First of June" in 1931, twenty-seven officers of the 1st Battalion were presented by Field-Marshal Sir Claud Jacob, on their return from foreign service, in the new uniform. Captain H. FitzM. Stacke, in his History of the Regiment, has referred to the efforts which were made after World War I to return to the traditional elongated star of the Garter as a cap-badge. An unimpressive round bronze badge with a scroll had crept into use, and it took a Regimental Committee three years to effect a return to the old eight-pointed star in silver, the removal of the scroll allowing for the lengthened shape to be reintroduced. In 1930 an effort was made to standardize the dress of officers as between the two Regular battalions. The 1st Battalion, for example, had been wearing no stars on the collar in blue patrol. Thus if an officer from the 2nd Battalion transferred to the 1st Battalion his collar displayed two empty holes where formerly stars had appeared. The 2nd Battalion wore two buttons on the cuff of their khaki jacket. The 1st Battalion did not. These and other anomalies were rectified by a Regimental Committee.

It remains only to collect a few reflections on some institutions and aspects of regimental life and place them on record for future generations.

The life of a battalion is the story of its movements from A to B, the battles in which it has been engaged, its reactions to Plymouth, Malta, Shanghai or Aldershot. But the story of a regiment embraces many activities in England which in the case of the Worcestershire Regiment are followed with intense and constructive criticism by all ranks. It is to satisfy this vital enthusiasm of the Regiment as a family in which both serving and retired personnel have a stake that comment on a few features of common interest is added.

Such agencies as *Firm*, the Old Comrades Association, and the Museum at Norton are symbols of a vitality which will endure into the days when warfare becomes a matter for the science laboratories. Even so men will surely always have the last word.

Perhaps the first tribute should be to *Firm*, without which it would indeed have been difficult to write this story. In November, 1922, the 2nd Battalion started a journal, *The Green 'Un*. The first editor was Lieutenant E. H. Knott, of the Army Educational Corps, and the Commanding Officer at the time received a letter of encouragement and congratulation from the Colonel of the Regiment, General Sir George Higginson.

It seems curious to record that the necessity for a magazine to cover the activities of all battalions and the Regiment as a whole had not made itself felt previously. The need was not met until 1927, when the first issue of *Firm* appeared in November of that year. It happily coincided with the appointment of Field-Marshal Sir Claud Jacob as Colonel. It was perhaps not so much a case of the need for a Regimental Magazine not being appreciated as the practical difficulty of finding an editor with the necessary time and capacity to give to the work. For the first issue, Captain Crawford, a retired officer, volunteered to make a start. But his work in civilian life assumed such dimensions that he was unable to spare the time for a second number. Thus it was that a whole year passed before the second copy of *Firm* appeared in November, 1928. From that month onwards the Regimental Magazine has appeared regularly as a quarterly except for the duration of World War II. Even so, under various editors and in spite of paper shortage, it struggled on until May, 1941. There was then a gap until November, 1945. From the point of view of an author searching for material for a History, the issues during the war were of limited value since the demands of the censor meant the elimination of all names, dates and places even though it might be only a matter of an inter-company game of football. Subscriptions were maintained during the war years, and the first "peace" edition emerged in no way inferior to the pre-war standard. The annual subscription has remained at five shillings. Since its inception the printing of the magazine has been in the capable hands of the Messenger Company in Bromsgrove, who have produced a quality of print and paper of the highest standard. The form of the layout has not materially altered since 1927, with an Editorial, sections for Battalion and Company notes, notes on sport and individual contributions. The editor has rightly felt that contributions are not so much to be judged by their literary infallibility as by the manner in which they reflect the life of the Regiment.

The present editor, Colonel S. W. Jones, took over from Major Pereira in October, 1948, and in his hands the Regimental Magazine continues to constitute the link by which all members of the Regiment, past and present, are enabled to keep in touch with each other and with the movements of the Regular Battalion in its adventures abroad.

No mention of *Firm* would be complete without a reference to Major H. FitzM. Stacke for the labour and interest he continually gave to the magazine. His series of articles describing the actions which won Victoria Crosses for the Regiment were only one of his welcome contributions of research into past history.

Bound copies of *Firm* are kept in the Regimental Museum : and it is to the Museum that we turn for a very complete supplement to the Regimental Magazine in the study of history. To a layman the scope of the Museum and the care with which it is maintained come as something of a surprise : and if an outside comment were permitted it might be to the effect that such an institution lies so far from the centre of the city of Worcester, whose citizens should share facilities to view those many exhibits connected with the history of a Regiment which to a real degree is their proud possession. The Museum is, of course, open to the public, and a new Worcester Guide Book is to draw attention to it.

From such a wealth of material, it is difficult to pick out relics of particular interest. Exhibits range from an officer's sash of the 29th dating from the American War of Independence to the 75 mm. mountain gun captured at Maram Spur in Burma by the 7th Battalion in 1944. This, together with other Japanese weapons, was brought home by C.S.M. J. J. White, of Kidderminster, in the face of much opposition from Railway Transport Officers and Embarkation Staffs.

The portraits include Eric Kennington's splendid pastel work of Private Hunt, D.C.M., of the 1st Battalion, and J. P. Beadle's action picture of Gheluvelt. There is also a fine work by Matania of the battle of Neuve Chapelle. The artist is, of course, known for his vivid illustrations in the *Sphere* over a number of years. There is Sir Hubert Rance's flag flown by him as Governor of Burma, an emblem of British authority which will presumably never fly again. There is the Nazi flag captured by the 8th Battalion in France and a khidmatgar's belt to commemorate the association of the 2nd Battalion with the 6th Gurkha Rifles from 1942 to 1946. Perhaps one of the most striking exhibits is the bronze statuette, "The Sentry," by the late C. S. Jagger, who served with the Worcestershire Regiment in World War I and who used men of the Regiment as his models. "The Sentry" is a replica of his War Memorial at Paddington Station. His more familiar work is the impressive artillery memorial at Hyde Park Corner. These are but a few of the 1,400 exhibits which cover every phase of the life of the Regiment from the days of Farrington until 1950. Finally there is an excellent display of medals.

The Museum was started in the Depot Mess in embryo in 1933, and once again Major Stacke was responsible for its initiation, some badges and other relics left to the Officers' Mess by the late Colonel Everard being used as the nucleus of the collection. It was first housed in the Officers' Mess.

It is, however, Major H. P. E. Pereira whom we must thank for its subsequent expansion and layout ; and it was he who managed its affairs from 1944 to 1948, when he left to take up an important appointment as curator of the Scottish United Services Museum at Edinburgh.

In 1935 the Museum moved to the Keep. During the war it was housed in temporary hutments outside the Depot. But since the war it transferred to the top floor in Farrington block, where there is space to display exhibits in a manner in which they can be studied without that bewilderment which results when trophies are heaped together in close confusion. There is now a small but steady income from the friends of the Museum which enables medals and trophies to be purchased in the open market.

Until April, 1950, it was under the careful eye of Mr. Frank Lester, who as the guardian of so much history and tradition became known to many hundreds of the Regiment, past and present.

It was a tragedy that such a faithful servant of the Regiment was to be denied the experience of the reunion of April, 1950, for he died on 14th April, 1950, after an illness which he had faced with great courage and of which few were aware. Mr. Lester joined the Regiment in 1892, being posted to the 2nd Battalion on The Curragh in Ireland. After seeing service in South Africa and France he was wounded in November, 1918, and after a long period in hospital came to live in a regimental cottage outside Norton Barracks in 1926, taking charge of the Museum in 1935 when it was moved to the Keep. He was buried with full military honours at Norton churchyard, and it is good to know that a memorial in the Museum he loved so much will serve to remind future generations of a great servant of the Regiment.

The work of the Worcestershire Regiment's Association continues to play a vital part in the welfare and resettlement of all who have ever served with the Regiment, wherever they may be and whenever they are in need. It has been questioned whether in an era of National Insurance in a welfare state there is still scope for the work of a Regimental Association. The figures leave no room for doubt. In 1949 there were 521 applications for all types of assistance and advice, of which 399 were met. Grants and loans totalled £2,300. In distributing relief it is emphasized that the object is always to assist good men in the fundamental belief that God helps those who help themselves. The Association is, in fact, not merely a Society for dispensing charity.

On 1st September, 1949, the Association which formerly was universally known as the Worcestershire Regiment's Old Comrades Association changed to its present designation. In a letter the President, Lieut.-Colonel Sir John Reddie,[2] set out the reasons for the change. The old title, it seemed, was unpopular with the younger members who associated it with the veterans of the South African War! Sir John Reddie stressed that a change in the title involved no change in policy; and welfare, resettlement and comradeship continue to be the concern of the Association. Nevertheless, in spite of an official new name, old habits linger on, and the words "Old Comrades" are frequently in use in moments of forgetfulness! The offices of the Association are at 5, Foregate Street, Worcester.

A link which might in other circumstances have developed for the benefit of future generations of the Regiment is that which exists between the Regiment and three battalions of local cadets. They total about 700, the object being to prepare youth for national service. But apart from the wearing of the Regimental cap-badge by cadets, the link is a slender one. Cadets pass on to the Mercian Brigade and any domestic interest which might have developed is lost in vaguer claims on their loyalty.

Norton Barracks has been the scene of many ceremonial parades, symbols often of milestones in the regimental life. Indeed, the author's first introduction to Norton in September, 1949, is coloured by a memory of the band of the Coldstream Guards, who were in Wor-

---

[2] Lieut.-Colonel Sir J. Reddie, C.B., D.L.

cester for recruiting purposes, marching and counter-marching in full dress in front of Charlemont Block facing the Green. Here, only those prominent occasions are recalled which mark the more vital stages of constant regimental evolution.

The delivery up of the Colours of the 1st Battalion from the Cathedral in Worcester on 20th February, 1946, is perhaps an outstanding ceremony of recent times. For it marked an occasion on which the county of Worcestershire was able to express its gratitude and affection not only for the Battalion but for the Regiment which bore its name.

A special altar had been set up at the foot of the choir steps. At three o'clock in the afternoon the procession of the choir and Cathedral clergy made its way slowly from the Regimental Chapel of St. George to the altar. To the words of the 98th Psalm the brilliant splash of colour moved through the Cathedral and the Colours were laid on the altar.

At the time the Battalion was in Germany and so the Colours were taken over by a detachment of officers and men who had come to claim them. In solemn terms the Dean handed over the Colours and was in turn thanked by the Commanding Officer, Lieut.-Colonel C. P. G. Wills. The lesson was read by the Colonel of the Regiment, and a roll of drums heralded the National Anthem. There followed the Blessing. The Colour party rose and, to the Regimental Slow March, the Colours were marched down the aisle to the west door. There were many that day in the congregation who had shared the hopes and tragedies of Keren and Tobruk, who had known the comradeship of prison camps and who fought from Normandy into Germany. These men will have sensed that queer elation at the sight of the symbol of so much diverse heroism in distant lands, in the great Cathedral Church of their home town.

Outside, the people of Worcester had their opportunity to pay their tribute as the Colours were taken to the Drill Hall in Silver Street, there to be cased before being flown to Germany.

To the Dean of Worcester there is a debt of gratitude for the care he had lavished on a ceremony which in every

COLONELS OF THE REGIMENT

(*a*) General Sir George Higginson, G.C.B., G.C.V.O., 1893-1927.
(*b*) Field-Marshal Sir Claude Jacob, G.C.B., G.C.S.I., K.C.M.G., 1927-1938.
(*c*) Brigadier-General G. W. St. G. Grogan, V.C., C.B., C.M.G., D.S.O., 1938-1945.
(*d*) Brigadier B. C. S. Clarke, D.S.O., 1945-1950.
(*e*) Lieut.-General Sir Richard Gale, K.B.E., C.B., D.S.O., M.C., 1950.

detail reflected his purpose to complete a labour of love.

Over a year later, on 16th July, 1947, Norton was the scene of another ceremony. Though without the impressive background of the Cathedral to mark the occasion, the laying-up of the Colours of the 2nd Battalion at Norton was a ceremonial parade of simplicity and sadness. The Battalion cadre under Lieut.-Colonel F. S. Ramsay were there to represent the officers and men who had so recently rung down the curtain on their last act in Burma. From Lieut.-Colonel Ramsay, the Depot Commander, Lieut.-Colonel Bryant accepted the Colours for custody to be laid up in the Officers' Mess until such a time as the 2nd Battalion are again called upon to uphold traditions which date from the year 1701.

Both escorts turned out in a manner worthy of the occasion, and the Colonel of the Regiment, who addressed the parade, was quick to comment on their high standard of drill. For him the parade was of personal appeal and significance.

Two months later the 2nd Battalion were again to remind us of their continuing identity. This time the ceremony was in London at the Royal Hospital, Chelsea. The Colours of certain regiments had for long been in the custody of the Governor of the Royal Hospital, and by command of the King they were returned to their units. In the case of the 2nd Battalion The Worcestershire Regiment the Colours had been presented on 10th November, 1816, at Portsmouth, on the anniversary of the battle of Nivelle. The Royal Hospital is an ideal setting for such an occasion, even though the scars of enemy action were still in evidence. The Colonel of the Regiment received the Colours, the King's Colour being handed over by Pensioner G. C. Murphy, D.C.M., who had joined the Army in 1882, coming to the 1st Battalion at Aden in 1896.

Another pensioner, Private W. Lamb, who had joined the 1st Battalion in 1886, was a witness at the ceremony, and the gathering of members of the Regiment included Lieut.-Colonels Watkins, Court, and Ramsay.

The Colours, faded and threadbare, now hang in the Regimental Museum. Their material lustre has vanished.

S

Yet their worn fabric tells a story of deeper significance than any later brilliance.

At some point the historian is faced with the choice of a date on which to close the present record of a great regiment : and in the present case there can be little doubt that 15th April, 1950, is as certain a landmark as would be found within the day-to-day events which comprise regimental history. The 1st Battalion were recently back from Germany and the opportunity was taken to concentrate several functions in one memorable day, a task which must have taxed the patience and capacity of the entire Depot Staff to the full. They rose nobly to the occasion and the day passed only too quickly for those hundreds of old comrades who had gathered from all corners of England to witness the parade on the county cricket ground, the ceremony in the Cathedral, and finally to dip into memories of the past for an hour or so in a great family gathering at Norton Barracks.

The afternoon opened with the presentation of silver drums to the Regiment by the Mayor,[3] coupled with the official grant of free entry to the city. The latter privilege was set out in a finely phrased resolution which was subsequently read out by the Town Clerk.

For an hour previously crowds had been gathering on the cricket ground. Fortunately, those responsible for arrangements were rewarded by the behaviour of the weather. In spite of ominous clouds the rain held off, while we were rewarded by the appearance of the sun at a moment when it was needed to lend that extra touch of warm colour which gave the ceremony a rich splendour rare in the modern days of drab mechanized ceremonial. Before the arrival of the Colours of the 1st, 2nd and 7th Battalions with the escort, furnished by the 1st Battalion, the band of the Cheshire Regiment entertained the spectators with light music, and for those privileged to witness the ceremony from the cricket pavilion the arrival of the Mayor and Corporation in full regalia was a spectacular diversion. Indeed, it is no reflection on subsequent events to say that the hat of the gentleman carrying the Mayor's sword of state was a constant source of astonishment for

---

[3] Alderman T. S. Bennett.

the more privileged spectators. It might well have been
lent for the occasion by the White Queen in "Alice in
Wonderland."

Punctually at 2.30 p.m. the Battalion, under command
of Lieut.-Colonel A. H. Gillmore, O.B.E., and Colour
parties marched on to the ground, led by the Band and
Drums in full dress. In his inspection the Mayor was
accompanied by the retiring Colonel of the Regiment, his
predecessor, Brigadier-General Grogan, and his successor,
Lieut.-General Gale.[4] Following the inspection, the Mayor
addressed the assembled company in a happy speech of
acknowledgement of the city of Worcester's appreciation
of the great services of their county regiment in two World
Wars. There was a brief summary of the great heritage
of two and a half centuries and a sober reference to the
grim demands of the international situation of today.

In reply Brigadier Clarke thanked the Mayor for the
city's magnificent presentation, adding that the drums
would serve as a reminder of the warm interest for the
comfort and welfare of the men of the Regiment displayed
by the city and county throughout long years of war.

But to the casual spectator more significant than the
details of a carefully-planned ceremonial was the spectacle
of a new generation of the Worcestershire on parade
receiving the tribute of their people in as fair a setting as
could be found. It was indeed a happy gesture of the sun
to shine out on a foreground of khaki and colour on the
green field, yet catch the mellow stone of the great
Cathedral which provided so glorious a background.

There followed a march through the town and some
2,000 Old Comrades fell in behind the Escort to the
Colours and marched through crowded streets, the Mayor
taking the salute in front of the Guildhall. Previously on
the cricket field a voice which sometimes coaxed and
sometimes threatened had had some difficulty in assembling a mildly difficult and light-hearted parade. But
once on the road behind a band, to the strains of the
march they knew so well, the Old Comrades shed the
years and were for a few minutes again the men of former
ceremonies of bygone days. In the new order, how wel-

_____
[4] See Appendix 1.

come it is sometimes to be reminded that a city, a county and its regiment are still one !

The parade marched on into the Cathedral, where the scene was laid for the unveiling of the Regimental War Memorial in St. George's Chapel and its dedication by the Bishop.

Great care had been taken to frame an impressive service covering the unveiling and dedication of the Memorial. After hymns and prayers the Colour parties which had taken post at the west end of the Cathedral moved to the Regimental Slow March up the nave to the Chapel entrance in the North Choir transept. Inside the Chapel the Colonel of the Regiment, after a short address, unveiled the Memorial, the Dean accepting it on behalf of the Cathedral and the Bishop adding his dedication. Brigadier Clarke briefly outlined the circumstances in which no less than a total of 579 officers and 10,308[5] other ranks had given their lives for their country in two world wars, and added that in remembering them others also who had suffered grievous bodily harm should not be forgotten. There followed the "Last Post" and "Reveille," and a memorable service closed with "Abide with Me," while finally the Colours, now at the choir steps, were lowered to the National Anthem.

The Memorial is simple but impressive in Hopton Wood stone of a light greyish-pink colour. It is surmounted by the Regimental Badge embossed and the Naval Crown and Irish Harp are at the base.

After the service there was a move to Norton Barracks, where tea was ready in a tent large enough to accommodate a circus. Here many old friendships were drawn out of their "cold storage" and experiences over the years exchanged. The outgoing and incoming Colonels of the Regiment made short speeches and, generally helped by beer, this happy reunion proved a great family party when many old friends could at last find out how fate had dealt with him or her since those more leisured days when friendships were not made in a hurry. "Those were the days" was indeed the background to the many memories refreshed on 15th April.

---

[5] World War I : Officers 505, other ranks 9,463 ; World War II : Officers 74, other ranks 845.

COLONELS OF THE REGIMENT

General Sir George Higginson, G.C.B.

In 1922, the year from which this record dates, General Sir George Wentworth Alexander Higginson, G.C.B., had already held the Colonelcy of the Regiment for twenty-nine years. Born on 21st June, 1826, he joined the Grenadier Guards in 1845 and served as Adjutant in the Crimean War. In Lady Butler's well-known picture, "The Roll Call," it is Higginson who figures in the foreground.

From the date of his appointment as Colonel in 1893 Sir George Higginson associated himself closely with every aspect of regimental life, and when he died on 1st February, 1927, there was no one actually serving with the Regiment who could remember the days before him. With the passing of a grand old soldier in his 101st year the work of one who had come to be regarded as an institution was ended.

Field-Marshal Sir Claud W. Jacob, G.C.B., G.C.S.I., K.C.M.G.

Sir Claud Jacob, who assumed the Colonelcy on 1st February, 1927, served his first two years of service in the old 29th Regiment before transferring to the Indian Army. Like many officers of the Indian Service, he was conscious of a great debt to the battalion of the British Army in which he had served his apprenticeship, and he welcomed the opportunity to repay that debt in identifying himself with every interest of the Regiment and devoting much time and thought to his duties as their Colonel.

He was born in 1863 of a long line of soldiers whose name is perpetuated in a fine cavalry regiment, Jacob's Horse. After education at Sherborne School and Sandhurst he transferred from the British Service to the Indian Staff Corps in 1884.

He saw service in the Zhob Valley Expedition, 1890, and again on the North-West Frontier in 1901. It was as Colonel on the General Staff that he arrived in France in 1914 with the Indian Expeditionary Force and in 1915 received command of the Dehra Dun Brigade. He continued to go from strength to strength, commanding the 21st Division and in May, 1916, assuming command of the 2nd Corps with the rank of Lieutenant-General.

As a Corps Commander he fought through the Somme battle in 1916, Passchendaele in 1917 and the hard fighting in 1918. After command of a Corps on the Rhine in 1919 he returned to India in 1920 as the late Lord Rawlinson's Chief of Staff, in which capacity the heavy burden of seeing through Lord Rawlinson's reorganization of the Indian Army fell on his shoulders. From 1924 to 1925 he commanded the Northern Command in India, acting in 1925 for a short period as Commander-in-Chief. During this period he was made A.D.C. General to His Majesty The King and was promoted to Field-Marshal in 1926.

Returning to England, he held the extremely important post of Military Secretary at the India Office from 1926 to 1930, and in 1938 he was appointed Constable of the Tower of London. Elsewhere is described the happy occasion when by good fortune the instalment of the Field-Marshal as Constable on 1st June, 1938, coincided with the 1st Battalion's responsibility for duty at the Tower of London.

In November, 1938, Sir Claud handed over his office. He should have retired in 1933 at the age of seventy, but, to the great joy of the Regiment, his tenure was extended by His Majesty for another five years.

After surrendering the Colonelcy, Sir Claud Jacob continued to take an active interest in the affairs of his Regiment throughout the war years, and it was good to see him at Harrow in 1943 when the 1st Battalion once again assumed its identity.

It would be difficult to assess in detail the many services he rendered. He was responsible for the restoration of the ancient Lion badge of the 29th and the motto "Firm" of the 36th to the centre of the Regimental Colour.

At his side Lady Jacob had quietly played her part as hostess with great charm and high sense of duty. To her the sympathy of all ranks of the Regiment went out when her husband in his eighty-fifth year died at King's College Hospital on 2nd June, 1948.

Brigadier-General G. W. St. G. Grogan, V.C., C.B., C.M.G., D.S.O.

In November, 1938, an old and distinguished officer of the Regiment was appointed as Colonel. General Grogan was born on 1st September, 1875, and first saw service with the West India Regiment in 1896. It was not until January, 1908, that he joined the Worcestershire Regiment as a Captain.

General Grogan's earlier service was of that varied nature which must appeal to all those who search for the old element of adventure in soldiering. In 1898 he was in operations in Sierra Leone and at Lagos in the following year. For five years from 1902 he served with the Egyptian Army.

Lieut.-Colonel Grogan's command of the 1st Battalion in France in World War I is described in detail by Captain FitzM. Stacke in his History of the Regiment. His leadership culminated in the action which was to win the Victoria Cross on the Bouleuse Ridge on

29th May, 1918. On that occasion only reckless bravery could save the day, and Colonel Grogan accepted the challenge. It is perhaps appropriate to quote the citation : "Shells, bombs and bullets struck all round him and presently his horse was shot ; but he mounted another horse and continued to ride along the firing line, cheering and encouraging his men, miraculously escaping death at every instant and inspiring all who saw him, both French and British." A picture by Gilbert Holiday recording the event is in possession of the Regiment at Norton Barracks. Subsequently he commanded the 23rd Brigade.

After the war from May until October, 1919, he commanded 238 Infantry Brigade in the Force operating in North Russia, later proceeding to India to command the 3rd Battalion.

It was his sad responsibility to disband the Battalion and lead a small cadre back to Gravesend, where they dispersed. Later he commanded the 5th Brigade at Aldershot. Brigadier-General Grogan retired in 1926 and in 1933 became a member of the distinguished Corps of Gentlemen-at-Arms. He was A.D.C. to the King from 1920 to 1926.

When in 1938 he succeeded the late Sir Claud Jacob as Colonel of the Regiment he was destined to serve his tenure throughout the strenuous war years of a Second World War. With memories of the value of the personal touch in war, he threw himself into the task of encouraging all units of the Regiment whether their duty lay at home or abroad. It would be invidious to single out any particular occasion from the many on which he was prominent in his devotion and interest for the Regiment and its welfare.

On reaching the age limit he retired on 28th August, 1945, when Brigadier Clarke assumed the Colonelcy. But he continued to take an active interest in all matters concerning the life of the Regiment, whether administrative or social ; and he was last seen participating in the great ceremonial parade on 15th April, 1950, at Worcester.

Brigadier B. C. S. Clarke, D.S.O.

On 1st September, 1945, Brigadier Clarke took over his responsibilities from Brigadier-General Grogan. There can be few officers who could claim a closer association of family and sentiment than Brigadier Clarke, for his father joined the 29th in 1868 and his mother was of the family of Ensign Vance who died carrying one of the Colours of the 29th at Albuhera. After Wellington College and Sandhurst, Brigadier Clarke joined the 4th (Militia) Battalion on 1st January, 1899, being granted a Regular Commission into the Regiment in 1903 after service in South Africa.

Brigadier Clarke was to see most of his service with the 2nd Battalion, and it must indeed have been hard for him as Colonel of the Regiment to face the decision which terminated the life of the old 36th. He followed the fortunes of the Battalion between the wars in

South Africa and India, where in 1912 he was appointed Adjutant. Returning with them to Aldershot in 1913, he served as Adjutant when the Battalion went to France in August, 1914, and fought with them at Mons, through the Ypres battles and at Gheluvelt. After the war at first the 3rd Battalion brought him to Dover and Dublin. But from 1922 onwards, with the exception of a spell of command at the Depot, he was destined to serve his time with the 2nd Battalion, which he commanded at Plymouth in 1929. It was his fortune to take his Battalion to Malta, where, in as happy a setting for routine soldiering as is possible to find, he was able to complete his four years' command.

In 1934 he was promoted Brigadier to command 145 Brigade, T.A., giving up command in 1938. In 1939 he held command of North Aldershot Area for two years until retired for age.

When succeeding to the Colonelcy of the Regiment in September, 1945, he assumed his duties at a period which perhaps, in view of the many drastic administrative decisions covering reorganization, demanded a more constant attention to regimental affairs than is the case in normal times. The circumstances of an officer in retirement are not such as to lighten the burden of duty, and Brigadier Clarke gave freely and unstintingly of his time and capacity. His last public function as Colonel of the Regiment has been recorded elsewhere when, on behalf of the Regiment, he received the presentation silver drums from the city of Worcester and unveiled the Regimental War Memorial on 15th April, 1950.

A few days later he laid down his responsibilities of office and handed on his duties to his successor. It was an appropriate occasion in that a Colonel of the Regiment who has long had a keen eye for ceremonial as a symbol of discipline and morale was able to witness his Regiment on a parade worthy of the many great occasions of the past.

Lieut.-General Sir Richard N. Gale, K.B.E., C.B., D.S.O., M.C.

Sir Richard Gale, who has succeeded Brigadier Clarke, joined the Worcestershire Regiment in 1915 and was for the major portion of the 1914-18 war attached to the Machine Gun Corps. It was as an officer of that fine Corps that he won the Military Cross. After the war he served with both the 3rd and 1st Battalions in India. In 1930 he received accelerated promotion into the Duke of Cornwall's Light Infantry. There followed a period on the Staff, first as Brigade Major at Ferozepore and later at the War Office.

World War II was to bring General Gale a rich and varied experience of command. After commanding a Battalion of the Leicestershire Regiment he was appointed to command No. 1 Parachute Brigade. In 1943 and 1944 he commanded the 6th Airborne Division, and in 1945 he commanded the 1st Airborne Corps. Thus the responsibility for vital aspects of the campaign in Normandy and Belgium was upon his shoulders. After the war he commanded the 1st Infantry Division and later was G.O.C., British Troops, in Egypt. His services in France had won him the D.S.O., and he was created C.B. in 1945 and a Commander of the Legion of Merit, U.S.A., in 1948. In the King's birthday honours, 1950, he was created K.B.E.

General Gale is now Director-General of Military Training at the War Office. The unpredictable character of international events more than ever throws a burden of heavy responsibility on the General Officer directing the training of the British Army, and it is therefore with pride and gratitude that the Worcestershire Regiment recognize the time and care that General Gale is able to devote to regimental matters in the midst of heavy duties.

COMMANDING OFFICERS

FIRST BATTALION

H. A. Fulton	1919—1923
L. M. Stevens, D.S.O.	1923—1927
W. F. O. Faviell, D.S.O.	1927—1931
J. F. Leman, D.S.O.	1931—1935
S. A. Gabb, O.B.E., M.C.	1935—1939
E. L. G. Lawrence, D.S.O., M.C.	1939—1942

SECOND BATTALION

C. M. G. Davidge, D.S.O.	1921—1925
F. P. Dunlop, C.B.E., D.S.O.	1925—1929
B. C. S. Clarke, D.S.O.	1929—1933
J. H. Pelly	1933—1937
C. Deakin, O.B.E.	1937—1940

SEVENTH BATTALION

F. M. Tomkinson, D.S.O.	1920—1922
E. F. du Sautoy, T.D.	1922—1928
G. G. Elkington, D.S.O.	1928—1932
W. R. Prescott, M.C.	1932—1936
R. H. Edwards, T.D.	1936—1939
J. Parkes, M.C., D.C.M.	1939—1940

EIGHTH BATTALION

W. R. Chichester, O.B.E.	1921—1923
W. E. L. Cotton, O.B.E., M.C.	1923—1927
A. V. Rowe	1927—1931
A. O. Needham, C.B.E., M.C.	1931—1935
E. M. Buck, M.C.	1935—1939

SUBSTANTIVE LIEUTENANT-COLONELS

D. Chesney, O.B.E.	1940—1942
R. H. M. Lee	1942—1944
P. W. Hargreaves, M.C.	1942—1945
S. W. Jones	1944—1947
J. O. Knight, D.S.O.	1945—1948
R. E. L. Tuckey	1947—
A. H. Gillmore, O.B.E.	1948—

WAR-TIME COMMANDERS

FIRST BATTALION

E. L. G. Lawrence, D.S.O., M.C.	... ...	1939—1941[1]
J. O. Knight, D.S.O.	...	1941—1942[2]
W. R. Cox (K.S.L.I.)		Jan. 1943—Sept. 1943
R. B. Moss, M.B.E.		Sept. 1943—Jan. 1944
A. R. Harrison		Jan. 1944—7 Aug. 1944
R. E. Osborne-Smith, D.S.O. (Northamptonshire Regt.)		Aug. 1944—Nov. 1944
A. W. N. L. Vickers (K.O.Y.L.I.)	...	Nov. 1944—Feb. 1945
M. R. J. Hope-Thomson, D.S.O., M.C. (R.S.F.)		

SECOND BATTALION

C. Deakin, O.B.E.	...	1937—1940
P. W. Hargreaves, M.C.		Nov. 1940—May 1943
B. C. Wilkinson (K.O.Y.L.I.)		May 1943—Nov. 1943
B. G. Symes, D.S.O., O.B.E. (Dorsets) ...		Nov. 1943—Oct. 1945
G. Mander-Jones (York and Lancaster Regt.)		Oct. 1945—Mar. 1946
J. O. Knight, D.S.O.[3]		May 1946—Sept. 1946
F. S. Ramsay		Dec. 1946—Sept. 1947

SEVENTH BATTALION

J. Parkes, M.C., D.C.M.	...	1939—June 1940
T. L. Molloy (Dorsets)		June 1940—Oct. 1941
R. V. C. Cavendish (Sherwood Foresters)[4]		Oct. 1941—Aug. 1942
E. F. S. Versfeld		Nov. 1942—Mar. 1944
A. A. J. Stocker, D.S.O. (S.W.B.)[5] ...		Mar. 1944—May 1944
C. A. Street (S. Staffs)[6]		June 1944—Feb. 1945
T. A. Irvine, D.S.O., T.D. (Cameronians)		Feb. 1945—Aug. 1945
J. B. Brierley, M.C.		Aug. 1945—Oct. 1945

EIGHTH BATTALION

J. Johnstone		Mar. 1939—Jan. 1943
R. B. Moss, M.B.E.		Jan. 1943—Sept. 1943
J. W. Hallowes, M.C. (K.S.L.I.) ...		Sept. 1943—July 1944
W. Vale (S. Staffs)		July 1944—Mar. 1945
A. R. Harrison		Mar. 1945—Aug. 1945

---

[1] Lieut.-Colonel W. R. Bucknall (Black Watch) commanded April—September, 1941.

[2] Lieut.-Colonel P. A. A. D'Oyle commanded the nucleus from Tobruk in Cairo, August, 1942.

[3] Major A. G. S. Edgar and Major G. G. H. Peace both commanded for short periods, 23rd September, 1946—19th December, 1946.

[4] Lieut.-Colonel J. P. O'B. Twohig, C.B.E., D.S.O. (Royal Inniskilling Fusiliers).

[5] Major J. B. Brierley, M.C., commanded for the period 23rd May, 1944, until 29th June, 1944.

[6] Killed in action. Battle of Dawete (Irrawaddy), 8th February, 1945.

NINTH BATTALION

J. Parkes, M.C., D.C.M.	Aug. 1939—Sept. 1939
R. H. Edwards, T.D.	Sept. 1939—Oct. 1939
W. R. Prescott, M.C.[7]	Oct. 1939—Oct. 1940
R. R. Cripps (Artists Rifles)	Nov. 1940—Sept. 1942
W. E. Tolley, M.C. (Royal Lincolns) ...	Sept. 1942—Jan. 1943
J. H. O. Wilsey, O.B.E., D.S.O.	Jan. 1943—Oct. 1943
K. G. Exham (Duke of Wellington's Regt.)	Oct. 1943—May 1944
M. M. A. Bryant	May 1944—July 1944
C. P. G. Wills, O.B.E.	Aug. 1944—July 1945
D. H. Nott, D.S.O., M.C.	July, 1945—Dec. 1945

TENTH BATTALION

A. R. Kettle (5th R. Inniskilling D.G.) ...	Aug. 1939—Sept. 1939
D. Chesney, O.B.E.	Sept. 1939—Nov. 1940
A. T. Burlton	Dec. 1940—Jan. 1942
C. P. G. Wills, O.B.E.	Jan. 1942—Aug. 1944
D. J. Stevens	Aug. 1944—Oct. 1944
C. W. D. Chads (Green Howards) ...	Oct. 1944—Nov. 1944

ELEVENTH BATTALION

E. B. de Courcy-Ireland, M.B.E., M.V.O.	June, 1940—July 1940
C. V. W. Court, M.C.	July, 1940—May 1941
W. R. Cox (K.S.L.I.)	July 1942—Dec. 1942

TWELFTH BATTALION

A. P. Watkins, M.C.	June 1940—Mar. 1942

POST-WAR COMMANDERS

FIRST BATTALION

C. P. G. Wills, O.B.E.	July 1945—June 1946[8]
R. E. L. Tuckey	July 1946—Jan. 1949[9]
A. H. Gillmore, O.B.E.	Mar. 1949—

SEVENTH BATTALION

S. H. C. Stotherd (Cheshire Regt.) ...	Nov. 1945—Jan. 1947
T. A. M. Bolland (R.I.F.)	Jan. 1947—Feb. 1947
H. J. L. Lattey, T.D.	Mar. 1947—

EIGHTH BATTALION

J. O. Knight, D.S.O.	Aug. 1945—Feb. 1946

---

[7] Major R. G. Minchin officiated in command from 8th October to 8th November, 1940.

[8] Major A. H. Nott acted in command 3rd June, 1946—7th July, 1946.

[9] Major J. W. C. Williams, D.S.O. (N. Staffs) acted in command 28th January, 1949—3rd March, 1949.

HONOURS AND AWARDS, 1939-1946

THE MOST EXCELLENT ORDER OF THE BRITISH EMPIRE

COMMANDER

Brigadier J. H. O. Wilsey, D.S.O. ...	Western Europe	...	24.1.46

OFFICERS

Lieut.-Colonel L. A. Bishop	... Western Europe	...	2.8.45
Lieut.-Colonel M. J. Glenn ...	... Italy	...	13.12.45
Lieut.-Colonel R. H. M. Lee	... Home Forces	...	19.10.44
Lieut.-Colonel J. Milner ...	... Home Forces	...	1.1.46
Lieut.-Colonel C. P. G. Wills	... Home Forces	...	1.1.44

MEMBERS

Lieut. I. G. Bain	Prison escape	...	29.6.44
Capt. A. C. L. Bennett	Italy	...	13.12.45
Lieut. St. J. C. Brooke-Johnson ...	Special Air Service	...	23.1.47
Major G. C. Cave	India ...	...	14.6.45
Major D. N. Cronin	Home Forces	...	1.1.46
Lieut. (Q.M.) A. H. Cooper ...	Middle East	...	16.4.42
Major R. A. C. Du Vivier	Western Europe	...	24.1.46
Capt. W. J. Field	Sicily ...	...	23.3.44
Major E. J. Haywood	Caribbean ...	...	1.1.46
Sub-Conductor V. G. Morris ...	Burma ...	...	8.2.45
Lieut. (Q.M.) J. R. Mountford ...	Burma ...	...	6.6.46
Major L. W. G. Rice	Home Forces	...	1.1.46
Major P. T. C. Rolt	Burma ...	...	11.9.45
Major D. K. Sadler	Italy	...	13.12.45
Major J. W. B. Stuart	Italy ...	...	13.12.45
Major the Rt. Hon. T. H. P. Touchet, Baron Audley	India ...	...	14.6.45

THE BRITISH EMPIRE MEDAL

Cpl. J. W. Goldwhite	Prisoner of War	...	18.4.46
C.S.M. P. T. Ryal	Middle East	...	6.1.44
Sergt. E. Stupple			
C.Q.M.S. E. Sterry	Home Forces	...	1.1.44

THE DISTINGUISHED SERVICE ORDER

Major W. O. Churchill, M.C. ...	Mediterranean	...	15.3.45
Major P. H. Graves Morris, M.C. ...	Burma ...	...	26.4.45
Major P. G. Hall	Western Europe	...	21.6.45
Major T. F. Hughes	Western Europe	...	3.5.45
Lieut.-Colonel J. O. Knight ...	Middle East	...	13.8.42
Major D. H. Nott, M.C.	Middle East	...	30.12.41
Major J. D. Ricketts	Western Europe	...	5.4.45
Brigadier J. O. Wilsey	Western Europe	...	29.3.45

THE MILITARY CROSS

2/Lieut. E. W. B. Berry	France and Belgium	20.8.40
Lieut. J. F. Betts	France and Belgium	20.12.40
2/Lieut. T. J. Bowen	Middle East ...	18.7.41
Major J. B. Brierley	Burma	28.6.45
Lieut. W. O. Churchill	Middle East ...	23.3.44
Lieut. C. N. Cross	Prison escape ...	9.12.43
Lieut. R. H. Clark	Western Europe ...	7.6.45
Lieut. M. J. Campbell	Burma	17.1.46
Lieut. R. L. Dray	Middle East ...	16.4.42
,, ,, (bar)	Middle East ...	24.9.42
Lieut. R. F. B. Evans	Middle East ...	26.8.43
Lieut. J. C. B. Ellis	Italy	24.2.44
Capt. L. J. Elkington	Burma	22.4.35
Major H. Elliott	Burma	31.8.44
Lieut. R. N. Fellows	Western Europe ...	21.8.45
Major A. J. Francis	Italy	8.3.45
Major P. H. Graves Morris	Middle East ...	30.12.41
Major A. J. Gutch	Western Europe ...	19.10.44
Major C. E. Garrett	Western Europe ...	19.10.44
Lieut. C. A. Hershman	Middle East ...	19.8.43
2/Lieut. J. J. Horton	Middle East ...	24.9.42
Lieut. A. F. Holyoake	Italy	21.8.45
2/Lieut. F. N. Lymes	Middle East ...	5.11.42
Lieut. R. Morgan	Western Europe ...	22.3.45
Capt. P. G. B. Martin Smith ...	Italy	2.8.45
Major D. H. Nott, M.C. (bar) ...	Middle East ...	24.9.42
2/Lieut. J. D. Plumley, M.M. ...	Burma	17.1.46
Lieut. D. A. T. Phillips	Burma	27.7.44
Lieut. D. J. Pullen	Western Europe ...	14.2.45
Lieut. J. D. Reynolds	Italy	13.1.44
Major F. A. Rowley	Burma	15.11.45
2/Lieut. A. D. Steel	France and Belgium	20.8.40
Major K. M. Scott	Burma	19.4.45
Capt. I. S. Spalding	Burma	12.7.45
Lieut. A. Smith	Italy	26.4.45
Major F. G. Thomson	Burma	28.6.45
Major E. R. W. Tooby	Burma	6.6.46
Lieut. T. E. Watt	Burma	27.7.44

THE DISTINGUISHED CONDUCT MEDAL

5253132 Sergt. W. T. St. C. Bull ...	Burma	6.6.46
5248112 C.S.M. J. Dumolo	Eritrea	16.4.42
5255533 C.S.M. S. Hubbard ...	Western Europe ...	24.1.46
5251041 Pte. M. Hunt	Middle East ...	5.11.42
5247965 Pte. H. Newman	Middle East ...	31.12.42
5249567 C.S.M. J. White	Burma	5.10.44

THE MILITARY MEDAL

4856723 Pte. W. Burbridge	France and Belgium	3.9.40
5257681 Pte. G. Bromwich	Western Europe ...	1.3.45
5101525 Pte. T. Bagshaw	Burma	28.6.45
5050102 Sergt. J. H. Bratton	Burma	15.11.45
5123931 Pte. L. R. Barnes	Burma	16.1.46
5116757 Cpl. D. Beeson	Escaping	9.11.44
5254227 Pte. J. Clark	Burma	2.8.45
4926571 Pte. P. C. Cox	Western Europe ...	21.12.44
5252820 Pte. C. Dayus	Western Europe ...	29.3.45

5249620 L./Cpl. L. Davies	Western Europe ...	12.7.45
3714070 Pte. R. J. Edwards		21.2.46
5255506 Sergt. R. F. Edwards ...	Western Europe ...	12.4.45
5252554 L./Cpl. D. Flowers ...	France and Belgium	20.8.40
5251607 Pte. D. Goodchild	Middle East ...	24.9.45
5258245 Sergt. G. Guest	Western Europe ...	1.3.45
5254906 Sergt. A. Greatrix	Western Europe ...	21.12.44
5252486 Pte. R. Hodgetts ...	Escaping	9.11.44
5251439 Cpl. M. B. Hughes ...	Escaping	26.6.45
4982401 Sergt. W. Jennings ...	Western Europe ...	1.3.45
5254069 Pte. R. F. Jones	France and Belgium	7.3.41
3242885 Sergt. W. Kelly	Middle East ...	16.4.42
5351411 Pte. J. Keohane	Middle East ...	29.11.40
C./Sergt. W. Lawton ...	Burma	22.3.45
5436899 Pte. R. Lugg	Western Europe ...	1.3.45
5251082 Cpl. E. S. Lock	Burma	21.2.46
5249721 Pte. D. Morgan	Middle East ...	16.4.42
4914275 Cpl. R. Mason	Western Europe ...	12.7.45
13090232 Cpl. M. McGinty	Burma	19.4.45
5251416 Pte. A. T. Manders ...	Middle East ...	19.8.41
5249419 Sergt. A. E. Miller ...	Middle East ...	30.12.41
5952113 Cpl. J. Metcalf	France and Belgium	20.8.40
5253563 Pte. D. Nash	Special Ops. ...	3.2.44
5254043 Sergt. J. Norton	Western Europe ...	24.5.45
5257811 Sergt. G. H. Oakley ...	Western Europe ...	22.3.45
4197320 L./Cpl. T. Owen	Escaping	7.1.43
5254864 Cpl. T. Plumley	Burma	22.6.44
5257827 L./Cpl. A. H. Palmer ...	Western Europe ...	1.3.45
5250269 Sergt. S. G. Phillips ...	Middle East ...	29.4.42
5248138 L./Cpl. F. E. Pearcey ...	Escaping	9.11.44
1553806 Pte. V. W. Rosser	Western Europe ...	24.5.45
5252454 Pte. L. J. Rhodes	Burma	21.2.46
5256794 Pte. J. A. E. Riley	Burma ... ...?	22.6.44
5257400 Sergt. A. L. Sanders ...	Western Europe ...	22.3.45
6234291 Sergt. E. Stupple	Western Europe ...	19.10.44
14419045 Cpl. A. Stacey	Western Europe ...	1.3.45
1700083 Sergt. N. Stokes	Western Europe ...	22.3.45
5260155 Cpl. A. P. Scott	Western Europe ...	3.5.45
5506394 Sergt. A. E. Shiner ...	Burma ...	6.6.46
5248160 Pte. W. E. Sheldon ...	Middle East ...	18.7.41
5247980 Pte. G. Stephens	Middle East ...	19.8.41
5252596 Sergt. S. W. Wood ...	Western Europe ...	22.3.45
14424131 L./Cpl. A. E. White ...	Western Europe ...	3.5.45
4191752 Sergt. E. Worsley	Burma	16.1.46
5250676 Sergt. J. H. Williams ...	Burma	6.6.46
5252596 Sergt. S. Wood	Western Europe ...	22.3.45
787157 Sergt. J. L. Winter ...	Middle East ...	24.9.42

MENTIONS IN DESPATCHES

Capt. H. M. Barker	Burma	9.5.46
Lieut. A. J. Booth	Western Europe ...	22.3.45
Lieut. F. B. T. Brady	Escaping	27.4.44
Major R. Bucknell	Western Europe ...	9.8.45
Major C. H. C. Beresford ...	Burma	27.9.45
Lieut.-Colonel J. B. Brierley, M.C.	Burma	10.1.46
Capt. H. V. Barnard	Burma	10.1.46
Capt. M. B. Cooke	Burma	26.4.45
Capt. P. H. Crooke	Italy	23.5.46
Lieut. (Q.M.) A. H. Cooper, M.B.E.	Middle East ...	1.4.41

Capt. T. B. Carr	Italy	24.8.44
2/Lieut. G. P. P. Chesshire	France and Belgium	20.12.40
Capt. R. G. Dewdney ...	Italy	29.11.45
Capt. R. L. Deverell	Burma	19.7.45
Capt. M. T. Dixon	Italy	24.8.44
Major G. H. Day	France and Belgium	20.12.40
Capt. D. H. Evans	Burma	10.1.46
Capt. M. R. Ellis	Burma	9.4.46
Capt. J. D. Farrer	France and Belgium	10.3.42
Capt. I. T. Fisher	Burma	19.9.46
Major H. Guiton	Middle East ...	13.1.44
Capt. D. E. Green	Western Europe ...	22.3.45
Brigadier A. H. Gillmore	Burma	26.4.45
Capt. D. Harrison	Burma	10.1.46
Capt. D. B. Haslehust	Middle East ...	30.12.41
		30.6.46
	Prisoner of War ...	31.1.46
Lieut.-Colonel B. G. T. Hawkes ...	Western Europe ...	4.4.46
Major R. H. Hornsby, M.B.E. ...	Burma	9.5.46
Lieut.-Colonel A. R. Harrison ...	Western Europe ...	22.3.45
Lieut.-Colonel J. C. Home	Burma	5.4.45
Capt. P. G. Harding	Western Europe ...	9.8.45
		4.4.46
Capt. R. W. Harding	Burma	19.9.46
Major J. H. Hunter	Italy	11.11.45
Major S. W. Jones	France and Belgium	20.12.40
Major K. R. H. James	Escaping	27.7.44
	Western Europe ...	4.4.46
Capt. N. V. Jones	Western Europe ...	4.4.46
Lieut.-Colonel J. Johnstone ...	France and Belgium	20.12.40
Lieut. J. C. Leak	Burma	10.1.46
2/Lieut. K. G. Leigh	Prisoner of War ...	21.2.46
Major J. A. E. Miller	Western Europe ...	8.11.45
Lieut. E. R. Middleton	Italy	29.11.45
Major F. N. Nicklin	Burma	19.9.46
Major D. H. Nott, D.S.O., M.C. ...	Middle East ...	30.6.41
Lieut. P. D. O'Malley	Burma	28.10.42
Lieut.-Colonel J. Parkes, M.C., D.C.M.	France and Belgium	20.12.40
Capt. H. L. Preedy	Burma	19.9.46
Capt. L. M. Rudge, M.C., M.M. ...	France and Belgium	20.12.40
Major J. W. B. Stuart, M.B.E., M.C.	Middle East ...	15.12.42
	Italy	6.4.44
Major E. D. Schluter	Prisoner of War ...	5.12.46
Lieut. P. Stevenson	Italy	23.5.46
Colonel G. B. M. Scutt	Western Europe ...	4.4.46
Lieut. E. S. Spalding	Burma	19.7.45
Capt. J. A. Sandys	Burma	19.7.45
Major D. N. Sadler, M.B.E. ...	Italy	27.11.45
Major M. A. Staniforth	Western Europe ...	2.8.45
Major E. G. Theophilus	North Africa ...	23.9.43
Capt. E. W. Tooby	Burma	10.1.46
Major P. S. Tipple	Italy	23.5.46
Major R. E. L. Tuckey	Middle East ...	30.12.41
		30.6.42
		15.12.42
Lieut. A. F. S. Veasey	Escaping	20.9.45
Lieut. R. A. Weeks	Prisoner of War ...	31.1.46
Capt. D. Y. Watson	Western Europe ...	4.4.46
Brigadier J. H. O. Wilsey, C.B.E., D.S.O.	Western Europe ...	8.11.45
Major G. E. D. Whitaker	Western Europe ...	8.11.45
Major A. G. O. Williams	Western Europe ...	8.11.45

Lieut. P. Ward Jackson ...	...	Middle East ...	15.12.42
5245830 R.S.M. G. Ackerman	...	Italy	23.5.46
5258144 Pte. B. Barlow ...	...	Western Europe ...	22.3.45
511776 S./Sergt. R. G. Blood	...	Italy	2.6.45
5249236 Pte. W. E. Bishop	...	Prisoner of War ...	20.12.45
5253452 Sergt. F. J. Bate ...	...	France and Belgium	20.12.40
14259083 L./Cpl. A. G. Broom	...	Burma	19.7.45
3717127 L./Cpl. R. Burkhill	...	Burma	19.7.45
			9.5.46
3972361 Cpl. A. Beach ...	...	Burma	19.9.46
7143450 C./Sergt. A. Carey ...	...	France and Belgium	20.12.40
5245971 L./Cpl. E. Corfield ...	...	Middle East ...	30.12.41
			30.6.42
5258587 C./Sergt. R. J. Chad	...	Middle East ...	6.4.44
5248372 Pte. W. E. Cotterell	...	Middle East ...	30.6.42
5252820 Pte. C. Dayus ...	...	France and Belgium	30.12.40
5249749 Sergt. H. Drew ...	...	Western Europe ...	9.8.45
4460048 Sergt. W. J. Dart ...	...	Burma	19.7.45
5252537 Sergt. F. R. Diston	...	Western Europe ...	4.4.46
5244557 C./Sergt. S. C. Dyke	...	Middle East ...	30.12.41
5566480 C./Sergt. C. Dowdell	...	Middle East ...	30.12.41
1635466 Sergt. S. Drummond	...	Burma	9.5.46
5105903 Pte. R. Ellis	...	Middle East ...	30.6.42
5246897 R.S.M. E. L. Griffiths	...	Paiforce	23.12.43
862466 Pte. H. Green ...	...	Prisoner of war ...	14.11.46
5190884 Cpl. J. Grimes ...	...	Burma	19.9.46
4927882 Cpl. J. R. Green ...	...	Burma	19.7.45
			10.1.46
5246615 Sergt. H. Hodgetts ...	...	Western Europe ...	22.3.45
5257031 Pte. W. Hare ...	...	Escaping	26.6.45
5341930 Sergt. J. Huggett ...	...	N. Africa	16.9.43
		N. Africa	23.9.43
		Italy	11.1.45
5258274 C./Sergt. H. C. Harrison ...		Western Europe ...	4.4.46
5249156 Sergt. F. C. Harrold	...	Burma	19.9.46
885921 Pte. E. J. Hughes ...	...	Prisoner of War ...	14.11.46
5255533 Sergt. S. Hubbard ...	...	Italy	24.8.44
5253009 Pte. S. Jones... ...	...	France and Belgium	20.12.40
5379229 Pte. E. Jewkes ...	...	Middle East ...	13.1.44
14425775 Pte. W. G. T. Johnson	...	Western Europe ...	22.3.45
5248218 C.S.M. H. Knox ...	...	Middle East ...	30.12.41
3242885 Sergt. W. Kelly ...	...	Middle East ...	30.12.41
5249989 Sergt. D. G. Lloyd	...	Middle East ...	30.6.42
5506730 Sergt. A. Lingard ...	...	Burma	19.9.46
5252797 Pte. W. Lloyd ...	...	Prisoner of War ...	21.2.46
5249457 Pte. A. C. Lucking ...	...	Western Europe ...	8.11.45
Sergt. J. V. Lacey ...	...	Burma	26.4.45
5249759 R.Q.M.S. P. Marsh...	...	Middle East ...	13.1.44
14630028 Pte. D. Minshull ...	...	Western Europe ...	10.5.45
5257806 Pte. A. Morris ...	...	Western Europe ...	10.5.45
4197133 Pte. R. K. McGawley	...	Burma	2.8.45
5254455 Sergt. S. A. Morris	...	Burma	10.1.46
			19.9.46
5250732 Sergt. G. Millership	...	Burma	19.7.45
5255142 C.S.M. C. W. Munt	...	Burma	19.9.46
2717408 R.S.M. D. McCabe...	...	Middle East ...	30.6.42
5254043 Sergt. J. T. Norton	...	Western Europe ...	9.8.45
5252065 Pte. L. Owens ...	...	France and Belgium	20.12.40
5722151 P.S.M. J. F. Purdy	...	Middle East ...	30.6.42
3714065 C.S.M. J. Pearson ...	...	Burma	19.9.46
5253221 Cpl. J. Pratt ...	...	Burma	9.5.46

T

4921576 Pte. C. Poole	Burma	19.7.46
5253960 R.S.M. W. C. M. Parry ...	Burma	5.4.45
5258373 Pte. L. Proctor	Western Europe ...	8.11.45
5249736 C.S.M. J. Pitt	France and Belgium	20.12.40
5254187 L./Cpl. A. Reeve	Middle East ...	13.1.44
5258543 Pte. L. Redley	Middle East ...	13.1.44
5257390 L./Cpl. T. Rudge	Italy	23.5.46
873902 Pte. R. S. Robinson ...	Burma	19.9.46
5251852 Sergt. P. R. Reynolds ...	Middle East ...	6.4.44
1815309 Pte. J. D. Seaborne ...	Burma	19.9.46
5258422 Sergt. V. H. Smythe ...	Western Europe ...	23.3.45
5258441 Sergt. H. F. Sabin	Western Europe ...	22.3.45
6234291 Pte. E. Stupple	Middle East ...	30.12.41
5249218 Cpl. G. Smith	Middle East ...	30.12.41
		15.12.42
3972930 C.S.M. W. Truelove ...	Burma	9.5.46
5253038 Sergt. F. Taylor	Burma	9.5.46
5256633 Pte. G. Wilmer	Middle East ...	30.6.42
5257126 Pte. J. Walton	Western Europe ...	22.3.45
5250676 Sergt. J. H. Williams ...	Burma	10.1.46
5499296 C./Sergt. K. J. White ...	Burma	19.9.46
5248084 C.S.M. F. Wright	Burma	19.9.46
4917754 Cpl. T. W. M. Yates ...	Western Europe ...	4.4.46

The following past officers of the Regiment were awarded decorations:

Major-General R. N. Gale, C.B., O.B.E., D.S.O., M.C., Western Europe
Brigadier H. U. Richards, C.B.E., D.S.O., Burma
Brigadier E. C. Pepper, C.B.E., D.S.O., North Africa and Western Europe
Major C. P. Vaughan, D.S.O., Burma
Colonel E. F. Du Sautoy, O.B.E., Home Guard
Major L. J. Vicarage, M.B.E., India

The dates given throughout are those of the "London Gazette"

ROLL OF HONOUR, 1939-1945

OFFICERS

Major J. J. Abbott	Norway	40
2/Lieut. M. C. G. Alcock	U.K.	15.12.42
Capt. F. E. Baker	East Africa ...	5.5.41
Lieut. E. J. Banner	U.K.	23.8.45
Capt. F. W. Baylis	France and Belgium	23.5.40
Lieut. A. J. Booth	Western Europe ...	7.8.44
Major J. S. Boyt	Burma	20.3.45
Capt. E. S. J. Brazier	Burma	30.4.44
Lieut. G. E. R. Brewer	Middle East ...	15.11.43
Major W. H. Broome	Western Europe ...	30.9.44
Lieut. I. R. Chadwick	India	19.1.43
Capt. A. H. Cooper, M.B.E.	South Africa... ...	31.8.42
Capt. F. T. Coulcher	Western Europe ...	30.12.44
Lieut. The Earl of Coventry	France and Belgium	27.5.40
Lieut. T. O. Cranko, M.C.	Western Europe ...	19.6.44
2/Lieut. J. S. Crossley	U.K.	19.4.45
Lieut.-Colonel C. Deakin, O.B.E. ...	U.K.	8.3.44
Capt. R. N. A. Dingley	Western Europe ...	27.6.44
Lieut. M. E. Drake	Burma	6.1.45
Major R. L. Dray, M.C.	Italy	3.7.44
Major G. J. Dunstall	U.K.	19.3.42
Capt. J. D. Farrar	France and Belgium	29.5.40
Lieut. S. J. R. Fraser	Italy	29.1.44
Capt. R. B. Frith, M.C.	Eritrea	17.3.41
Major M. A. Gibbins	Western Europe ...	25.9.44
Lieut. R. H. Gillard	Western Europe ...	7.10.44
Capt. E. L. R. Gilson	Italy	16.10.44
2/Lieut. D. G. Goodwin	France and Belgium	26.5.40
Capt. A. E. Haines	U.K.	1.11.43
Lieut. T. E. Hancox	Western Europe ...	10.4.45
2/Lieut. J. C. Hares	Middle East ...	19.5.42
Capt. G. Hayton	Western Europe ...	14.9.44
Lieut. G. B. Hingley	France and Belgium	20.5.40
Lieut. J. B. Howley	Italy	16.5.44
Lieut. P. E. Hulme...	Western Europe ...	28.6.44
Lieut. C. A. Humphries	Western Europe ...	18.11.44
Lieut A. A. A. E. Hudson (Gordon Highlanders, attached 2nd Battalion) ...	Burma	21.1.45
2/Lieut. S. F. Ibbetson	France and Belgium	26.5.40
Lieut. J. H. Jackson	Western Europe ...	20.11.44
Capt. D. C. Johnson	Italy	17.8.44
Lieut. A. C. J. Kennagh	Burma	14.11 43
Capt. P. W. Kerans	Eritrea	25.3.41
Lieut. E. A. Lawton	Western Europe ...	6.4.45
2/Lieut. D. H. Lunt	France and Belgium	40
Capt. G. W. MacDonald	France and Belgium	29.5.40
Lieut. W. P. MacGregor	U.K.	30.1.45
Capt. J. K. G. Marshall	Western Europe ...	7.8.44

Capt. R. A. W. Miller	...	...	Western Europe	... 28.8.44
2/Lieut. P. C. W. Monahan	...	...	France and Belgium	26.5.40
Lieut. D. B. Moore	...	...	North Africa	... 27.12.42
2/Lieut. J. W. Morgan	...	...	N.W. Frontier	... 12.8.40
Capt. R. R. Noakes	...	...	Sicily ...	... 5.8.43
Capt. T. M. H. Pardoe	...	...	Hong Kong	... 16.12.41
Lieut. D. A. T. Phillips, M.C.	...	...	Burma	... 14.3.45
Major P. O. C. Ray	...	...	Eritrea	... 17.3.41
Major J. C. Scott ...	...	...	India	... 8.9.45
Lieut. J. F. Sheldrake	...	...	Western Europe	... 1.7.44
Capt. A. D. R. Smith	...	...	Western Europe	... 24.7.44
Lieut. B. S. Smith ...	...	...	India	... 16.5.44
Lieut. R. B. Smurthwaite ...	...	...	Middle East	... 6.4.43
Major M. M. Souper	...	...	Western Europe	... 24.9.44
Lieut. R. S. Spicer	...	...	Western Europe	... 13.7.44
Major A. D. Steel, M.C.	...	...	Italy ...	... 10.11.44
Lieut. D. B. Steward	...	...	Middle East	... 43
Lieut. W. A. B. Temple	...	...	Western Europe	... 16.6.44
Major E. G. Theophilus	...	...	North Africa	... 25.1.43
Capt. E. J. Townsend	...	...	Western Europe	... 13.2.45
Capt. C. Tyrwhitt ...	...	...	Malaya	... 15.2.42
Lieut. A. H. Watkins	...	...	Burma	... 11.4.44
Capt. N. Watkins ...	...	...	Western Europe	... 29.9.44
Lieut. D. G. Webb	...	...	Burma	... 19.12.44
Major P. Weston ...	...	...	Western Europe	... 23.7.44
Lieut. J. Woodward	...	...	Burma	... 19.5.44
Lieut. D. G. Wye ...	...	...	Western Europe	... 27.6.44
Capt. R. Young	...	...	Burma	... 8.2.45

OTHER RANKS

14517428 Pte. W. D. Abbott	...	...	Burma	... 22.3.44
5259544 Pte. T. Adams ...	...	...	Western Europe	... 11.1.45
5050150 Pte. L. Adams ...	...	...	Western Europe	... 19.11.44
5249282 Pte. F. Adams ...	...	...	Western Europe	... 9.8.44
5046216 Pte. J. W. Adams	...	...	Middle East	... 12.42
5257882 Pte. J. Allchurch	...	...	Western Europe	... 30.7.44
5385054 Pte. S. H. G. Allen	...	...	France and Belgium	5.40
5258511 Pte. J. Allen	...	...	Middle East	... 14.6.42
4197190 Pte. W. Allen	...	...	France and Belgium	5.40
4913329 Cpl. J. W. Allsebrook	...	...	France and Belgium	26.5.40
6341660 Sergt. F. C. Amey	...	...	Middle East	... 18.3.41
5257881 Pte. J. E. Appleby	...	...	Western Europe	... 19.11.44
5248082 Pte. A. Archer	...	...	Eritrea	... 17.3.41
5253780 Pte. G. A. Ashcroft	...	...	Burma	... 22.1.45
5253994 Pte. H. E. Askew	...	...	U.K. ...	... 26.2.41
14596143 Pte. W. Aspbury	...	...	India	... 6.12.44
4856754 Pte. H. Aston	...	...	France and Belgium	6.40
5249316 Pte. E. L. Atthews	...	...	Western Europe	... 25.9.44
5258022 Pte. F. B. Attwood	...	...	Western Europe	... 27.6.44
5255296 Pte. R. Ayling ...	...	...	Western Europe	... 16.8.44
5258149 Pte. F. G. Bache	...	...	Western Europe	... 9.8.44
5257676 L./Cpl. M. W. Baldwin	...	...	Western Europe	... 7.7.44
5249944 Pte. S. L. Ball ...	...	...	Western Europe	... 1.7.44
4197129 Pte. R. Ball	...	...	France and Belgium	5.40
5251531 Pte. L. A. Ballard	...	...	Burma	... 17.6.44
5249109 Pte. A. E. W. Band	...	...	Middle East	... 14.6.42
5255459 Pte. G. E. Banninge	...	...	U.K. ...	... 9.10.40
5258141 Pte. F. Barker ...	...	...	Western Europe	... 19.11.44
5253122 Pte. S. J. Barley	...	...	Burma	... 26.2.45

5253691 Pte. L. H. Barnes	... ...	France and Belgium	29.5.40
3784226 Pte. J. F. Barnett	... ...	Western Europe ...	5.7.44
5117771 Pte. J. T. Barrett	... ...	Middle East ...	31.3.41
14730479 Pte. A. Bartley ...	...	Burma	16.3.45
1617993 Pte. R. Bassett	... ...	U.K.	14.9.45
5254067 Cpl. B. N. Bastock	... ...	Western Europe ...	13.7.44
5251664 Pte. F. Bateman	... ...	Middle East ...	7.6.42
5498968 L./Cpl. J. D. Bath	... ...	Burma	22.1.45
5252856 Pte. J. E. Batty	... ...	France and Belgium	5.40
5571079 Cpl. R. Beasant ...	... ...	France and Belgium	6.40
5260638 Pte. G. D. Beddoes	... ...	U.K.	9.6.42
6084622 Cpl. C. C. Bedwell	... ...	Middle East ...	19.12.42
4039668 Pte. H. L. Beecham	... ...	Burma	8.2.45
5250093 Sergt. A. L. Belcher	... ...	Middle East ...	30.6.42
5248096 L./Cpl. G. W. Bellamy	...	Burma	12.12.44
5248016 Sergt. F. Bennett	... ...	Burma	12.2.45
4197351 Pte. J. Bennett ...	... ...	France and Belgium	5.40
5341920 Cpl. F. J. Biddle	... ...	India	23.5.44
3596534 Sergt. T. Bigrigg	... ...	Middle East ...	14.6.42
14699990 Pte. A. Bisbey ...	...	Burma	13.2.45
5248236 Pte. W. E. Bishop	... ...	Middle East ...	40.7.44
5254136 Cpl. W. H. Bishop	... ...	Burma	11.4.44
2077577 Pte. B. Bishton ...	... ...	India	7.6.44
4914624 Pte. G. E. Blount	... ...	France and Belgium	22.5.40
5118007 Pte. C. Bodycote	... ...	Eritrea	26.1.41
5117591 Pte. J. J. Bolton	... ...	Burma	23.1.45
4918824 Pte. G. E. Bonsall	... ...	Burma	21.1.45
5384569 Pte. H. J. Boodle	... ...	France and Belgium	5.40
5247818 Sergt. J. L. Bostock	... ...	Eritrea	17.3.41
5243761 C.S.M. A. A. Bott	... ...	France and Belgium	21.5.40
14572612 Pte. H. C. Bottrill	... ...	Western Europe ...	29.6.44
14553303 Pte. E. A. Boughton	... ...	India	10.6.44
5251646 Pte. J. J. Boucher	... ...	Eritrea	24.9.39
4918236 Pte. J. H. Boulton	... ...	Western Europe ...	12.2.45
3964417 Pte. D. J. Boundy	... ...	Burma	7.1.45
5252993 Pte. F. H. Bourne	... ...	France and Belgium	5.40
5247561 L./Cpl. F. Bowater	... ...	Western Europe ...	18.8.44
5252993 Pte. F. H. Bourne	... ...	France and Belgium	5.40
5247561 L./Cpl. F. Bowater	... ...	Western Europe	18.8.44
1437277 L./Cpl. R. F. Bowden ...	...	Western Europe ...	27.3.45
14745158 Pte. G. A. Bowen	... ...	Burma	26.2.45
5052474 Pte. L. T. Bowkett	... ...	Western Europe ...	9.2.45
5052474 Pte. L. T. Bowkett	... ...	Western Europe ...	9.2.45
5259546 Pte. L. Box ...	... ...	Western Europe ...	10.7.44
5248349 Pte. D. Boxley	... ...	India	2.9.42
5255098 Pte. W. B. Boyden	... ...	U.K.	3.11.41
14751296 Pte. G. Bradford	... ...	Burma	19.2.45
5258125 Pte. W. Bradley	... ...	U.K.	1.5.41
14771755 Pte. W. Bradley	... ...	Burma	8.6.46
14654219 Pte. R. Bradley	... ...	Western Europe ...	21.7.44
14654228 Pte. W. D. Braggins	... ...	Western Europe ...	9.8.44
5250218 Cpl. W. Bratt ...	... ...	Western Europe ...	28.8.44
5255428 Pte. A. A. Bratton	... ...	Western Europe ...	28.6.44
3651648 Cpl. J. Brennan	... ...	Middle East ...	17.3.41
5253614 Pte. D. H. Brewer	... ...	France and Belgium	5.40
5109902 Pte. F. W. E. Brickles ...	...	Western Europe ...	27.6.44
5251532 Cpl. R. A. Britt	... ...	Eritrea	27.5.41
5253891 Pte. N. V. Brittain	... ...	Burma	4.4.45
5435383 Pte. F. Brittain ...	... ...	Middle East ...	9.9.41
5506473 Pte. F. W. Broad	... ...	Burma	8.2.45
14730539 Pte. A. Brooks ...	... ...	Western Europe ...	3.5.45

4197391 Sergt. T. Brookes	... ...	Burma	13.4.44
14577361 Pte. F. L. Brookes	... ...	India	21.11.44
4918443 Pte. H. Brooks ...	... ...	Burma	22.1.45
5248103 Sergt. A. H. Brookes	... ...	U.K.	16.5.41
5249294 Pte. E. D. E. Brooks	... ...	Eritrea	4.6.41
5252118 Pte. G. F. Brooks	... ...	France and Belgium	5.40
5253731 Pte. F. Brookes	... ...	U.K.	7.8.40
14718206 Pte. R. G. Broughton	...	Western Europe ...	25.9.44
5259120 L./Sergt. T. Brough	...	Western Europe ...	4.7.44
5257895 Pte. A. Brown ...	... ...	Western Europe ...	27.6.44
5256893 Pte. C. Brown ...	... ...	Western Europe ...	1.8.44
5045927 Pte. E. L. Brown	... ...	Middle East ...	8.6.42
4197222 Pte. G. Brown ...	... ...	France and Belgium	26.5.40
5253630 Pte. H. Brown ...	... ...	France and Belgium	21.3.40
5255458 Pte. H. W. Brown	... ...	Burma	8.2.45
1690428 Pte. J. W. Brown	... ...	Burma	20.1.45
14699570 Pte. W. Brown ...	... ...	Burma	28.2.45
14416719 Pte. A. J. Bryant	... ...	Western Europe ...	16.8.44
14718362 Pte. C. T. Burman	... ...	Burma	4.6.45
4460028 Cpl. J. Burn ...	... ...	Burma	23.2.45
5249755 C.S.M. H. G. Burton	...	U.K.	6.5.44
5252048 Pte. H. Busby ...	... ...	U.K.	13.5.44
6029690 Pte. B. J. Bush ...	... ...	Burma	23.11.45
14551686 Pte. L. T. Butland	... ...	Western Europe ...	8.8.44
5247661 Pte. W. E. Butler	... ...	At sea	17.6.40
5249951 Pte. E. J. Cadwallader	...	Western Europe ...	27.6.44
5257910 L./Cpl. F. Cairns	... ...	Western Europe ...	27.6.44
14423720 Pte. W. R. Cambrook	...	Western Europe ...	6.11.44
4197110 Pte. W. Carroll	... ...	France and Belgium	29.5.40
5246459 Pte. R. J. Carter	... ...	France and Belgium	5.40
5252623 Pte. J. Carter ...	... ...	France and Belgium	5.40
5571091 Pte. H. A. V. Carter	... ...	France and Belgium	22.5.40
14529300 Pte. J. Cartwright	... ...	Western Europe ...	26.8.44
4918839 Pte. W. Casey ...	... ...	Western Europe ...	24.9.44
5249922 L./Cpl. R. E. Castle	... ...	Eritrea	5.2.41
5256894 Pte. W. Caunt ...	... ...	Middle East	14.6.42
5253604 Pte. W. A. Challis	... ...	France and Belgium	5.40
5250526 Pte. J. H. Chamberlain	...	U.K.	1.8.41
5248910 C.S.M. A. E. Chapman	...	Burma	8.2.45
5252566 Pte. J. W. Chapman	...	France and Belgium	21.5.40
5341983 L./Cpl. E. W. Chapman	...	U.K.	25.9.43
7684821 Pte. W. Chatterton	...	Middle East ...	17.11.42
5258259 Pte. D. Chatterton	...	Western Europe ...	25.9.44
4197354 Pte. H. Cheetham	...	France and Belgium	5.40
4196637 Pte. J. Cheevers	...	Burma	11.4.44
14301908 L./Cpl. P. A. Chudleigh		U.K.	13.2.45
5249444 C./Sergt. A. W. Church	...	Iceland	23.8.41
14585208 Pte. W. T. Churm	...	Burma	4.6.45
5254867 L./Cpl. S. G. Clark	...	U.K.	24.9.44
4918172 Pte. D. T. Clarke	... ...	Western Europe ...	1.10.44
5258515 Pte. A. P. Clarke	... ...	At sea	14.11.42
5117281 Pte. W. J. Clarke	... ...	Eritrea	17.3.41
5251632 Pte. E. Clee ...	... ...	Middle East ...	30.1.41
5258158 Pte. K. Clews ...	... ...	Western Europe ...	4.7.44
5342125 Cpl. D. D. Cocklin	... ...	U.K.	12.5.44
5257515 Pte. P. S. Cocks	... ...	India	20.9.44
5256446 Pte. H. A. Coe ...	... ...	U.K.	23.12.41
5247830 Pte. T. Coley ...	... ...	U.K.	27.7.40
5256450 Cpl. B. Collier	... ...	Western Europe ...	19.11.44
5260600 Pte. W. G. E. Collins	...	India	31.5.44
5727045 Pte. E. I. Coney...	... ...	France and Belgium	40

7344266 Pte. R. C. Conway	... ...	Western Europe ...	27.3.45
5252972 L./Sergt. H. O. Cook	... ...	Burma	8.2.45
14640582 Pte. A. G. Cooke	... ...	Western Europe ...	28.8.44
5248579 Sergt. W. T. Cooper	... ...	France and Belgium	25.5.40
5258191 Pte. E. H. Cooper	... ...	Western Europe ...	10.7.44
4197380 Pte. S. Cope ...	... ...	France and Belgium	5.40
5258171 Pte. S. C. Cope ...	... ...	Western Europe ...	9.8.44
14738135 Pte. F. R. Corbett	... ...	Burma	13.2.45
14324957 Cpl. A. R. G. Corke	... ...	Western Europe ...	24.11.44
5258180 Pte. H. Cornwell	... ...	U.K.	17.8.41
14986302 Cpl. D. M. Cox	... ...	Burma	10.6.46
14421248 Pte. G. H. Cox	... ...	Western Europe ...	27.8.44
5251435 Pte. W. E. Cox	... ...	Western Europe ...	15.4.45
5183886 Pte. S. D. Cozens	... ...	At sea	14.11.42
5260660 Pte. E. G. Craythorn	... ...	U.K.	9.6.42
1530054 Pte. T. Crerar ...	... ...	U.K.	28.3.46
5256900 Pte. T. Creswick	... ...	Eritrea ...	23.9.43
5251214 L./Cpl. T. G. Croft	... ...	France and Belgium	29.5.40
5249458 Pte. F. Cross ...	... ...	Western Europe ...	16.8.44
5571101 Pte. W. M. Currant	... ...	France and Belgium	40
2717693 Pte. T. J. Curtin	... ...	Burma	20.3.45
4919973 Pte. F. E. Curtis	... ...	Middle East ...	14.11.42
4915690 Pte. D. Dalloway	... ...	France and Belgium	25.5.40
5250320 Pte. W. Dalton ...	... ...	India	14.7.40
4923679 Pte. B. Darby ...	... ...	Burma	8.2.45
5251346 Pte. J. Darby ...	... ...	Middle East ...	7.9.39
5252621 L./Cpl. L. G. Darby	... ...	France and Belgium	24.5.40
14740233 Pte. C. E. Davies	... ...	Burma	13.2.45
5254978 Cpl. G. O. Davies	... ...	Western Europe ...	27.3.45
5379317 Pte. H. Davies ...	... ...	Middle East ...	26.1.41
14640590 Pte. J. E. Davies	... ...	Western Europe ...	16.8.44
4125772 Pte. J. Davies ...	... ...	U.K.	20.12.40
5252593 Pte. W. H. Davies	... ...	Western Europe ...	29.10.44
5258041 Pte. J. Davies ...	... ...	Western Europe ...	15.8.44
5249412 L./Cpl. R. Davies	... ...	Middle East ...	42
5257290 Pte. T. H. Davies	... ...	U.K.	1.12.45
5254234 Pte. W. Davies ...	... ...	Burma	8.2.45
4077581 Cpl. D. V. Davis	... ...	U.K.	2.5.45
5255314 Pte. W. J. Davis	... ...	Western Europe ...	1.7.44
2656340 Pte. W. H. Davis	... ...	U.K.	18.12.41
4978458 L./Cpl. G. E. Dawson	... ...	Burma	12.6.44
5181511 Pte. J. Day ...	... ...	Burma	5.4.45
5252061 Pte. T. Deakin ...	... ...	France and Belgium	12.7.40
4541905 Pte. E. A. V. Degerlund	... ...	U.K.	12.1.42
5681116 Pte. G. W. Dellarocca ...	... ...	India	9.9.43
5250527 Pte. E. Dellaway	... ...	India	18.7.42
14397837 Pte. F. Dent ...	... ...	Western Europe ...	9.8.44
7597895 L./Cpl. W. G. Denton ...	... ...	Western Europe ...	25.7.44
4197134 Pte. T. W. Dibley	... ...	France and Belgium	5.40
3765879 C.S.M. J. Dodd	... ...	East Africa ...	13.6.44
3445679 Pte. J. Dolan ...	... ...	France and Belgium	40
5253141 Pte. W. J. Donnon	... ...	France and Belgium	29.5.40
5258208 Pte. H. A. Dorricott	... ...	Western Europe ...	23.9.44
5246596 Pte. S. Dovey ...	... ...	Middle East ...	25.12.44
5118020 Pte. G. W. Downes	... ...	Eritrea ...	17.3.41
14585888 Pte. F. Draycott...	... ...	Western Europe ...	27.6.44
5250603 Pte. S. W. Drew	... ...	Western Europe ...	15.8.44
5102937 Pte. W. J. Drinkwater ...	... ...	Western Europe ...	27.6.44
14542412 Pte. G. H. Dumbleton ...	... ...	Western Europe ...	22.11.44
5258065 Pte. H. Dunn ...	... ...	Western Europe ...	24.11.45
14577466 Pte. G. Dupree	... ...	Western Europe ...	27.6.44

5255499 Cpl. A. H. Dutton	... ...	Burma	4.4.45
5249153 Bdsmn. F. J. Dyason	... ...	Eritrea	1.4.41
14571445 L./Cpl. P. J. Ebbutt	... ...	Western Europe ...	4.8.44
6203386 Pte. W. J. Edgington	... ...	Western Europe ...	27.8.44
5571108 Pte. P. S. Edmonds	... ...	France and Belgium	22.5.40
14442193 Pte. J. H. Edmunds	... ...	Burma	26.3.45
5253599 Pte. L. W. Edwards	... ...	France and Belgium	14.3.45
5284925 Pte. A. G. Elkins	... ...	France and Belgium	22.5.40
14542166 Pte. F. Ellson ...	... ...	Burma	4.5.44
5258797 Cpl. P. J. Evans	... ...	Burma	23.1.45
14629748 Pte. S. C. Evans	... ...	Western Europe ...	31.7.44
4913144 L./Cpl. F. W. A. Evans	...	Burma	8.2.45
5250055 Pte. F. G. Evans	... ...	Europe	27.12.41
5250063 Pte. G. F. Evans	... ...	Western Europe ...	1.8.44
6252578 Pte. D. Evans ...	... ...	France and Belgium	5.40
14505599 Pte. L. S. Everard	... ...	Burma	8.2.45
14689068 Pte. A. D. E. Everfield	...	Western Europe ...	27.8.44
5258522 Pte. L. Farmer ...	... ...	Middle East ...	15.8.44
5250267 Pte. R. Farmer ...	... ...	Western Europe ...	6.1.45
4197205 Pte. W. Faukes	... ...	France and Belgium	27.5.40
5334706 Pte. W. Faulkner	... ...	Western Europe ...	16.8.44
5260612 Pte. W. A. Faulkner	... ...	Burma	24.1.45
5385372 Pte. F. H. Faulkner	... ...	France and Belgium	40
5735553 Pte. W. T. Fereday	... ...	Western Europe ...	15.3.45
5251092 Pte. A. Fidoe ...	... ...	France and Belgium	22.5.40
5248902 Sergt. S. T. Fidoe	... ...	France and Belgium	21.5.40
5248958 Pte. H. E. Finch	... ...	Middle East ...	12.1.43
14657839 Pte. T. H. Finchett	... ...	Burma	12.4.45
14577478 Pte. C. C. Fisher	... ...	Western Europe ...	7.7.44
4914742 Pte. T. F. Fisher	... ...	France and Belgium	5.40
5251145 Pte. F. C. Fisher	... ...	Middle East ...	12.42
5255118 L./Sergt. H. Fisher	... ...	U.K.	10.1.45
5246991 Sergt. H. Fitzgerald	... ...	India	19.4.41
5253927 Pte. J. T. Fleetwood	... ...	U.K.	2.4.40
13051439 Pte. F. Fletcher	... ...	Western Europe ...	11.6.44
5618891 Pte. T. G. Foot ...	... ...	Western Europe ...	15.4.45
5257731 Pte. F. B. Footman	... ...	Western Europe ...	27.8.44
5254844 Pte. H. Ford ...	... ...	Middle East ...	14.6.42
5056202 Pte. G. E. Forrester	... ...	India	30.12.44
5253302 Pte. R. W. Foster	... ...	France and Belgium	5.40
5254814 Pte. J. Fradgley	... ...	India	9.6.44
5257737 L./Cpl. A. E. Frampton	...	Western Europe ...	27.6.44
5251984 Pte. K. G. Franklin	... ...	Burma	13.5.44
5251778 Pte. C. J. Franklin	... ...	France and Belgium	5.40
14360461 Pte. C. F. Franklin	... ...	Burma	15.4.44
5252362 Pte. H. C. Freemantle	... ...	France and Belgium	20.1.41
14886593 Pte. R. E. French	... ...	U.K.	13.1.46
5253453 Pte. T. W. French	... ...	France and Belgium	5.40
5253574 Pte. F. J. French	... ...	France and Belgium	5.40
5258235 Pte. A. J. Fudge	... ...	Western Europe ...	27.6.44
5249658 C./Sergt. J. W. Fudger	...	Burma	20.12.44
5117020 Pte. J. F. Fullerton	... ...	Eritrea	17.3.41
5117885 Pte. W. Gamble	... ...	Middle East ...	28.11.41
5571116 Pte. B. E. Gant ...	... ...	France and Belgium	29.5.40
14700002 Pte. J. T. Garbett	... ...	Burma	15.4.45
14385509 Pte. K. Gardiner	... ...	Western Europe ...	19.11.44
5260223 Pte. J. R. Gardner	... ...	Burma	14.3.45
5253670 Pte. L. A. Gardner	... ...	India	12.8.40
5108915 Pte. J. Gardner	... ...	Eritrea	17.3.41
5254627 Pte. G. A. Garford	... ...	Burma	24.2.45
4914629 Pte. W. H. Gasson	... ...	France and Belgium	5.40

5257931 Pte. W. George ...	Western Europe ...	9.8.44
5248020 Pte. A. H. George	Middle East ...	25.1.41
5257930 Pte. J. Gibson ...	Western Europe	8.8.44
5253626 Pte. P. C. Gilbert	France and Belgium	16.5.40
5257744 L./Cpl. H. Gill	Western Europe ...	9.8.44
4928546 Pte. G. Goddard	Burma	22.1.45
5780389 Pte. H. J. W. Goddard	India	4.11.45
5256014 Pte. B. Golding ...	Western Europe ...	27.8.44
5260619 Pte. E. Golga ...	Burma	11.4.44
5257012 Pte. J. R. Gollins	India	4.3.43
3717253 Pte. A. L. Goolding	Burma	27.4.44
5053187 Cpl. E. Gordon	Western Europe ...	17.4.45
5107004 Pte. E. Gough ...	France and Belgium	26.5.40
1439404 Pte. T. W. Gnosill	Burma	28.2.45
5571121 Pte. G. Graham	France and Belgium	29.5.40
5257752 Pte. W. Grainger	Western Europe ...	27.8.44
5253156 L./Cpl. S. Grazier	France and Belgium	5.40
5117806 Pte. J. S. Greaves	Eritrea	6.7.41
5258254 Sergt. F. J. Green	East Africa ...	28.11.43
5251763 Pte. J. R. Green	U.K.	28.8.42
4613380 Pte. L. Green ...	Western Europe ...	8.8.44
5882391 L./Cpl. J. Green	Burma	4.5.44
3911710 Pte. R. Greenhow	Burma	10.4.45
5385068 L./Sergt. W. Gregory ...	Burma	14.4.44
5571122 Pte. H. F. Gregory	France and Belgium	5.40
5253636 Pte. J. W. Griffiths	France and Belgium	6.12.40
14708247 Pte. W. Guest ...	Western Europe ...	19.11.44
14552681 Pte. T. G. Guest	Western Europe ...	20.11.44
5249697 L./Cpl. J. L. F. Guest	U.K.	23.9.40
5244262 L./Cpl. E. J. Gunnell ...	France and Belgium	29.5.40
5257155 Pte. S. Hadlington	Western Europe ...	23.11.44
5252663 Pte. N. E. J. Halford ...	Western Europe ...	13.7.44
5247844 Pte. A. Hall ...	Eritrea	17.3.41
5256560 Pte. R. J. C. Hall	Burma	8.5.44
5059247 Pte. A. T. Hall	Burma	22.1.45
14499273 Pte. N. W. Hall	Western Europe ...	11.7.44
5251344 Pte. T. Hall ...	Middle East ...	29.11.42
3971199 Pte. P. Hammond	Burma	9.2.45
5252903 Pte. R. W. Hammond ...	France and Belgium	24.5.40
5117893 Pte. D. Hannan	Eritrea	5.5.41
14421897 Pte. W. S. L. Hansford	Western Europe ...	1.8.44
5258618 Pte. C. W. Hanshaw ...	Burma	22.1.45
5248078 Sergt. A. H. Harcourt	Burma	9.5.44
5255552 L./Cpl. F. R. M. Hardeman ...	Burma	8.5.44
5257939 Pte. S. Harding	Western Europe ...	9.8.44
2558287 Pte. H. E. Harding	Western Europe ...	20.11.44
5251326 Pte. F. Hardman	France and Belgium	29.5.40
5251433 L./Cpl. A. J. Hardwick	Eritrea	17.3.41
5250941 Pte. J. Hargreaves	Eritrea	1.2.41
4917724 Pte. B. Harris ...	Burma	16.6.45
14596533 Pte. S. J. Harris...	Western Europe ...	19.7.46
5382828 Pte. F. L. Harris	France and Belgium	24.5.40
5571127 Pte. D. R. Harris	France and Belgium	27.5.40
5504225 Cpl. S. R. Harrison	Burma	3.3.45
5247696 L./Cpl. J. H. Harrison	At sea	14.11.42
5253171 Pte. H. Hartshorn	France and Belgium	20.5.40
5571129 Pte. H. A. Hartwell	U.K.	16.11.39
14625268 Pte. S. A. Harvey	Western Europe ...	19.11.44
14389069 Pte. E. Harvey ...	Burma	2.3.45
5258023 Pte. H. Hathaway	Western Europe ...	16.8.44
5251424 Pte L. A. Hawker	Middle East ...	21.11.42

5256229 Pte. F. Hawkes	Burma	1.9.45
4541949 Pte. G. Hawkin ...	Western Europe	24.9.44
14630223 Pte. A. K. Hawley	Burma	19.3.45
14754168 Pte. H. F. Head...	Western Europe	27.3.45
4042611 Pte. G. A. J. Heaton	Western Europe	27.8.44
4197227 Pte. K. Helliwell	France and Belgium	29.5.40
5250813 Pte. C. Hemming	France and Belgium	21.5.40
5253060 Pte. C. Hemming	Western Europe	18.11.44
14446449 Pte. G. T. Henn	India	19.6.45
5260435 L./Cpl. W. T. Hewitt ...	Western Europe	25.9.44
5249255 Sergt. E. S. Hickman ...	Western Europe	2.7.44
5250565 Pte. H. S. Higgs	France and Belgium	6.40
4919983 Pte. A. Hill	Middle East	20.8.44
5247113 Sergt. J. A. Hill	France and Belgium	5.40
5253176 Pte. B. W. Hill	Burma	25.7.44
5258278 Sergt. W. H. Hockley ...	Western Europe	27.8.44
5248766 Pte. E. Hodgetts	France and Belgium	21.5.40
5258268 Pte. M. Hodgkins	Western Europe	7.8.44
5117897 Pte. R. Holgate ...	Middle East	1.2.41
14748142 Pte. W. G. Holt...	Burma	12.2.45
5253900 Pte. R. L. Holt	Middle East	42
5247981 Pte. T. K. C. Holton	Middle East	8.6.42
5250884 Pte. P. Hope	Eritrea	12.5.41
5256650 Pte. A. J. Hope ...	Western Europe	16.4.45
14431358 Cpl. J. E. Horten	Western Europe	12.2.45
5254290 Cpl. G. G. Houghton ...	At sea	14.11.42
5256259 Pte. W. Howard	U.K. ...	19.4.41
14577491 Pte. K. T. Howells	Western Europe	9.8.44
5260433 Pte. S. Howells ...	U.K. ...	11.8.42
5252222 Pte. L. Howes ...	France and Belgium	27.5.40
5256196 Pte. W. H. Howlett	Middle East	43
14918695 Pte. C. H. Hubbard	U.K. ...	22.12.45
5571135 Pte. F. H. Hughes	France and Belgium	5.40
5251104 Sergt. S. G. Hughes	Burma	20.3.45
4191591 Pte. R. Humphreys	Burma	24.2.45
1477945 Pte. J. G. Humphries ...	Western Europe	5.8.44
5247943 Pte. F. Humphries	Middle East	14.6.42
4114550 W.O.I J. Hurd ...	Western Europe	16.8.44
5254027 Pte. W. A. Hurst	Burma	8.1.45
14699690 Pte. E. Hutchins	Western Europe	16.8.44
14491880 Pte. A. J. W. Ingleby	Western Europe	27.3.45
5257034 Pte. W. H. Ingram	Western Europe	16.8.44
5252516 Pte. L. F. Ingram	France and Belgium	21.5.40
4032435 Cpl. V. N. H. Ives	Burma	27.1.45
5252853 Pte. J. Jack	U.K. ...	14.1.40
14529318 Pte. D. A. Jackson	Western Europe	12.8.44
3717169 Pte. W. E. Jackson	Burma	12.5.44
5251052 Pte. T. W. Jacobs	Eritrea	18.3.41
5256045 Pte. F. Jakeman	U.K. ...	14.9.42
5248276 Pte. W. E. Jakeway	Middle East	11.44
5252496 Pte. E. W. James	France and Belgium	5.40
5254775 Cpl. A. O. James	Western Europe	8.8.44
14565712 Pte. E. J. James	Western Europe	8.8.44
5251033 Pte. E. I. Janes	Middle East	28.11.41
5254284 Sergt. F. Jarvis	Burma	26.2.45
5247020 Sergt. D. H. T. Jaynes	At sea	14.11.42
5179943 Cpl. C. D. Jefferies	U.K. ...	8.3.45
5571143 Pte. C. F. Jeffery	France and Belgium	6.40
14228154 Pte. L. A. Jelfs	Burma	19.6.44
5258682 Pte. R. Jenkins ...	Western Europe	16.8.44
4856434 L./Cpl. I. Jevons	Western Europe	19.11.44

5257949 Pte. S. W. Jew ...	Western Europe ...	8.8.44
3971291 Pte. H. Jewell ...	Burma	20.3.45
5253181 Pte. C. Jewkes	France and Belgium	6.40
5251579 Pte. F. Jewkes ...	U.K.	15.5.40
5259057 Pte. L. S. Johnson	Burma	7.1.45
5056238 Pte. A. Johnson	Burma	21.1.45
14596363 Pte. G. Jones ...	Burma	29.12.44
14718392 Pte. J. O. Jones	Western Europe ...	27.3.45
4193275 L./Cpl. D. Jones	Burma	30.11.44
14585240 Pte. S. N. Jones...	Western Europe ...	14.8.44
14593710 L./Cpl. W. G. F. Jones	Western Europe ...	14.8.44
14438903 Pte. W. J. Jones...	Western Europe ...	7.8.44
4201026 Pte. T. Jones ...	U.K.	5.12.41
4858995 Pte. J. Jones ...	France and Belgium	21.5.40
5247890 Pte. E. Jones ...	Western Europe ...	9.8.44
5249107 Pte. P. H. Jones...	France and Belgium	24.5.40
5252385 Pte. A. E. M. Jones ...	France and Belgium	5.3.40
5253009 L./Cpl. S. Jones	India	2.8.44
5257777 Pte. C. Jones ...	Western Europe ...	9.8.44
5257956 Pte. W. Jones ...	U.K.	27.9.43
5258294 Pte. E. Jones ...	Western Europe ...	26.8.44
846028 L./Cpl. T. W. Jones	India	6.7.40
5126351 Pte. J. W. Jones...	Burma	18.12.44
14565797 Pte. F. Jones ...	Burma	21.1.45
4913385 W.O.II H. Jones ...	Burma	20.12.44
14850388 Pte. S. A. Jones	Ceylon	23.8.46
5255135 Pte. E. C. Jordon	U.K.	6.10.40
5258295 L./Sergt. A. L. Jordon	Western Europe ...	25.9.44
5341874 Pte. D. H. Jordon	Western Europe ...	5.7.44
5252491 Pte. L. F. Juggins	France and Belgium	5.40
5257039 Pte. W. T. Jukes	U.K.	4.12.41
14745175 Pte. T. M. A. Kell	Burma	13.2.45
14577290 Pte. J. C. Kendall	Western Europe ...	9.8.44
5250370 Sergt. D. H. Kerrigan	Western Europe ...	26.8.44
3453495 Pte. J. Kerton ...	Western Europe ...	25.9.44
5253579 Pte. F. Key ...	France and Belgium	29.5.40
5253189 Cpl. J. S. Kibble	Burma	19.5.44
5258308 Pte. J. Kinnersley	U.K.	22.12.41
5253187 Pte. C. Kirk ...	Middle East ...	27.12.42
14321068 Pte. A. E. Kiss ...	U.K.	8.2.43
5250344 L./Cpl. G. S. Knight ...	India	26.7.40
5252824 Sergt. G. G. W. Knight	Burma	19.12.44
5254531 Pte. L. C. Knight	Western Europe ...	19.2.45
3908482 Pte. J. T. Knott...	U.K.	30.12.40
5260249 Pte. J. Knott ...	Burma	15.4.44
14376804 Pte. W. E. Kyte...	Burma	20.3.45
5253191 Cpl. S. Lambert	France and Belgium	5.40
5250943 Pte. W. H. Lampitt	Middle East ...	11.42
4925383 L./Cpl. G. Lane	Burma	15.4.45
5249708 C./Sergt. A. E. L. Lane	Malaya	6.9.43
5252895 Pte. T. A. J. Lane	France and Belgium	41
5244193 Cpl. A. P. Langfield	France and Belgium	29.5.40
5504284 Cpl. A. Langhorn	Burma	15.5.45
5250299 Pte. N. C. Langley	South Africa... ...	1.12.40
5248337 Pte. F. Lappage	Middle East ...	1.2.41
1100219 Pte. J. T. Law ...	Western Europe ...	19.11.44
5255581 Pte. R. E. Lawrence	U.K.	25.7.40
14629944 Pte. J. S. Lawton	Burma	22.1.45
5254340 Pte. C. Lea ...	Italy	5.10.43
5256060 L./Cpl. F. Lee ...	Middle East ...	11.44
5248634 Pte. G. T. Lee ...	At sea	42

5256756 Cpl. J. E. Lee ...	...	Western Europe ...	23.7.44
5254059 Pte. L. T. Leighton	...	France and Belgium	40
14654303 Pte. G. Lench ...	...	Burma	8.2.45
5118035 Pte. R. S. Lennon	...	Eritrea	18.3.41
5339330 L./Cpl. C. V. Levy	...	Burma	9.5.44
5252509 L./Cpl. R. Lewis	...	Western Europe ...	11.7.44
5253467 Pte. L. B. Lewis	...	Burma	19.6.44
5251266 Pte. H. Lippitt ...	...	France and Belgium	20.5.40
4918284 Cpl. R. Lithgow	...	Western Europe ...	25.9.44
5257954 Pte. J. S. J. Littlewood...	...	Western Europe ...	16.8.44
5258316 Pte. W. Little ...	...	Western Europe ...	19.11.44
5253750 Pte. H. H. Lloyd	...	France and Belgium	29.5.40
6030050 Pte. C. Locke ...	...	Burma	19.5.44
5251238 Pte. S. F. Lockyer	...	Western Europe ...	19.11.44
1544853 Pte. T. F. Lomas	...	Western Europe ...	19.11.44
4197111 L./Cpl. A. Lomax	...	France and Belgium	22.5.40
5257792 Pte. C. W. Long	...	Western Europe ...	28.8.44
14758019 Pte. M. Lovelock	...	Western Europe ...	17.2.45
5254725 L./Cpl. E. Loveridge ...	...	Burma	24.2.45
5257784 Pte. J. Lowe ...	...	Western Europe ...	7.7.44
5257791 Sergt. K. V. Lowe	...	Western Europe ...	24.9.44
5252998 Pte. B. C. Lucas	...	France and Belgium	6.40
4968182 Pte. D. J. Lyons	...	At sea	24.5.40
5350500 L./Cpl. R. W. A. Macey	...	Western Europe ...	16.2.45
5253448 Pte. L. L. Malbut	...	France and Belgium	6.40
5571152 L./Cpl. W. R. Manns ...	...	France and Belgium	2.2.40
5252130 Pte. H. Mantle ...	...	France and Belgium	5.40
5345495 Pte. B. F. Marchant	...	Western Europe ...	15.4.45
14719795 Pte. P. Marlow	...	India	5.9.45
1463788 Pte. C. Marsden	...	Burma	20.3.45
5258632 Pte. J. H. Marshall	...	Western Europe ...	19.11.44
14575974 Pte. F. E. Marsh	...	Western Europe ...	29.9.44
5253612 L./Cpl. J. Marsh	...	Burma	9.5.44
14625329 Pte. S. J. Marsh	...	Western Europe ...	10.8.44
5258324 Pte. W. Marson	...	U.K.	17.12.40
5249984 Sergt. A. G. Mathlin	...	Middle East	13.7.40
5258335 Pte. W. Matthews	...	Western Europe ...	30.6.44
5253419 Pte. C. A. May	...	France and Belgium	5.40
5250774 Pte. J. May ...	...	India	24.9.43
4915679 Pte. C. Mayes ...	...	France and Belgium	20.5.40
5252559 Pte. D. P. McDornell ...	...	France and Belgium	29.5.40
5251311 Pte. T. A. McElhone	...	India	30.3.44
5259732 L./Cpl. H. E. McFarland	...	Burma	21.1.45
6769526 Cpl. S. A. McGregor ...	...	Burma	14.3.45
5258356 Sergt. W. G. McKay ...	...	Western Europe ...	7.8.44
2718886 Pte. C. McKea ...	...	Middle East ...	4.11.41
5258343 Pte. L. W. G. Meadows	...	Western Europe ...	6.7.44
5253203 Pte. J. Menzies	...	France and Belgium	21.5.40
5258350 Pte. C. L. Mercer	...	Western Europe ...	27.6.44
14572734 Pte. W. G. Morrison ...	...	Western Europe ...	9.8.44
5251606 Sergt. J. L. Michaels ...	...	Middle East ...	7.4.41
14708839 Pte. F. Middleton	...	Western Europe ...	9.8.44
14795014 Pte. R. H. Miles	...	U.K.	30.6.45
5256351 Pte. N. Miller ...	...	Burma	8.2.45
5252755 Pte. S. J. Millington ...	...	France and Belgium	21.5.40
5252925 Sergt. F. E. Millman ...	...	Burma	14.4.45
5246956 L./Sergt. T. Mills	...	France and Belgium	6.40
5253064 L./Sergt. S. W. Mills	...	France and Belgium	22.5.40
14748162 Pte. H. Millward	...	Burma	12.2.45
5252660 Pte. D. Mitchell	...	France and Belgium	5.40
5258331 Pte. G. A. G. Mobley ...	...	U.K.	5.12.41

5256070 Pte. A. R. Mogg	... ...	U.K.	15.8.41
5257803 Pte. W. Moore ...	... ...	Middle East ...	7.6.42
14725128 Pte. H. Moreton	... ...	Burma	28.2.45
5256074 Pte. T. P. Morgan	... ...	East Africa ...	5.5.41
5244619 Sergt. T. H. Morris	... ...	France and Belgium	29.5.40
5252765 Pte. W. H. Morris	... ...	France and Belgium	5.40
5257058 L./Cpl. A. J. Morris	... ...	Burma	7.5.44
5256582 Pte. L. E. Moseley	... ...	East Africa ...	12.5.41
14756609 Pte. B. G. Mott	... ...	Western Europe ...	9.3.45
5507671 Pte. A. J. L. Mourant ...	...	Burma	5.6.44
5248535 Pte. A. Muir ...	... ...	India	4.1.45
5251406 Pte. W. Mullett	... ...	Middle East ...	1.2.41
4915706 Pte. G. Mulloy	... ...	France and Belgium	20.5.40
5055094 Pte. T. Mulvihill	... ...	Western Europe ...	13.10.44
5258345 Cpl. M. J. Murphy	... ...	Western Europe ...	20.8.44
5252231 Pte. A. W. Murray	... ...	France and Belgium	5.40
5571156 Cpl. J. Must ...	... ...	Western Europe ...	16.8.44
5253445 Pte. E. Nabbs ...	... ...	France and Belgium	25.8.40
14681695 Pte. A. Neale ...	... ...	Western Europe ...	24.9.44
5251399 Pte. R. Neale ...	... ...	Eritrea	17.3.41
14423270 Pte. G. H. Neil ...	...	Western Europe ...	9.8.44
14588580 Pte. L. Newell ...	... ...	Western Europe ...	9.8.44
5180893 L./Cpl. L. S. Newell	... ...	Europe	19.8.42
6976739 Pte. T. Newell ...	... ...	Middle East ...	5.6.42
5254177 L./Cpl. N. Newey	... ...	Burma	26.2.45
5251403 Pte. C. Nicholls	... ...	Middle East ...	12.4.41
5257364 Pte. J. Nock ...	... ...	Burma	20.6.44
5252391 Pte. J. V. Noke ...	... ...	France and Belgium	5.40
14673107 Pte. R. W. Norman	... ...	Western Europe ...	7.8.44
5248936 Cpl. H. North ...	... ...	Eritrea	19.3.41
4915650 Pte. H. Norton	... ...	France and Belgium	26.5.40
5571162 Pte. E. J. Oakford	... ...	France and Belgium	5.40
5257811 Sergt. G. H. Oakley	... ...	Western Europe ...	16.4.45
5252615 Pte. W. A. Oakley	... ...	France and Belgium	5.40
14388717 Pte. D. J. Oakley	... ...	Western Europe ...	27.8.44
4747298 Pte. G. Ollier ...	... ...	Burma	14.4.44
3975978 Pte. D. O'Neill	... ...	Burma	4.6.45
6103296 Pte. W. Orridge	... ...	East Africa ...	26.8.40
5249047 Sergt. S. G. L. Packer ...	...	Middle East ...	16.9.42
7962691 Pte. A. E. Packman	... ...	Western Europe ...	16.8.44
14423096 Pte. W. W. Packman	... ...	Western Europe ...	19.11.44
5248015 Sergt. R. Paddick	... ...	Middle East ...	42
5499468 Pte. E. A. G. Painter ...	...	Burma	11.2.45
5116941 Cpl. B. A. Palmer	... ...	Middle East ...	14.6.42
5258379 Cpl. S. H. Palmer	... ...	Western Europe ...	15.8.44
5251398 Pte. W. H. Panther	... ...	Middle East ...	11.42
4201244 Pte. J. Park ...	... ...	India	27.12.43
2026613 Pte. T. Park ...	... ...	U.K.	19.8.45
5251361 Cpl. L. C. Parkes	... ...	Eritrea	17.3.41
5251631 Pte. R. E. C. Parker	... ...	Middle East ...	23.2.42
5252580 Cpl. H. Parkes ...	... ...	Western Europe ...	17.2.45
5571164 L./Cpl. E. Parkinson	... ...	France and Belgium	6.40
4854684 Pte. J. H. Parr ...	... ...	France and Belgium	29.5.40
5059132 Pte. A. Parsonage	... ...	Burma	21.1.45
5250032 Pte. A. E. Partridge	... ...	France and Belgium	26.5.40
14341213 Pte. R. E. Partridge	... ...	Burma	7.1.45
5253967 Pte. F. W. Payne	... ...	Middle East ...	11.42
5956348 Pte. J. E. Payne	... ...	Middle East ...	6.42
5249884 Sergt. W. J. Peacock	... ...	West Africa ...	26.12.44
5571167 Pte. C. C. Peake	... ...	France and Belgium	29.5.40
5177586 Sergt. H. R. Pearce	... ...	Middle East ...	11.42

14216762 Pte. E. T. Pearce	Western Europe	20.12.44
5250940 Pte. W. E. Pearson	India	5.7.40
4915785 Pte. J. H. Pennell	France and Belgium	5.40
4615275 Pte. G. G. Penrose	France and Belgium	29.5.40
5252394 Pte. T. Percy	France and Belgium	6.40
5125346 L./Sergt. F. C. Perkins	Burma	29.5.45
5254137 L./Cpl. J. W. T. Perkins	Burma	15.4.44
4920043 L./Cpl. S. A. Perkins	Middle East	15.8.44
5247369 Pte. F. E. Perry	Middle East	20.6.42
6912139 Sergt. T. W. Pettyfor	Burma	28.4.44
4928610 Pte. H. Petty	Burma	22.1.45
5254621 Pte. G. A. Phipps	U.K.	23.3.43
14499485 Pte. P. V. Pingree	U.K.	17.2.44
5500695 Pte. W. C. Pink	Burma	9.2.45
5251368 Pte. J. Piper	Middle East	14.6.42
7963272 Pte. J. E. Pirie	Western Europe	19.11.44
5249828 Pte. J. Pitt	Burma	21.5.44
5254631 Pte. H. B. Plant	U.K.	16.5.43
14673114 Pte. F. J. Platt	Western Europe	8.8.44
5242937 C./Sergt. H. Pleabance	Middle East	2.3.45
5258382 Cpl. K. Poade	Western Europe	29.6.44
5249327 Pte. C. F. Pocock	East Africa	9.5.41
861705 Pte. C. Poole	Eritrea	26.1.41
5253215 L./Cpl. W. E. Postings	France and Belgium	5.40
5253577 Pte. E. Potts	France and Belgium	29.5.40
5256091 Cpl. O. J. Pound	Western Europe	4.8.44
4862604 Pte. P. J. Powdrill	Western Europe	25.9.44
5250563 Pte. E. D. Powell	France and Belgium	5.40
5571171 Pte. S. D. Poxon	Western Europe	6.11.44
549769 Pte. B. T. Poyner	Western Europe	24.9.44
14541916 Pte. G. H. Poyner	Burma	28.2.45
5256094 Pte. A. Pratt	Middle East	6.5.45
5248348 Cpl. A. Preece	Eritrea	17.3.41
14428566 Pte. H. Preston	Western Europe	6.11.44
5252483 Pte. F. Price	France and Belgium	5.40
5254341 Pte. J. H. Price	India	27.3.45
5254661 Pte. F. Price	Italy	10.43
5250554 L./Cpl. E. Price	France and Belgium	40
4197242 L./Cpl. D. Price	France and Belgium	2.12.44
14565811 Cpl. D. W. Priest	Western Europe	27.8.44
5248109 Cpl. A. W. Pring	East Africa	5.5.41
4914347 L./Cpl. C. T. Pringle	Italy	19.3.44
5257979 Pte. H. Pritchard	Western Europe	27.6.44
5384804 Pte. R. A. Prowting	France and Belgium	6.40
5247615 L./Cpl. J. Purcell	Middle East	11.9.40
14529394 Pte. D. Purslow	Western Europe	17.2.45
14785305 Pte. D. Quinlan	Western Europe	9.3.45
5252958 Pte. A. Ralph	France and Belgium	5.40
4341614 L./Cpl. H. Ramster	Eritrea	10.5.41
5248247 Pte. J. H. Randall	Middle East	18.3.41
5251621 Pte. W. Randle	Eritrea	17.3.41
5251782 Pte. D. Randle	France and Belgium	5.40
5243814 Pte. A. R. Randle	France and Belgium	20.5.40
4039472 Pte. D. Ratcliffe	Burma	18.3.45
5253733 Pte. F. C. Rawlins	France and Belgium	5.40
4616526 Pte. H. Rawlings	France and Belgium	5.44
5259750 Pte. C. H. W. Rawlings	Burma	29.5.42
5116947 Cpl. L. H. Rayner	Middle East	14.6.45
14446485 Pte. D. Reay	Burma	28.5.45
5259749 Pte. H. J. Rees	U.K.	23.9.44
14711451 Pte. W. Rees	Western Europe	24.9.44

5249943 Pte. H. Reeves ...	Western Europe	...	14.7.44
13054473 Pte. W. Reid ...	Western Europe	...	12.8.44
14559799 Pte. E. A. Rentoul	Western Europe	...	19.11.40
5253225 Pte. J. S. Revitt	France and Belgium		5.42
5256610 Pte. J. A. Rhodes	Middle East	...	14.6.41
5110047 Pte. A. E. Richards	U.K.		14.11.40
5252387 L./Cpl. W. A. Richards...	France and Belgium		6.40
5253697 Pte. W. A. Richards	France and Belgium		29.5.40
5254308 Pte. J. W. Richards	Western Europe	...	14.8.44
4203321 Pte. W. D. V. Richards	Burma ...	...	1.3.45
5334639 Pte. A. J. Richardson ...	Western Europe	...	8.44
5258080 Sergt. G. H. Ridler	Western Europe	...	24.9.44
5250483 Drummer E. Riley	Eritrea ...	...	17.3.41
5256794 Pte. J. A. H. Riley	Burma ...	...	7.5.44
14388719 Pte. O. H. Roberts	Western Europe	...	9.8.44
5255352 Pte. D. Roberts	U.K.		28.8.40
5251771 Pte. W. Robinson	France and Belgium		5.40
7915967 Pte. A. Robinson	India ...	...	23.9.45
14542099 Pte. H. N. Rockall	Western Europe	...	28.8.44
5257838 Pte. T. J. Rodda	Western Europe	...	27.3.45
5258420 Pte. C. D. Rogers	At sea ...	...	6.8.44
5248331 Pte. J. A. Rogers	Eritrea ...	...	17.3.41
5252600 Pte. W. E. Rollinson	France and Belgium		21.5.40
5249629 Sergt. G. W. Rone	U.K.		7.9.44
5257833 Pte. E. Roper ...	Western Europe	...	27.8.44
4914486 L./Cpl. V. Round	Burma ...	...	20.1.45
4918285 Pte. A. Rowe ...	Western Europe	...	19.11.44
14438183 Pte. W. F. Roxby	Western Europe	...	9.8.44
5117924 Pte. A. Rubin ...	Eritrea ...	...	31.3.41
5250423 Pte. E. Ruff	France and Belgium		29.5.40
5258398 Pte. L. Russell ...	U.K.		20.1.44
3310533 W.O.I A. C. Rutty	India ...	...	12.9.41
14682619 Pte. A. E. Ryall	Burma ...	...	19.12.44
4197344 Pte. J. Ryan ...	Burma ...	...	8.3.45
5258078 Pte. F. Ryan ...	Western Europe		27.6.44
5253230 Pte. L. H. Sabin	France and Belgium		5.40
5258441 Sergt. F. Sabin	Western Europe	...	25.11.44
14676458 Pte. R. Salisbury	Western Europe	...	27.8.44
5248799 W.O.II G. E. Salt	U.K.		23.2.42
5248174 L./Cpl. O. Salt	Middle East	...	6.42
5251154 Pte. W. Sanders...	India ...	...	27.7.41
5254807 Sergt. P. H. Saunders ...	Burma ...	...	15.4.44
5256118 Pte. W. Saunders	East Africa	...	5.5.41
5254225 Cpl. E. C. Sawyer	Western Europe	...	9.8.44
1511506 Pte. R. Scott ...	Western Europe	...	9.8.44
4915773 Pte. F. Seeley ...	France and Belgium		18.5.40
4928627 Pte. A. Shade ...	Burma ...	...	22.1.45
14588462 Pte. P. B. Shakespeare ...	Western Europe	...	10.8.44
850729 Pte. A. Shaw ...	Burma ...	...	16.6.45
14497341 Pte. C. C. Shaw...	Western Europe	...	23.11.44
5254178 Pte. J. W. Shaw...	U.K.		1.1.44
4541856 Cpl. A. Shay ...	Burma ...	...	20.3.45
14708198 Pte. W. G. Shepherd ...	Western Europe	...	27.8.44
4197291 Pte. F. Sheridan	France and Belgium		20.9.43
5249415 Pte. J. R. Siddall	Eritrea ...	...	17.3.41
14723136 Pte. J. Silverman ...	Burma ...	...	17.3.45
5251357 Pte. W. A. Simmons ...	Eritrea ...	...	21.3.41
14745306 Pte. S. Siverns ...	Burma ...	...	28.3.45
4925181 Sergt. C. E. Skidmore	Western Europe	...	25.9.44
5259638 Pte. A. J. Slatcher	Burma ...	...	20.1.45
5117933 Pte. W. Slater ...	Middle East	...	42

4614423 Pte. F. Slingsby	France and Belgium	29.5.40
6106560 Pte. P. C. Smewing	Western Europe	18.7.44
5253106 Pte. A. Smith	France and Belgium	6.40
5254182 Pte. A. H. Smith	Western Europe	27.3.45
6103339 Pte. A. Smith	Western Europe	9.8.44
5257990 Pte. B. Smith	Western Europe	27.8.44
6100291 Pte. G. A. Smith	Western Europe	27.8.44
5247955 Sergt. H. Smith	U.K. ...	13.4.42
14585410 Pte. H. A. Smith	U.K. ...	4.12.43
5257993 Cpl. J. W. A. Smith	Western Europe	9.8.44
5252163 Pte. J. C. Smith...	France and Belgium	10.6.40
4909744 Sergt. L. Smith	Burma	11.4.44
14380864 Pte. S. Smith	Western Europe	27.3.45
5250379 L./Cpl. R. F. Smith	Burma	14.4.45
5252821 Pte. W. H. Smith	France and Belgium	5.40
5957185 Pte. W. H. R. Smith	Middle East	9.6.42
5050862 Pte. J. A. Snape...	Western Europe	19.11.44
5254106 Pte. B. R. Sollis	Western Europe	18.7.44
5249272 W.O.II C. Southwood ...	Western Europe	7.44
14629908 Pte. D. A. Southwick	Burma	5.6.45
5125661 Pte. D. R. Spares	Burma	28.4.44
5253240 Pte. A. Spencer	France and Belgium	28.5.40
5250799 Pte. S. Stacey	Western Europe	1.4.45
13041577 Pte. H. Stanley	Western Europe	22.10.44
14747355 Pte. W. Statham	Burma	5.4.45
4928628 Pte. J. W. Statham	Burma	3.2.45
5258432 Pte. R. P. Stimson	Western Europe	16.8.44
4615225 Pte. D. Stone	France and Belgium	5.40
5256690 Pte. F. R. Stone	Burma	8.2.45
14654360 Pte. B. Storey	Western Europe	15.8.44
5251259 Sergt. A. J. Strain	France and Belgium	21.5.40
4912720 Sergt. R. C. Strange	Western Europe	30.7.44
4925029 Pte. V. Stromboli	Burma	8.1.45
5250754 Pte. F. W. Sturdy	India	6.7.40
5506413 Pte. H. Sutton	Burma	22.1.45
5251805 Pte. L. Sutton	At sea	24.5.40
1594112 Pte. G. Swift	Western Europe	19.11.44
4854842 Pte. A. L. Swift	France and Belgium	6.40
5112860 Cpl. A. R. Swindale	Eritrea	14.5.41
5257407 L./Sergt. E. C. Swindells	Middle East	14.11.42
5506415 Pte. H. R. Sykes	India	18.12.44
5117941 Pte. C. E. Sykes	Middle East	14.6.42
5248155 Bdsmn. W. H. Tainton	Middle East	26.8.40
5252569 Pte. W. G. T. Taylor ...	France and Belgium	5.40
5252605 Pte. L. Taylor	France and Belgium	5.40
5252613 Pte. S. J. Taylor	France and Belgium	27.6.40
5254532 Pte. H. M. Taylor	Middle East	11.42
5245983 Pte. W. Taylor ...	Norway	28.4.40
5248311 Pte. E. W. Taylor	Middle East	11.42
14669105 Pte. A. Taylor	Western Europe	24.7.44
14552997 Pte. A. C. Taylor	India	5.6.45
4197342 L./Cpl. H. Taylor	France and Belgium	5.40
5571195 Cpl. E. C. Tester	France and Belgium	30.5.40
4915748 Pte. E. Thomas	France and Belgium	5.40
4199634 Pte. A. J. Thomas	Burma	7.1.45
5258470 Pte. L. Thomas	Western Europe	19.11.44
5049247 Pte. G. Thompson	Middle East	14.6.42
5257998 Pte. W. J. Thompson	Western Europe	9.8.44
5253245 Cpl. A. G. Thompson	France and Belgium	9.5.45
5254397 Pte. J. A. Thompson	Burma	8.6.44
4863473 Pte. J. W. Thompson	Burma	26.2.45

3456774 Pte. H. Thornley	... ...	India	17.5.44
5251816 Pte. C. J. Thornton	... ...	Burma	13.4.44
5253947 Pte. R. C. Thornton	... ...	India	22.9.42
5575270 Sergt. L. Thumwood	...	Burma	8.2.45
5258461 Pte. R. E. F. Tildesley		U.K.	16.6.44
5246052 W.O.II H. S. Tillman	...	France and Belgium	14.8.45
5248729 Pte. J. T. Tilt ...	... ...	France and Belgium	29.5.40
5253104 Pte. G. B. Timney	... ...	France and Belgium	26.6.44
5251934 Pte. P. Toland ...	... ...	Middle East ...	4.11.42
14740805 Pte. G. E. Tolley	... ...	Burma	2.3.45
7011450 Pte. R. J. Toman	... ...	Middle East ...	7.1.45
4912992 Cpl. H. Tomlinson	... ...	Burma	20.6.44
5256681 Cpl. E. R. Tonks	... ...	Western Europe ...	31.7.44
5106505 Pte. G. Tovey ...	... ...	Eritrea ...	18.2.41
5250342 Pte. L. Tovey ...	... ...	Western Europe ...	19.11.44
5254884 Pte. H. Tracey ...	... ...	Burma	8.2.45
14426422 Pte. L. H. Treadgold	...	Western Europe ...	27.8.44
1706670 Pte. H. L. Tredwell	...	Western Europe ...	18.11.44
5252675 Pte. E. J. Trigg	... ...	France and Belgium	5.40
5249252 Pte. W. Tropman	... ...	India	1.2.44
5248616 Pte. G. E. Troth	... ...	Western Europe ...	16.8.44
5571198 Pte. A. J. Trueman	...	France and Belgium	29.5.40
5499810 Pte. D. A. Tuck	... ...	Western Europe ...	27.6.44
5571199 Pte. F. G. Tuck...	... ...	France and Belgium	29.5.40
14588467 Pte. E. P. Turbutt	...	Burma	19.12.44
5254801 Pte. F. W. Turley	...	U.K.	27.12.41
5255659 Pte. J. E. Turner	...	India	8.3.43
5252761 L./Cpl. A. C. Turner	...	France and Belgium	6.40
4915577 Pte. J. H. Turner	... ...	India	25.10.45
5257445 Pte. T. J. Twigger	...	Middle East ...	2.11.42
5248795 Cpl. B. F. Tyler	... ...	France and Belgium	29.5.40
14565728 L./Cpl. F. Upton	...	Burma	29.12.44
5257421 Pte. R. Vale ...	... ...	Middle East ...	8.11.42
5258476 Pte. E. Veal ...	... ...	Western Europe ...	27.3.45
5118056 Pte. F. R. Vernalls	...	Middle East ...	42
5770314 Sergt. R. Vincent	...	East Africa ...	5.5.41
4918273 Sergt. J. B. Vlummer	...	Western Europe ...	3.10.44
5503485 Pte. H. E. Wadham	...	Burma	13.2.45
5253661 Pte. E. Wadley ...	... ...	India	4.6.41
4623315 Pte. T. R. Waites	...	Western Europe ...	19.11.44
7938897 L./Cpl. A. K. Walbey	...	Burma	29.5.45
14496639 Pte. G. A. Walker	... ...	Western Europe ...	28.3.45
764284 Sergt. J. H. Walker	...	France and Belgium	29.5.40
14683120 Pte. R. A. Wall ...	...	Western Europe ...	13.7.44
5247787 Pte. A. Wallace ...	...	Eritrea ...	18.3.41
5571345 Pte. H. F. Wallis	...	France and Belgium	29.5.40
4197175 Pte. A. Walmsley	...	France and Belgium	23.5.40
14552753 Pte. H. F. Walsh	...	Western Europe ...	21.11.44
5346428 Pte. P. W. Walters	...	Western Europe ...	19.11.44
14397534 L./Sergt. H. A. Ward	...	Western Europe ...	24.9.44
5109063 Sergt. J. H. H. Ward	...	Middle East ...	42
5252890 Pte. A. G. Wardle	...	India	28.7.41
5245694 W.O.II H. L. Warman...		France and Belgium	6.40
5250962 Pte. J. Warner ...	...	Middle East ...	10.12.42
6349988 Pte. C. F. Warren	...	Western Europe ...	19.11.44
5499874 L./Cpl. G. E. F. Wart	...	Burma	8.2.45
14654577 Pte. J. W. Waters	...	Western Europe ...	10.8.44
5257435 Pte. R. G. Watson	...	Burma	6.5.44
5055354 Pte. W. T. Watson	...	Western Europe ...	30.9.44
5253041 Pte. J. W. Waugh	...	France and Belgium	5.40
5504002 Pte. J. Way ...	... ...	India	6.12.43

U

5257136 Pte. E. Webb		Western Europe	27.8.44
5243579 W.O.II H. A. Webb		France and Belgium	6.40
2751773 Pte. W. T. Webb		France and Belgium	28.5.40
5499551 Pte. C. W. Weston		Burma	22.1.45
2024001 Pte. G. A. Whaley		Middle East	31.12.42
5256155 Pte. J. Whatsize		Middle East	11.42
5252100 Pte. W. L. A. Wheeler		France and Belgium	21.5.40
2033595 Pte. C. H. Whiles		Burma	19.3.45
5251617 Pte. J. A. Whitaker		Middle East	2.4.44
5257423 Pte. J. W. White		Western Europe	8.8.44
5250058 Drummer C. H. White		France and Belgium	23.5.40
5254767 Pte. L. R. White		Burma	8.5.44
5243547 Sergt. L. A. White		West Africa	11.6.41
5247080 Pte. C. M. P. White		U.K.	17.1.43
5251353 Cpl. R. Whitehall		Eritrea	19.3.41
3651726 Pte. G. White		Eritrea	17.3.41
5258496 Pte. C. Whitehouse		Western Europe	8.8.44
6103380 Pte. R. G. Whitehead		Western Europe	29.3.45
14424566 Pte. R. L. Whittingham		Western Europe	19.11.44
6103419 Pte. L. A. Wilcox		Western Europe	1.8.44
4915695 Pte. G. W. Wild		U.K.	10.10.40
5252492 Pte. P. V. Wilkes		France and Belgium	7.3.40
5248177 L./Cpl. F. C. J. Wilkes		Middle East	10.12.40
5056574 Pte. W. L. Wilkins		Western Europe	25.9.44
5253887 Pte. A. Wilkinson		France and Belgium	29.5.40
5259921 Pte. E. Wilkinson		Burma	9.3.45
5253256 Pte. D. S. Willetts		France and Belgium	28.5.40
5257871 Pte. A. E. J. Williams		Western Europe	1.7.44
5503192 Pte. C. T. Williams		Burma	12.2.45
4202274 Pte. D. F. Williams		Burma	2.3.45
4198263 Cpl. E. R. Williams		Burma	4.6.45
4197128 Pte. G. R. Williams		Burma	11.4.44
14730532 Pte. W. Williams		Burma	16.2.45
5248066 Pte. W. P. Williams		Eritrea	17.3.41
4855535 Pte. C. Willis		France and Belgium	5.40
2087819 Pte. F. Wilmot		India	31.12.44
14577344 Pte. A. E. Wilson		Burma	25.1.45
5251512 Pte. E. J. Winwood		France and Belgium	29.5.40
5254388 Pte. J. W. Wood		Burma	23.1.45
2043547 L./Sergt. V. C. Wood		Burma	8.2.45
5251586 Pte. R. Woodall		U.K.	7.9.45
4197224 Pte. T. W. Woodward		France and Belgium	6.40
5250737 Pte. A. E. Woodward		Western Europe	25.9.44
5250002 Cpl. A. B. Woolley		India	17.2.40
13048978 Pte. W. H. Woolner		Middle East	17.6.42
5379271 Sergt. R. Worboys		Middle East	10.10.41
5256152 Pte. N. Worgan		U.K.	21.1.42
5188211 Pte. S. Worgan		U.K.	20.1.42
4855231 Pte. J. Worthington		France and Belgium	21.5.40
5117954 Pte. B. Wright		Middle East	12.12.40
5255674 Pte. W. W. Wright		Burma	15.2.45
4912946 Cpl. C. E. Wright		France and Belgium	26.5.40
5248363 Sergt. J. W. Wyatt		Middle East	2.4.42
5251647 Pte. V. F. Wyer		Middle East	25.12.41
5251711 Pte. W. H. Wykes		France and Belgium	10.6.40
5258570 Pte. L. Yardley		Middle East	1.8.42
5240838 W.O.I S. A. Yarnold		France and Belgium	5.40
5253665 Pte. A. E. Yeomans		France and Belgium	6.40
5256671 Pte. W. L. York		Middle East	11.42
5249173 Pte. N. Young		France and Belgium	6.40
5258571 Pte. F. C. Young		India	23.9.42

INDEX

Aachen, 69, 70
Abbassia Barracks, Cairo, 16
Abbott, J. J. : Lt., 102, 109 ; Capt., 7 n.
"Able" Ridge, 128, 129, 130
Abyssinia, 28
Acqua Col, 22
Acroma, 34, 35, 40, 41, 43
Adam, Gen. Sir R., 236
Adderbury, 220
Addis Ababa, 29
Aden, 257
Adlestrop, 170
Adowa, 28
Adyar, River, 115
Afferden, 76
Afghanistan, 114
Agheila, 33
"Agility 1," Exercise, 99
"Agility 2," Exercise, 99
Agny, 162, 163
Agordat, 20, 21, 22
Ahlhorn, 78
Ahmedabad, 171
Ahmednagar, 171
Akbar, Moghul Emperor, 5
Akrabad, 3
Akureyri, 241
Alamah, 21
Aldershot, 10, 12, 13, 18, 234, 249, 251
Alexander, Maj., 53
Alexandra Barracks, Maymyo, 152, 153
Alexandria, 30, 32, 41
Alfonso, H.M. King, of Spain, 108
Alice Holt Wood, 11
Allahabad, 2, 3, 4, 5
Altcar, 201
Amba Alagi, 28, 29, 30
Amba, Mt., 22
Amelinghansen, 90
American Zone, Germany, 96
Amesbury, 216
Amiens, 163
Amtoing, 166
Andaman Islands, 171
Andelst, 68
Aosta, Duke of, 29, 30, 197
Aradura spur, 177
Arakan, The, 174, 175
Ardennes, 72
Arkwright, Maj.-Gen. H. R. B., 100 n.

Armentières, 210
Arnhem, 67, 68
Arnholt, 77
Arras, 163
Arromanches, 49
Aschen, 66
Ashbrook, 227, 228
Ashburnham beaches, 240
Ashdown, 45
Ashebyin, 136
Ashridge, 237
Asmara, 28, 30
Assam, 118, 173
Atbara, 17, 18
Atlantic Ocean, 240 ; Battle of, 220
"Atlantic," Exercise, 222, 228
Auchinleck, Sir C., 197
Aunggon, 121
Ava, 188, 191
Ava bridge, 190
Ava fort, 190
Avelin, 209, 210

Bad Harzburg, 83, 84
Badminton tunnel, Gloucestershire, 226
Bailey, D. R. C. : Lt., 120, 121, 124, 125 ; Maj., 120 n.
Bain, Brig. G. A., 116, 125
Bain, Lt. I., 44
Baker, Brig. E. E. F., 235
Baker, Capt. F. E., 29
"Baker" Ridge, 128, 129, 130
Bald Hill, 29
Ballycastle, 221, 222
Balmoral Show Ground, Belfast, 227
Bambecque, 211, 212, 213, 219
Bandal, 194
Bangalore, 114, 116
Banmauk, 119, 121
Bann, River, 223
Bannister, Capt. J., 53, 60
Bannu, 113
Bardia, 41, 42
Barentu, 20, 21, 22
Baron, 56
Bauchem, 71
Baumeweg, 79
Baw, 123
Bayeux, 49, 57, 66
Beadle, J. P., 253
Bedford, 235
Bedfordshire, 217